Interacting or Interfering?

Interacting or Interfering?

Improving interactions in the early years

Julie Fisher

Mc Graw Hill Education   Open University Press

Open University Press
McGraw-Hill Education
McGraw-Hill House
Shoppenhangers Road
Maidenhead
Berkshire
England
SL6 2QL

email: enquiries@openup.co.uk
world wide web: www.openup.co.uk

and Two Penn Plaza, New York, NY 10121-2289, USA

First published 2016

A catalogue record of this book is available from the British Library

ISBN-13: 978-0-33-526256-4
ISBN-10: 0-33-526256-2
eISBN: 978-0-33-526257-1

Library of Congress Cataloging-in-Publication Data
CIP data applied for

Typeset by Aptara, Inc.
Printed and bound by CPI Group (UK) Ltd, Croydon, CR0 4YY

Praise for this book

"Julie Fisher gives a characteristically clear, grounded and extensively referenced exposition of how adults can best support young children's learning. Her book is based on direct observation and thoughtful conversations with reflective practitioners who work with children from birth to seven, and is thus deeply convincing. Each chapter builds logically on earlier points, and has an effective summary and provocative questions for all involved in early years education and care. Politicians, inspectors and parents as well as practitioners, academics and students could all learn from the detailed explanations and subtle inspirations to be found in this timely book."

Wendy Scott OBE, President of TACTYC, UK

"Few people are able to write with such depth, clarity and authority on a subject of such critical importance to understanding Early Years pedagogy. Julie Fisher's reputation as one of our most influential and respected experts is further enhanced by this timely and significant book which explores the contexts, issues and challenges of effective interaction. Both theoretical and practical, it manages to combine a rich evidence base with a clear insight to reflective and impactful practice. I have no doubt that this will become a seminal text for all those working with young children."

Jan Dubiel, National Development Manager at Early Excellence, UK

"Julie Fisher's new book Interacting or Interfering? focuses on the importance of adult-child interactions in pre-school settings. There are many strengths in this book that will make it essential reading for early childhood practitioners in initial and continuing professional development courses. The book draws on a research project on Adult-Child interactions, and provides some fascinating documentation of everyday events in early childhood settings, focusing on children from birth to five. This documentation is used as a stimulus to provoke reflective analyses of the data, and to ask critical questions of our own communication practices and interactions with children. These questions are not posed as a 'to do' list, but to provoke the deep reflection that we know is essential to high quality interactions that support children's thinking, enquiry, creativity and playfulness.

For early childhood specialists teaching in post-graduate programmes, and for researchers, the research evidence will be of interest, particularly as Julie supports her assertions with reference to sound scholarship, drawing on a range of perspectives that are relevant in ECE – child development, pedagogical theories, psychotherapy, language, communication and literacy. She traces many ideas back to the original research to present a synthesis of key theories that are used as analytical tools in thinking critically about the data. This book is very real, in that it presents the voices and perspectives of children and of practitioners as they grapple with important questions about their own practices and ECE policies. Julie's work will be relevant in many countries as the vignettes, and the questions she poses, resonate across different cultures and contexts."

Dr Elizabeth Wood, Professor of Education, University of Sheffield, UK

To the inspirational members of the
Oxfordshire Adult-Child Interaction Project (2010–14).
My thanks go to you all.

Contents

Preface   *xiii*

Acknowledgements   *xvii*

1   The importance of interactions for young children's learning   **1**
Introduction   1
Different definitions of 'effectiveness'   1
Interactions in the home   4
Why interactions matter   7
Why interactions matter to children entering school   9
Why interactions matter to practitioners   11
Summary   15

2   Interacting with babies and toddlers   **17**
Introduction   17
The foundations of interactions   18
The development of interactions   22
Summary   34

3   Knowing the child well   **35**
Introduction   35
Focus on babies and toddlers   36
What practitioners need to learn about children   37
The importance of the Key Persons Approach   40
The impact of knowing children well   42
Talking to someone and not everyone   45
Analysing your own practice   46
Transcripts 3:1; 3:2   47
Summary   51

4   Environments conducive to conversation   **52**
Introduction   52
Focus on babies and toddlers   52
Emotional space   53
 - for the child   53
 - for parents and carers   54
 - for practitioners   55

Physical space	56
- place	57
- noise and light	58
- position	59
- stimulation	60
- time	61
- experiences	61
Analysing your own practice	63
Transcripts 4:1; 4:2	64
Summary	67

5 Tuning in to the child — **69**

Introduction	69
Focus on babies and toddlers	69
The child as a learner	70
Strategies for tuning in to children	72
Working out what a child is thinking is more valuable than looking at what they are doing	78
Deciding when and whether to interact can be the difference between interacting and interfering	80
Analysing your own practice	81
Transcripts 5:1; 5:2	81
Summary	84

6 Who leads the learning? — **86**

Introduction	86
Focus on babies and toddlers	86
The benefits of learning alongside an adult and learning independently	87
Independent learning is not abandoned learning	89
Interactions in adult-led, adult-initiated and child-led contexts	91
The purpose of an interaction	93
The balance between adult-led and child-led learning	93
Who leads the learning?	96
Analysing your own practice	98
Transcripts 6:1 to 6:4	98
Summary	106

7 Sustaining effective interactions — **108**

Introduction	108
Focus on babies and toddlers	108
Initiating conversations	109
Sustaining interactions	111
Consolidating, extending and provoking thinking	117
Analysing your own practice	122
Body language	122
Analysing your own practice	123
Tone of voice	123

Transcripts 7:1 to 7:7 124
Analysing your own practice 124
Summary 125

8 Interacting with children who might not want to interact 127
Introduction 127
Focus on babies and toddlers 128
Reluctant talkers 128
Children with autism 132
Children with English as an additional language (Eal) 134
Signing as a form of communication 137
Analysing your own practice 138
Transcripts 8:1; 8:2 139
Summary 142

9 Questions that work and questions that don't 144
Introduction 144
Focus on babies and toddlers 144
Why do we ask questions? 145
Who asks the questions? 146
Transcripts 9:1 to 9:4 147
Different types of questions 149
Using questioning as control 152
Children's answers 152
Questions that work and questions that don't 154
Alternatives to questioning 155
Analysing your own practice 158
Transcripts 9:5 to 9:6 159
Summary 162

10 The attributes of effective practitioners 163
Introduction 163
Focus on babies and toddlers 163
The attributes of effectiveness 164
The importance of reciprocity 171
Interacting not interfering 174
Analysing your own practice 175
Transcript 10:1 178
Summary 180

Appendix: The Oxfordshire Adult–Child Interaction Project 2010–14 182
References 185
Index 195

Preface

This book is a celebration of the reflective practice of a group of Oxfordshire early years educators who challenged their practice, and sometimes their beliefs, to explore the question 'What makes an effective interaction with young children?'

Interacting with young children is at the heart of daily practice for all early childhood educators, and yet the Oxfordshire practitioners readily admitted that rarely did the issue arise on a staff meeting agenda and rarely had any of them closely analysed their own practice in order to improve their interventions in young children's learning.

The drive to undertake the research that forms the bedrock of this book came from my work as Early Years Adviser in one of England's largest local authorities. The Oxfordshire Early Years Team was responsible for the quality of teaching and learning in both the schools and settings in our county educating children within the Early Years Foundation Stage (EYFS). One way in which this was achieved was through a quality assurance scheme that required, among many other things, that a judgement be made about the quality of interactions in a setting. In discussion about this as an advisory team we realized that, while sharing many principles in common, what we were looking for by way of 'evidence' of quality varied quite substantially. We determined to see whether we could come to a more consensual view about what constitutes an effective interaction within the context of the early years of learning.

The Oxfordshire Adult–Child Interaction Research Project ran from 2010–14. The details of participants, aims and methodology are in the Appendix to this book, but suffice to say here, that there have been many challenges in representing the project within the pages of this book. The first has been that much of the effectiveness of an interaction rests on the body language and tone of voice of the practitioner. These non-verbal aspects of communication are almost impossible to capture through words on a page. Although most chapters have transcripts* to exemplify findings, they are inevitably without the many subtle nuances of communication that come from a raised eyebrow or a disrespectful tone of voice. Secondly, a book of this length can never carry all the transcripts needed to exemplify every point or finding from the research material. Nevertheless, I have tried to select transcripts from across the age range, from baby-rooms to Year 2 classes, to give a sense of the depth of our analysis with each age group.

The main concern of the research participants was that writing down the findings of the project would inevitably oversimplify some of the complexities of the issues that had been discussed over many, many months. Because of the subtleties of chemistry,

---

*All names used in the transcripts have been changed.

non-verbal communication and intersubjectivity, any attempt to describe an interaction through words rather than through the visual evidence of the DVD material ran the risk of giving readers an impression that improving interactions is more straightforward than it is. To try and reduce the likelihood of misrepresenting the project findings in this way, the project material has been developed into in-service training material and shown to practitioners across the country. Even up until the present time, a range of practitioners – from within and outside the project – have helped find words and phrases that best explain the various characteristics of an effective interaction.

The single biggest impact on the practice of the project participants was the filming of interactions in each setting and the subsequent discussions about practice. Being able to reflect on what practitioners actually do when they interact with children – rather than what they think they do – makes a critical contribution to the action research process. Change is unlikely to take place unless a practitioner sees the need for it, and the DVD footage gave each participant some 'personal training' moments when they could review their own practice and set their own targets for improvement. As a result of the project, several schools subsequently introduced filming all staff as part of their staff development programme and have reported the impact this has had on the quality of learning and teaching. It is important to note that being filmed takes a bit of getting used to, both for children and practitioners. Before the commencement of the project I spent time 'filming' in each classroom so that the children would get over smiling and dancing and other responses to a video camera being close by and so that, those who were old enough or sufficiently interested, could ask all the questions they wanted to. From the practitioners' perspective, the first set of footage prompted concerns about what individuals sounded like, or looked like – but this faded over time. The next concern was how much each practitioner spoke and how much they dominated the interactions. Because of this, the next batch of footage had many practitioners struck silent, concerned that they would talk too much and drown out the voice of the child. So it wasn't until the third or fourth set of filming that interactions were at their most relaxed, genuine and natural.

When the Oxfordshire Project began, the intention was to focus purely on interactions in child-led situations. The project participants believed that these scenarios posed the greatest challenge to practitioners and, that if we could identify the features of effective interactions in child-led situations, our project would have immense benefit. However, as time went by, it became apparent that the quality of an interaction in a child-led situation, is inextricably bound up with the quality of interactions in adult-led learning (one reason why there are separate chapters and sections for babies and toddlers is that 'adult-led' learning, by the definition used in this book – see Chapter 6 – is irrelevant). Through analysis of the project DVD material, one could observe that practitioners often 'interfered' with children's child-led learning, often hijacking it for their own ends, because they didn't teach what needed teaching well enough in an adult-led session. By making adult-led learning shorter, sharper, more focused, but effective, practitioners were left feeling more confident about following the thinking and purposes of the child, when supporting child-led learning. In the end, the Oxfordshire Project studied interactions in both adult-led and child-led situations.

There are two major findings from the Oxfordshire Adult-Child Interaction Project that need to be shared at this stage of the book, but which will be addressed in detail later on. The first is that practitioners talk too much; they certainly ask too many questions and they get more practice in speech, language and communication than children do. The second is that there are strategies that encourage children to talk that are still inadequately understood or applied in settings. The main one being the impact of making a comment or a statement rather than (always) asking a question. Throughout the project, participants worked on responding to children's thinking rather than interrogating it. They focused on maintaining the threads of thinking between adult and child rather than risk breaking these threads with questions that, more often than not, were posed for the practitioner's benefit rather than the child's.

The early drafts of this book revealed the need to treat those children who are non-communicators and non-verbal communicators separately. Not because the behaviour of effective practitioners alters significantly – it does not – but because the theory relevant to interactions with children who have ways other than words to send signals and messages demands something more specialist. Chapter 2 is, therefore, devoted to 'Interacting with Babies and Toddlers'. In addition, each subsequent chapter has a separate section at the beginning, entitled 'Focus on babies and toddlers', to show how all of the project findings are relevant to these youngest children. Chapter 8 considers 'Interacting with children who might not want to interact' and examines the strategies that a range of specialists, as well as practitioners, have found effective in supporting the speech, language and communication of reluctant talkers.

Chapters 1 and 2 in this book give theoretical overviews of the importance of adult-child interactions: Chapter 1 focusing mainly (but not exclusively) on children age 3+ and Chapter 2 being dedicated specifically to children from birth to age 3. Chapters 3–10 each address one key finding from the Oxfordshire Adult-Child Interaction Project. Each of these chapters then contains:

- theory underpinning the particular finding with which that chapter is concerned
- issues relevant to babies and toddlers
- practical implications and messages taken from analysis of the project DVD material
- prompts with which to analyse your own practice
- transcripts to exemplify the key messages of the chapter (numbered according to the chapter in which they are contained) and
- points for reflection.

We hope you find the book valuable, provoking and inspiring

Terminology

Throughout the book the pronoun 'he' is used when referring to the child and 'she' when referring to practitioners.

The term 'adult' is used when the text could refer either/and to a parent, carer or educator.

In the transcripts, the contribution of the adult is abbreviated consistently as 'A' whether referring to teachers, carers or early years practitioners.

Acknowledgements

My greatest thanks go to the Oxfordshire practitioners (named below), and the children in their settings, who took part in the Adult-Child Interaction Project from 2010–14. Your commitment to the project has been extraordinary, and your insights and reflections have inspired me – and countless others now – to improve the quality of interactions with young children.

As the Oxfordshire Project progressed, other practitioners in different local authorities contributed to our thinking and to the outcomes of the project. I would particularly like to pay tribute to the inspirational Tess Robson and her staff at Tachbrook Nursery School, but also acknowledge the countless practitioners on in-service courses around the country who have reflected on the Oxfordshire material and contributed to the final content of this book.

The project has been enriched by a steering group who remained loyal to the project and its participants throughout the four years of our research. Sue Vermes, head-teacher at the time of The Slade Nursery School and Children's Centre in Oxford, has been the most wonderful source of wisdom, principle and challenge. Her contributions always smoothed the rough edges of our thinking and ensured that children's interests remained central to the project's outcomes. Sally Thomas, an early years consultant with whom I had the privilege of working in Oxfordshire, deepened our understanding of the specialist years of birth to three and gave unfailingly of her time to discuss and research this aspect of our project so that our findings were robust. Mary Wild was a constant support and committed participant from Oxford Brookes University, always encouraging the dissemination of our work so that others could question the project's methodology and findings, thereby improving the contribution that this research would ultimately make. Alongside these steering group colleagues I was privileged to have external support from Elizabeth Wood, who was an inspiring mentor and critical friend, keeping me focused throughout the research phase of the project and supporting me to find my way through the emerging data.

Writing this book has proved a challenge. Trying to capture in print what is a very dynamic and transformational act creates all sorts of problems. Transcripts are not as vibrant as DVD footage; the outcomes of multifaceted discussions (and disagreements) appear all too unproblematic when trapped on the page; there is always the danger of making something that is complex and intricate appear straightforward and mechanistic. So I am indebted to all those who read various drafts of different chapters, and the book in its entirety, to ensure that the messages I give are clear, but do not oversimplify the challenge of engaging in effective interactions with young children. My grateful thanks go to Bethan Baldwin, Sue Hale, Megan Hale, Anne O'Connor,

Shane Page, Dorothy Selleck, Louie Suthers, Nick Swarbrick, Sally Thomas and Sue Vermes. In addition I want to thank Fiona Richman, who has been my commissioning editor at Open University Press since Starting from the Child was first published in 1996, and has been unstinting in her support, encouragement and advice in the writing of this book.

Finally, I want to acknowledge the contribution of my family in helping me see this book through to publication. Everyone at home – David, Sophie and Pepa – has had to make space for the time that writing takes and to be patient with my passion for seeing this project through to the end.

The Oxfordshire Adult-Child Interaction Project Participants *(and the schools and settings they worked in when the project took place)*

Bethan Baldwin	Headington Quarry Foundation Stage School
Megan Carberry	Rose Hill Primary School
Amanda Doy	Ladygrove Park Primary School
Janet Duffin	Lydalls Nursery School
Sarah Hall	Stockham Primary School
Fleur Holmes	Cholsey Primary School
Helen Johnson	Rose Hill Children's Centre
Anthea Kentish	The Town Nursery, Chipping Norton
Samantha Kirk	Grandpont Nursery School and Children's Centre
Shane Page	Oxford Brookes Day Nursery
Sally Pursell	The ACE Centre, Chipping Norton
Jacque Rafferty	St Marys CE (A) Primary School, Banbury
Sarah Read	Comper Foundation Stage School and Children's Centre
Maria Thorpe	The Slade Day Nursery
Sophie Tierney	Northbourne CE (A) Primary School
Helen Tyne	The Batt CE (A) Primary School
Katy Walsh	Caldecott Primary School
Helen Watson	Rose Hill Children's Centre

1

The importance of interactions for young children's learning

> Nothing matters more than stopping, listening and responding positively to the young child

Introduction

Interactions with young children are profoundly important for supporting and extending their learning. They are so much a part of the daily experience of both practitioners and children that it is easy to assume that they come about readily and naturally. The research in this book challenges this assumption. It would seem that something about the role of educator – as opposed to parent, carer or interested adult – puts pressure on practitioners to say things, and say them in ways, that are sometimes unnatural and often unhelpful. Why is this? Well, research into interactions between adults and young children in a variety of contexts suggests that by adopting the role of educator, adults sometimes force their own agenda onto children at an age when children are often highly motivated and driven by an agenda of their own, and do not welcome the interference!

This book examines the interactions that take place between early childhood educators and the children, from 6 months to 6 years, with whom they work. It explores both adult-led and child-led contexts and asks how interactions in these different situations can be made more natural, more purposeful and more effective – for children and for practitioners. This first chapter explores, in detail, why interactions are so important for young children's learning and development.

Different definitions of 'effectiveness'

There have been many attempts to identify the elements that lead to effective interactions between practitioners and children. But these are hugely dependent, of course, on the author's or researcher's definition of 'effectiveness'.

In the influential study of under fives in Britain in the 1980s (Bruner 1980; Wood et al. 1980), Bruner describes the challenge of trying to achieve what he calls

connected discourse (conversation) to occur. At the time, he and his colleagues were looking for a simple exchange between the adult and child where there was at least a three-element exchange on a single topic: A talks to B, B replies and then A responds to B's response. Of 9600 half-minute periods observed, Bruner reports that only 2 per cent contained such conversations.

In Tizard and Hughes' (1984) famous study of the difference between the interactions children and adults have in the home and at school, the authors analysed what they term **passages of intellectual search**, characterized by persistent questioning on the part of the *child* and the process of relating the adult's answers to existing knowledge. They found that mothers were more responsive to the questions of the child than teachers in schools and that mothers built more effectively on their child's existing knowledge, understanding and language.

The government-funded project 'Studying Pedagogical Effectiveness in Early Learning' (DfES 2002a) claimed that effectiveness is a result of the adult and child operating from a shared frame of reference that the researchers refer to as **'a mutual learning encounter'**, which includes not only the relationships and interactions between a practitioner and a child but also between the practitioner and the child's family.

Around a similar time, Siraj-Blatchford and her colleagues in their report on 'Researching Effective Pedagogy in the Early Years' (DfES 2002b) introduced the term **sustained shared thinking** (or what Bruner termed **joint involvement episodes:** Bruner 1966) to describe 'an episode in which two or more individuals 'work together' in an intellectual way to solve a problem, clarify a concept, evaluate activities, extend a narrative etc. Both parties must contribute to the thinking and it must develop and extend.' This research identified that the quality and quantity of episodes of sustained shared thinking were contingent upon the qualifications of the practitioners in the different settings within their study.

More recently (2008), Robin Alexander's research project 'Talk for Learning' has drawn on Gordon Well's use of the term 'dialogic inquiry' to speak specifically about **dialogic teaching**, which he describes as the exchange between adult and child which formulates the extent and manner of the child's cognitive development. Dialogic interactions he conceives as collective, reciprocal, supportive, cumulative and purposeful. In 2007, Mercer along with Karen Littleton adopted the term **interthinking** to describe how teachers and primary/secondary age children work together to solve problems, 'combining their intellects in creative ways that may achieve more than the sum of the parts.' (2007: 4).

These different terms describing the nature of interactions are not exclusive, but they demonstrate in their different ways how researchers and educationalists have attempted to capture the complexity that characterizes an effective educational exchange between a practitioner and a child. Throughout the duration of the Oxfordshire Adult-Child Interaction (ACI) Project, the participants discussed whether there was a project definition of 'effectiveness' that would adequately describe the findings of our research. All of the terms cited above seemed helpful at some level or other in describing the nature of an interactive episode, but most did not offer an adequate yardstick, against which judgements could be consistently made, as to whether an interaction was actually 'effective' or not. One major purpose behind the Oxfordshire

Project was to enable early years practitioners and those making judgements about the quality of their practice (headteachers; advisory staff; managers; Foundation Stage coordinators) to make evaluations about 'effectiveness' against criteria that were straightforward to apply yet rigorous to achieve. In analyzing the project's DVD material it seemed there were three criteria that were consistently applied to the judgement of 'effectiveness':

- For an interaction to be 'effective', learning has to be **enhanced**. This alone was seen as problematic for practitioners working with young children, as 'enhancing' could be appropriate in an adult-led context but sometimes result in overwhelming the child's agenda when activity was child-led (see Chapters 5 and 6).
- For an interaction to be 'effective' it has to be enhanced **by the practitioner**. This may seem obvious. But the DVD footage taken as part of the Oxfordshire research showed that on many occasions learning was enhanced by other children; by the environment or by the child's own independent enquiry. In an 'effective' interaction the practitioner must make a contribution. The contribution made by the practitioner might be cognitive, emotional, social, dispositional or metacognitive (see this chapter), but if the practitioner intervenes or interacts without any discernible impact on learning or development, then that interaction is clearly unhelpful or unnecessary.
- For an interaction to be 'effective' the child's experience must be **positive**. This helped strengthen our analysis of the difference between the role of the practitioner in adult-led and in child-led situations (see Chapter 6) and ensured that 'enhancing' did not become 'hijacking'. In addition, some of the interventions of some practitioners in our DVD footage had a negative impact on children. There were examples of children being confused, ignored, put down and criticized – none of which were outcomes that anyone would want from any adult-child interaction. So it was necessary to add that what the child gains must be positive (see Chapter 10).

By the conclusion of the project, these three criteria had fused together to create a key question (see Figure 1.1) which the project participants asked each time some DVD footage was analysed in order to begin making judgements about whether the contribution of the practitioner was appropriate, relevant and worthwhile. This key question is used to analyse the transcripts that accompany the chapters of this book.

As I have suggested, it is important to clarify that 'something positive' might not always refer to something cognitive. In keeping with the project participants'

'Did the child gain something positive from this interaction that s/he would not otherwise have had?'

Oxfordshire Adult-Child Interaction Project 2014

Figure 1.1 Key Question with which to analyse an interaction

commitment to the development of the whole child, 'something positive' might be cognitive, social, emotional, dispositional or, indeed, metacognitive. For example:

Cognitive: 'If you hold it up higher it will run down faster.'

Social: 'Maybe if you take the pen and make a chart on the board then everyone will get a turn?'

Emotional: 'Yes, your mummy went to work didn't she and then she's going coming back to collect you.'

Dispositional: 'That's great, because do you know, you couldn't do that on Monday and you've practised so hard that now it looks easy!'

Metacognitive: 'I need to think a bit about that. You're good at remembering, but sometimes I have to write things down.'

This key question gave the project participants a starting point for analysing their own practice as well as the practice of others, and also helped managers and headteachers to focus on the characteristics of early learning in order to analyse the quality of teaching in their school or setting.

Interactions in the home

I have already suggested that an inherent part of the challenge for early years educators, engaged in interactions with young children, is to 'bring about learning', when many more natural conversations – those that occur at home, for example – do not have that objective driving them. It seems, from the evidence of the Oxfordshire Project DVD material, that the very act of 'being an educator' can sometimes distort the nature of an interaction so much that it inhibits the very learning it is trying to promote. So, to begin with, it is illuminating to consider what is known from research about the effectiveness of interactions in the home. Despite the fact that parents do not have a duty to educate, many do – and very successfully. So what can be learned from interactions in the home that might improve the quality of interactions in an early years setting?

In the 1970s and 1980s a considerable amount of influential work (e.g. Tizard and Hughes 1984; Wells 1985) challenged the assumption that the nursery or school was a place that somehow compensated for the poor language experiences of many children in the home (Bernstein 1971; 1973; 1977). This research found, on the contrary, that language and conversations in the home were almost always more effective for the children because of how well the parent knew their own child (see Chapter 3). No matter what the education of the mother or the conversational style of the family, this research showed that conversations in the home (most often with the mother) were frequently more effective in bringing about development than conversations in the nursery or school, *even if this was not their purpose.*

The researchers identified the following features of talk in the home:

- Home conversations **arise from the moment**. In other words they have meaning and significance for the child because they come out of what a child has chosen to do or what has grabbed the child's attention as they engage in everyday activity. At school, conversations are more likely to originate from the teacher and be about an agenda that the teacher deems to be relevant.
- Parents usually respond to their children by **developing the child's own interests.** Conversations in the home are more often instigated by children who make comments or ask questions to which parents respond rather than the parent choosing an agenda which they expect the children to follow.
- The parent is frequently **part of the context** in which the child is exploring or thinking. In Wells' study (1985) the researchers concluded that sharing a home and daily life together provided a shared focus of attention between parent and child so that the parent was more likely to understand the purpose of the child's activity or the reason for their questions. Similarly, Tizard and Hughes' (1984) study found that in the home much of the conversation and activity between adults and children concerned everyday life and was initiated by the child in response to happenings within the situation. The parent was then uniquely able to respond to the child because she/he too was part of the context.
- Parents **intuitively adjust their utterances** to the edge of their children's linguistic competence. Cross (1977), for example, suggests that because the mother knows the child so well their language is tuned to the child's language. Sometimes new words are introduced deliberately to introduce the child to new vocabulary. But more often than not the mother instinctively matches language to action in a way that the child understands and which supports their thinking.
- The responses of parents are **'contingent' on the competence of the child.** In experiments reported by Wood (1998) where mothers and their children were using

building blocks, if a child failed to complete the required action, the most effective strategy was to increase the help given and therefore decrease the level of control experienced by the child. Wood called these responses 'contingent' because the mother would change her level of control depending on her judgement of the success or failure of the child.

• In the home, **children asked the questions** and the adults are there to supply the answers, whereas both Tizard and Hughes, and Wells, noted that in nursery and school, teachers posed a series of questions which the child was expected to answer, rather than the other way round.

Wells (1985: 33) sums up these findings very succinctly:

What these findings all suggest, then, is that what is most important in the behaviour of the child's parents and other caretakers is sensitivity to his current state – his level of communicative ability and his immediate interests – and to the meaning intentions he is endeavouring to communicate.

These major research studies remind us that there are some crucial elements of effective conversations with young children in the home that should be considered by early childhood educators if their interactions are to be equally effective. This book seeks to examine these different elements in the chapters highlighted:

1 The child is known well (see Chapter 3).
2 The environment influences the nature of interactions and allows the adult and child to share a context (see Chapter 4).
3 Parents instinctively 'tune in' to their children and interactions are contingent upon the adult's adjustments to their child's competence (see Chapter 5).
4 Most of the time, parents are responsive to the child's agenda rather than the parent leading the child with an agenda of their own (see Chapter 6).
5 Interactions are sustained because of joint interest and involvement in experiences that are often 'of the moment' (see Chapter 7).
6 Children ask the questions and parents answer them (see Chapter 9).

Language learning in the home

While it is crucial for early years practitioners to appreciate the way in which parents interact with their children, it is also crucial to understand the impact of these interactions on children's learning and, in particular, their language learning. There is increasing evidence that the amount of oral language input received by the young child in the home has a marked effect on their communication development (Chapman 2000; Hart and Risley 2002). Because most children start to acquire a vocabulary of words in the second year of life (see Chapter 2), the child's home and family usually provide the circumstances for the emergence of language and word learning. What makes Hart and Risley's research so compelling is their claim that the difference between children living in homes where parents value talk for communication and where they do not, is 'not in the kinds of experiences they provided their children but in the differing amounts of those experiences' (p.xiv). Their findings reveal that, by the time the children in their study were 3-years-old, parent utterances per hour ranged from 34 to 783. This means that within a year (working on a 14-hour waking day) some children are exposed to 250 thousand utterances versus 4 million utterances (p.70). Fewer words per hour meant fewer of everything – questions, affirmations, explanations, connections. The only feature that increased in the homes where language was used less was prohibition. In homes where children heard less talk, they correspondingly heard more negative talk e.g. 'Don't'; 'Stop; 'Quit'. The children in homes where talk was not valued heard a prohibition twice as often as they heard affirmative feedback. Hart and Risley (p.158) suggest that the amount of talk between adult and child is only part of the reason for the effectiveness of interactions in the home. Their analysis showed that:

> parents who provide more of the fundamentals, larger amounts of diverse language experiences and more encouragement to learn, tend also to add the nuances. They tend to be more responsive: they listen and prompt relative to what the child has got to say more often than they try to interest the child in adult concerns. They tend to encourage autonomy. They ask for compliance rather than demand it. They tend to make language important: they name and explain everything whether or not the child cares or understands (yet).

In 2012, Rowe made a study of the factors that contribute most to a child's later vocabulary development. She studied the vocabulary of 50 young children when they were 18, 30, 42 and 54 months of age, as well as the amount (quantity) and type (quality) of words the parents used with their children. She found that:

- *Children's vocabulary at 30 months was influenced by the quantity of words parents used one year earlier* – children aged 12–24 months benefit from hearing lots of talk and many examples of words.
- *Children's vocabulary at 42 months was influenced by parents' use of a variety of sophisticated words one year earlier* – children aged 24–36 months had learned a lot of common vocabulary and were ready to learn more difficult words such as 'purchase' instead of 'buy' or 'weary' instead of 'tired'.
- *Children's vocabulary at 54 months was influenced by parents' use of narratives and explanations, one year earlier* – children aged 36–48 months benefitted from conversations about things that happened in the past (e.g. an outing they went on, something funny that happened at preschool etc) or something planned for the near future (e.g. a trip to see grandma) or providing explanations about things (e.g. answering children's 'Why?' questions).

Moving from non-verbal to verbal communication successfully is determined by the amount, as well as the quality of children's language experiences in the home and in their early childcare settings. Practitioners who understand the critical importance of language and communication prioritize the time they spend with children to interact with them by talking, listening and responding.

Why interactions matter

If asked about a key feature of high-quality early education, most early years practitioners would immediately answer 'play'. Far fewer would say 'talk'. Yet, as Mercer and Hodgkinson (2008: xi) remind us, talk as a medium of learning has been recognized as 'the most important educational tool for guiding development and for jointly constructing knowledge'. Every working day, early years practitioners spend time in conversation with children – even in baby rooms where infants do not yet have verbal language with which to respond. So how do practitioners construct their role in these interactions? Is it the same as a parent talking to a child? If not, then what is the role practitioners play, in guiding development, in jointly constructing knowledge and in extending thinking, without overwhelming the learning agenda of the young child?

The impact of poor communication skills

From birth to age five is a critical time for the development of children's speech, language and communication. Being able to speak clearly, to understand others, to communicate ideas and feelings and to interact are the building blocks of a child's development socially, emotionally and educationally (Lee 2008). The rate of language development in these first few years of life is, like many other aspects of young children's development, dramatic. Children move from non-verbal to verbal communication because the outcomes have such significance for them, because they see a clear purpose in the practice and improvement of their burgeoning skills (Robinson 2003), and through an innate desire to communicate and to make their own individual voice heard (Gopnik et al. 1999; Smith et al. 2010).

If a young child does not develop the basic skills of speech, language and communication – for whatever reason – they are likely to be disadvantaged for life. Communication is perhaps the most valuable of all life skills, relied on by humans whether in social, personal or professional contexts – and to start life without the power to make one's own voice heard has devastating consequences. A child who struggles to speak will often struggle to access the curriculum (Dockrell et al. 2008) and particularly struggle to write (Snowling and Stackhouse 2006; Dockrell et al. 2007). Children with poor speech, language and communication can become withdrawn or exhibit challenging behaviour within the primary school environment (Hart et al. 2004). Language difficulties can impact on emotional development (Lees and Unwin 1997) and many children can be socially withdrawn (McCabe 2005); they play alone and are less liked by others in their class (Coster et al. 1999).

Then, as these children mature into young people, research by the Communication Trust (www.thecommunicationtrust.org.uk/) reveals that two-thirds of 7- to 14-year-olds with serious behaviour problems have language difficulties; 40 per cent of 7- to 14-year-olds referred to child psychiatric services have a language impairment; 65 per cent of young people in young offender institutions have communication difficulties, and many 18-year-olds not in education, employment or training struggle to communicate well (Lee 2010) and have reduced life chances (Clegg et al. 1999).

How can we, as early childhood educators, not give speech, language and communication our closest attention? How can anything matter more than stopping to interact with a child?

Why interactions matter to children entering school

In his influential report on primary education in 2006, Jim Rose claimed that it is expected that when a child starts primary school, they will be able to understand much of what is said, express themselves clearly, share their feelings and make their needs known. This level of proficiency in speech, language and communication, he suggests, is 'central to children's intellectual, social and emotional development' (2006: 3). Yet in parts of the UK, particularly in areas of social disadvantage, upwards of 50 per cent of children enter school with speech, language and communications needs (Locke et al. 2002). Some of these children are unable to speak in sentences, understand simple instructions or listen and join in with conversations either socially or during school tasks (Basic Skills Agency 2002). Spoken language is the primary medium through which teachers teach and young children learn (Lee 2008), and yet many children are unable to access this medium successfully because their skills in speech, language and communication are insufficiently developed.

The range of children's vocabulary

As we have seen, there is plenty of evidence to show that it is the level of development in language and communication that is the greatest predictor of success in later life, not in literacy. It is *vocabulary* at age five which will predict how well children achieve at the end of both Key Stage 1 and Key Stage 2 (Feinstein and Duckworth 2006); *vocabulary* at age five which is a very strong predictor of the qualifications achieved at school-leaving age and beyond (Feinstein and Duckworth 2006); and *vocabulary* at age five which has been found to be the best predictor (from a range of measures at age 5 and age 10) of whether children who experienced social deprivation in childhood were able to 'buck the trend' and escape poverty in later adult life (Blanden 2006).

Why Communication and Language is a Prime Area of Learning

This is why Communication and Language is a Prime Area of learning in the Early Years Foundation Stage (DfE 2012) while Literacy is not. Babies and young children are 'primed for' the development of Communication and Language and, along with the other Prime Areas (Personal, Social and Emotional Education and Physical Development), Communication and Language is:

- *Time sensitive*
  If not securely in place between three and five years of age the skills will be more difficult to acquire later on and their absence may hold the child back in other areas of learning.
- *Universal*
  The skills occur in all communities and cultures... they are what human beings are primed to do.

- *Independent of the Specific areas*
  The skills in the Prime areas are not dependent on the Specific areas of learning for successful development.

(These helpful headings come from Moylett and Stewart: 2012)

Why children use language at school

Children use language to communicate at school for many of the same reasons they do at home.

Children use language in order to **build strong relationships**, both with adults in their setting and with their peers. When children transfer from the security of the home environment to the demanding world of school they seek strong secondary attachments to make them feel secure in this new and challenging place (O'Connor 2013). They often turn to adults, as they do at home, for affirmation, for security and for reassurance.

Children use language in order to **communicate their ideas and their feelings**. Those who have strong language skills are better placed to say how they feel and to put forward their ideas than those whose language and experience of communication is more limited (Dowling 2013). A wide vocabulary gives children greater capacity to put forward a point of view, to express an opinion and to justify actions than children who struggle to name the thoughts and feelings they are having.

Children use language to **think creatively and critically**. At first children understand ideas by trying them out with their bodies. But once children begin to use words they have a powerful new tool for thinking. Then they begin to hold ideas in their mind to think more flexibly about things that are not physically present – e.g. what could happen next, or what might happen differently (Goddard Blythe 2005; Robinson 2008).

Children use language **as a tool for learning** (Mercer and Hodgkinson 2008). They describe and explain and reason and argue. They articulate what it is to be a learner... 'I kept trying so it got easier.'; 'Can't work... gonna join these... this way.' Language gives children the capacity to work out how to relate what is new to what already exists in their understanding. Barnes (in Mercer and Hodgkinson 2008) explains that 'the flexibility of speech makes it easy for us to try out new ways of arranging what we know, and easy also to change them if they seem inadequate' (p.5).

Children use language to **become confident with the written word**. After all, literacy is simply a process of using a recorded form of communicating with words (Stewart 2012). Having a good vocabulary; understanding sentence structure; being familiar with the language of books; are all directly related to competency in reading and writing. We simply cannot talk with our children enough. The preparation for all aspects of written language develops through one-to-one conversation with a responsive adult and, when it happens, the introduction of the technical skills of reading and writing must be at a time when it is relevant and effective for the child and when their linguistic and physical skills are securely in place (Goddard Blythe 2005).

While literacy is not the sole reason (by any means) for children to develop their skills of language and communication it can be seen that, in the school context,

having poor skills in speech, language and communication leaves young children doubly disadvantaged.

1 They will have difficulty accessing the *thinking skills* needed to explain, suggest, reason and discuss.
2 They will have difficulty accessing the *language skills* needed to read and write with meaning.

Why interactions matter to practitioners

There are many children who start school disadvantaged by a system that relies so heavily on talk for learning. No early childhood practitioner should, therefore, underestimate how vital it is that the development of language and communication is seen as central to their role as educators. Even though communication and language is a Prime area of learning, there are currently many pressures in schools to prioritize literacy over all else on the curriculum. But, as experts in child development, all early years educators should help others, less informed than themselves, to understand that:

• Communication and language development needs to come before any formal introduction to literacy (the Prime before the Specific).
• Pressure to become literate too early in a child's development will not raise standards. It will lead to failure, frustration and demotivation. This is not the road to success.

- The development of young children's communication and language comes primarily from tuning in to conversations that are meaningful to the child (see Chapters 5 and 6), not merely in planning conversations that suit the purposes of the adult.

Building warm relationships

Interactions matter to practitioners for a number of reasons. Firstly, interactions (be they verbal or non-verbal) help **build warm relationships** with young children and, as all practitioners who work with young children are aware, these relationships are at the heart of the quality of learning that is subsequently co-constructed between the practitioner and the child. Roberts (2002) reminds us that babies and young children benefit from developing strong self-esteem in order to have the confidence to be a successful learner. This self-esteem arises from relationships in which the fortunate child receives unconditional acceptance for who they are and what they are trying to achieve. Stern (1985) suggests that parents compose an 'ongoing biography' for their baby that influences how they see their baby and, ultimately, how the baby sees himself. Roberts' weekly documentation of the lives and experiences of two families over two years demonstrates vividly how 'Every time the father smiles at the baby, every time the mother is there when needed, the baby knows more certainly that he or she is accepted.' (Roberts 2002: 5)

An infant's successful attachment to their primary carer enables the young child to separate with least trauma when starting nursery or school (O'Connor 2013). The young child's capacity to form relationships, with their peers as well as with practitioners, will enable them to be more relaxed about learning and, therefore, to be more successful in the school environment. Early years practitioners need to interact with warmth and attentiveness to ensure that they build strong relationships with each of their children as the bedrock of their social, emotional and educational well-being.

Getting to know and understand children better

Conversations and interactions with young children give practitioners the knowledge they need to **know and understand children better**. The advantage of being a parent or primary carer is the opportunity to see the daily development of children which, suggest Tizard and Hughes (1984) and Wells (2009), is one reason why the quality of interactions in the home is often superior to the quality in school and nursery school. Most parents are better able to respond to children's questions and tune in to their thinking because they know their children so well. Clearly most parents have fewer children to focus on than the practitioner in the nursery or classroom, so the greater number of children in an educational setting means that practitioners have to work hard to ensure each child is spoken to and interacted with in a variety of learning contexts (see Chapter 4). The Oxfordshire ACI Project found that practitioners need to be particularly alert to children who do not want to have conversations with them. Some children are very adept at avoiding interactions, and they are often the children who need them most (see Chapter 8). Children who have English as an additional language, children who are shy, children who are not used to communicating with an adult, children with language delay may all find interacting with practitioners stressful and challenging. However, these are the very children practitioners need to be most empathetic towards and work hardest with to build a communicative relationship.

Modelling language

Effective practitioners use interactions to **model language**. Siraj-Blatchford et al. (2002) suggest that learning that takes place through imitation is often a result of the young child's desire to 'be like' and/or 'to be liked by' the person imitated. In exploring his social learning theory, Bandura (1977) claims that 'virtually all learning phenomena resulting from direct experience occur on a vicarious basis by observing other people's behaviour' (p.12). He explains that if children do not have the opportunity to hear the linguistic utterances of models, it would be virtually impossible to teach them the skills that constitute a language. So, just by engaging in regular, meaningful interactions with young children, practitioners, like parents, have the opportunity to offer phonetic, semantic and grammatical models of language, as well as corrections, in a context in which the child is reciprocally engaged. Yet children do more than just absorb and repeat words and syntax that they have heard from others. They actively construct sets of rules that will enable them to generate an almost infinite variety of new sentences. Unfortunately, for those children who learn to speak English, the structure of the language is not straightforward. The child who learns 'I phoned', or 'I walked', then generalizes to 'I runned', only to be told that this is not correct. However Gopnik et al. (1999) suggest that looking at children's mistakes shows, paradoxically, that they are learning in an intelligent way, because the mistakes reveal how conscientiously they are trying to apply the rules they have learned.

Modelling thinking

Practitioners should use interactions to **model the process of thinking**. A great deal of human thought is, of course, linguistically based. So by giving young children the power of language, practitioners also enhance their capacity for thought. Hedges' (2012) work develops recent ideas that consider young children as 'life-theorisers' who are active agents in their own inquiry into the world in which they live. Hedges explores the concept of children's 'working theories' that 'represent the tentative, evolving ideas and understandings formulated by children as they engage with others to think, ponder, wonder, learn and make sense of the world in order to participate more effectively within it' (p.144). The work of the Russian psychologist Lev Vygotsky has been particularly influential in emphasizing the role of sociocultural theory in cognitive development (2012). For Vygotsky, cognitive development results from the internalization of language as a result of the social nature of human learning. Although he sees thought and language as separate systems from the beginning of life, they merge at around the age of three years to give the young child verbal thought, which Vygotsky sees as 'inner speech'. Effective practitioners model the process of thinking, understanding that the development of metacognition (knowing about knowing) needs to be made explicit if young children are to appreciate the impact their own efforts have over their capacity to be an effective learner. The work of the American psychologist Carol Dweck and her colleagues (e.g. 1976; 2012; Benenson and Dweck 1986; Heyman et al. 1992) on 'learned helplessness' demonstrates the crucial need for practitioners working with young children to give them confidence to take control over their efforts and to see failure as a result of lack of application rather than the result of external factors such as innate (and thereby 'fixed') intelligence. Modelling to a young child that 'thinking hard'; 'trying again' (after an error); 'finding an alternative solution', and so on, are all valuable strategies that can have an impact on learning, and give the child attitudes to emulate and imitate, which will ultimately be internalized as the child 'comes to believe about (themselves) and other people as cognitive processors' (Flavell 1976: 907).

Scaffolding

Effective practitioners use interactions to **scaffold learning**. The concept of scaffolding derives from Vygotsky's notion of the 'zone of proximal development' – i.e. the gap between what a child is able to achieve alone and what s/he can achieve with help from an adult (or a more knowledgeable and skilled peer). Vygotsky has argued that the capacity to learn through instruction is a fundamental feature of human intelligence (2012), and the support given by another, who is more knowledgeable and skilled, enables the child to move from dependence to independence in their learning. Wood et al. (1976) took this concept further when they coined the term 'scaffolding' to represent the stages which are identified by a skilled adult in breaking down the structure of a learning situation into manageable steps for the child. Recently, Van de Pol et al. (2010) proposed that scaffolding involves three characteristics: a) *contingency*: responsive, tailored or adjusted support; b) *fading*: gradual withdrawal of this support over time, and c) *transfer of responsibility*: eventual handing over of responsibility for the performance of the task by the learning.

For early years educators, the concept of scaffolding seems particularly relevant for adult-led learning where the practitioner has a clear sense of the planned outcomes for the child. The support of a skilled practitioner can be beneficial in helping the child make connections, supporting their emerging skills or understandings, and helping the child to stay focused on an objective. But scaffolding can also be highly appropriate when a practitioner is supporting a child to achieve their own outcomes in child-led situations. Wood (1998) has said that when the child is left alone to learn they are 'overcome by uncertainty', not knowing what to attend to and/or what to do. Those who work alongside very young children will not recognize that image of the helpless, incompetent child, particularly when exploring or investigating their own interests and fascinations. A skilled practitioner, who knows a child well, can support the child's individual attempts to acquire a skill or achieve a goal through judicious commentary, suggestions and questions (see Chapter 9). However, no child-led situation would see a child 'overcome by uncertainty' as the power of learning that derives from a child's personal agenda lies in their remarkable capacity to stay focused and know exactly what they are trying to achieve.

Affirming and consolidating children's learning

Practitioners use interactions to **affirm and consolidate children's learning**. All those who educate young children know that there is a danger in believing that children must be constantly 'moved on' to their 'next steps'. For young children busy trying to create an internal model of the world and how it works, and assimilating vast amounts of what is new into what is already tentatively known, there needs to be plenty of time spent practising, repeating, revisiting and rehearsing. At this age and stage neither skills nor concepts are learned by being rushed. Both require patient repetition in different contexts to ensure familiarity, consistency and security. If children are rushed, they often arrive at misunderstandings, caused by trying to comprehend something new without having understood sufficiently what went before. As I have explained elsewhere (Fisher 2002) the foundations of learning are like the foundations of buildings. If we are too anxious to see the finished product then we do not pay sufficient attention to the foundations, and the building ultimately collapses. Foundations have to be broad and deep; they have to be flexible; they must compensate for buildings that are under stress. Most important of all, foundations take longer to create than buildings, so it is vital that we resist the temptation to move children on too soon and attempt to build too high, before the foundations of learning are securely in place.

Extending children's knowledge and understanding

Practitioners also use interactions to **extend children's knowledge and understanding**. Interestingly, while the Oxfordshire DVD footage showed plenty of examples of practitioners supporting and consolidating learning, there were far fewer effective examples of learning being extended. This chimes with the findings of Ofsted's 2011 report on the impact of the EYFS (Ofsted 2011) that 'practitioners missed opportunities to encourage children to explain and extend their thinking'. The report suggests that this might be because practitioners 'simply did not allow time for children to think' (an issue that is explored frequently in this book). The Oxfordshire project analysis would also suggest that when practitioners start to extend learning they often shift the agenda away from the child and towards their own intentions, thus making the interaction less relevant and effective from the child's perspective. The questions and comments from the practitioner often tend to become forced or false (see Chapter 9) and consequently, because the practitioner is not building on the child's own thinking and ideas, have less impact on the child's learning and development.

In high-quality settings, extending children's learning is achieved in one of two ways. Firstly, by adding something to the environment (see Chapter 4) so that the continuous provision is enhanced by the addition of fresh resources or the bringing together of resources in fresh configurations (small world characters in the block area for example). Secondly, by the practitioner's interactions with the child as they add something fresh to the child's thinking, planting an idea, offering a suggestion, or posing a question that builds naturally on what the child has already said, but helps the child think more deeply or differently about the world.

SUMMARY

In this chapter we have seen powerful evidence for improving the quality of interactions in all settings. Research shows clearly and unequivocally that the young child's need to communicate and to interact with others is a prime force in their lives. How each child develops, and how well they manage socially, emotionally and education-ally, depends on the adults with whom they interact. Every practitioner who listens, responds and engages with a young child's attempts at communication will help improve the quality of their language as well as their interpersonal skills, and give them effective tools for thinking, reasoning, explaining and persuading. It is crucial, therefore, that practitioners working with young children, from babies onwards, give the children in their care the time to communicate and offer them a warm and attentive response to whatever they have to say.

Interactions matter. They matter to babies and to young children, they matter to practitioners, they matter to learning and development. In the coming chapters we will see how effective practitioners develop the quality of communication and language in their nurseries and classrooms and explore different elements of effective practice in order to help you reflect on and analyse the quality of your own interactions with children. The next chapter will focus specifically on interacting with babies and toddlers.

Self reflection

1   Can I explain why talk matters so much to young children in the EYFS?

2   Do children have sufficient opportunities to communicate with me for their own purposes (rather than just for mine?)

3   Do children 'gain something positive' each time I interact with them?

2

Interacting with babies and toddlers

'One of the most powerful influences on development is what happens between people.' (Hobson 2002)

Introduction

For babies who are fortunate, a loving communication with their parent begins from birth. This communication is not based, of course, on words, but the result of what Hobson (2002) describes as a 'veritable rainbow' of gestures, sounds and facial expressions. The infant comes into the world with 'built-in capacities for initiating, maintaining and terminating social interactions with others' (Emde 1989: 38). This non-verbal communication is vital for developing the close bond that is necessary for baby – and parent – to thrive, and will lead to the exchange and understanding of meanings on which so much of the baby's development will depend.

Goouch and Powell (2013: 83) suggest that, particularly in baby rooms, the need for talk is 'fundamental to brain development and learning and applies to both babies in daycare and their young carers'. Yet interactions with babies, and with toddlers who are not yet verbal, can be challenging for practitioners. Effective interactions rely on attentive adults who are alert to the signals and messages conveyed by infants who, with sounds, gestures and facial expressions are able to communicate so much in non-verbal ways. Being responsive to the signals and messages of these very youngest children relies on practitioners who view the babies in their care as effective communicators with a great deal to say. When communication depends on so many non-verbal cues, then practitioners have to be especially attentive to ensure that they interpret the infants' messages accurately. So many of a baby's future skills in speech, language and communication will depend on the responses of the adults with whom they first converse. This chapter focuses specifically on the demanding yet rewarding interactions that take place between babies and toddlers and the practitioners who care for them.

The foundations of interactions

Birth to 2 months

The 'social brain'
The significant advances in social development made by young children in the first two years of life stem from the newborn's 'basic attraction to other people' and their 'remarkable responsiveness to others' (Murray 2014). In her beautiful book, 'The Psychology of Babies', Murray explains the development of young children's social understanding through the use of picture sequences from video footage, which clearly demonstrate newborns' remarkable capacity and desire to interact with others.

Recognising voices
Long before they are born, babies hear and can recognize voices. After months in the womb their brains are already specially attuned to the sounds of the human voice and they can already recognize the voices of their own parents. After birth, it is known that babies pay more attention to human voices than other auditory stimuli (Karmiloff-Smith 1995; Blasi et al. 2011). They are drawn to voices and the faces that produce them, and very quickly learn to use their own voice to signal what they need.

Looking at faces
Newborn babies also like to look at faces or objects that resemble faces (de Hann et al. 2001). From birth, says Murray (2014), babies show a strong tendency to respond to any human characteristic concerned with making social connections. A baby's vision is just right to see a face when it is held in a carer's arms, while everything else remains blurred (Robinson 2009). In the first three months of life, babies find it difficult to turn their attention to any stimulus on the periphery of their vision, a state which is called 'sticky fixation'. This state, suggests Robinson, may actually support the baby's ability to familiarize itself with specific faces without the distraction of other visual stimuli.

Eye gaze
Being able to recognize others is not the only reason why babies pay particular attention to faces. Eye gaze direction is crucial in helping infants discover what others are attending to and in showing others what they themselves are attending to (Robinson 2008; Karmiloff-Smith 2010; Murray 2014). In the early months, babies will learn to follow others' gaze, to predict that something interesting must be attracting another's attention and look in the same direction. It is necessary first to establish mutual gaze. If the adult's face is already averted towards another location, the baby will not follow the direction of the gaze (Senju and Csibra 2008). The baby must first see the face looking directly at him (what psychologists call 'dyadic attention') before he will follow the averted eye gaze. Karmiloff-Smith suggests that this has important implications for shared attention and for object naming. If a practitioner establishes mutual gaze with the baby, then moves her eyes to an object and checks that the baby is looking in the same direction (what psychologists call 'triadic attention') she can then name the object: 'Look, yes, it's a tractor.'

Being held

When babies are held closely by their parent or by their Key Person (see Chapter 3), it has been found that their heart rates 'synchronise'. Robinson (2009) draws attention to the fact that most babies are held on the left-hand side allowing for this heart-to-heart connection. In caring for a distressed crying baby, Goldschmied and Jackson (1994) elaborate on the importance of carers regulating their own breathing to reduce stress and to regain their composure so that their agitation is not communicated to the baby in the tension of their hold. The authors recommend that practitioners 'listen intently, perhaps telling the baby in your quietest gentlest voice… give soft massage rather than agitated pats jiggling up and down and anxious chatter…' (p.76). Rocking or gently massaging a baby are all ways of communicating with a young infant that underpin early language development. When a carer holds out their arms asking the baby if they are tired or hungry, this initiates a 'conversation' which includes and involves the child (Manning-Morton 1994).

Touch

Robinson (2008: 54) suggests there is 'universal acceptance that as babies, soothing touching, confident handling and cuddles are a necessary part of care'. In the first few weeks after birth, much parent-baby communication takes place through touch. Contact occurs as parents bathe, feed, hold and stroke their infants, settling them to sleep or soothing them when they are distressed. Although these acts of touching do not always involve face-to-face engagement, Murray (2014: 9) suggests that there is, nevertheless, a kind of communicative exchange as parents 'adjust their touch to the baby's state and signals, and babies similarly adjust their behaviour in response'.

Touch is generally 'suffused with emotional meaning' (Robinson 2008: 49) and can convey anything from empathy to aggression. The experiences we have of being touched when we are very young stay with us and manifest themselves in our tolerance for touching and being touched as we get older. In some instances the baby may not be averse to touch in general, but may be adverse to who is doing the touching as not every adult finds touch in this emotional/caring sense easy or natural, and babies sense this. Goldschmied and Jackson (1994) advocated personalized care as an antidote to the intimate physical care of a child being handled by any and many different adults. Laying the foundations for the Key Person Approach, Goldschmied and Jackson say that real sociability comes through the experience of the reliable affection of a few close people. The authors address the sensitive issue of respectful touch in bathroom routines, saying that 'Our body image is something precious and entirely personal to each one of us and our attitude towards ourselves is deeply bound up with our early experiences at the hands of adults' (p.113).

Imitation

Imitation plays a powerful role, both physically and socially, in the interactions between infant and child. It is the existence of mirror neurons in the brain that allow a 'match' between what the infant sees and the establishing of a pattern of action within his or her motor or sensory systems (Robinson 2008). This capacity to imitate is all the more remarkable because the baby has yet to see his own face and, therefore, relies entirely on being able to match what he sees the other person do with what he feels of his own facial movement (Murray 2014). Trevarthen claims that 'all children are equipped by their nature with eagerness to learn in conscious collaboration' (2002: 17) and that 'the newborn imitates expressions of voice, face and gesture conversation-ally... and with anticipation of appropriate qualities of response' (p.22). Kaye suggests that, to begin with, there is asymmetry in the relationship between the parent and their baby that means any communication is at first created by the parent, who interprets the infant's expressive reactions 'as if' they were meaningful, which in time leads the infant to become 'an intelligent partner in intersubjective communication' (1982: 53). Whatever the motivation, and whoever leads the exchange, what these early face-to-face contacts do is help 'establish a sense of close emotional engagement and a 'conversational' setting, where the parent makes sense of their baby's expressiveness and communicates their empathy and understanding, laying the foundations for later, more obviously social, communication' (Murray 2014: 10).

Attunement

Interacting with babies goes way beyond a mere physical exchange. Researchers concerned with the impact of the emotional connectedness between parents or carers and babies, refer to the importance of 'attunement' whereby the carer 'lets the child know his or her emotions are met with empathy, are accepted and (if appropriate) reciprocated' (Rose and Rogers 2012: 41). When a baby is newborn then the urge to have his or her needs met is intense (Underdown 2007), and the parent's response to a baby's cries can help soothe and contain the baby's emotions. It is as though the parent 'takes on board' the baby's powerful feelings and, by communicating with touch, gesture and speech, makes them more manageable (Bion 1962). Winnicott (1960) describes how children become secure in their relationships when they are 'held in mind' by the important adults in their life. It is the way in which caregivers respond to an infant emotionally which determines how the infant ultimately views their own emotions and whether they perceive those emotions to be acceptable. Goleman (1995: 100) says that it is the 'countless repeated moments of attunement or misattunement between (carer) and child' which shape the child's emotional well-being.

Attachment

Ideally, says Underdown (2007: 41), 'infants learn that they can rely on the main adults in their social network to help alleviate their stress and to share their joy and sense of fun'. Because survival is the primary goal of the dependant infant, the infant turns to the parent as a source of security and protection. If the parent gives the infant the 'secure base' that they need, then the infant forms an attachment that has such an impact on the infant's well-being that these feelings of security and protection last into adulthood (Bowlby 1988; Gerhardt 2004). When the needs of the infant are met, this in turn brings satisfaction and pleasure to the parent and so the relationship between baby and adult continues to be strengthened. O'Connor (2013: 3) suggests that a baby's attachment to his or her parent comes from more than the adult just knowing that the baby needs care, but that 'the baby is triggering something within the parent's brain that provides the drive to respond and care for them'.

Sadly this is not the case for all children. Some parents are unable to respond in positive ways to the needs, let alone the distress, of their babies. A baby's cries for attention can trigger negative responses in a parent, or a practitioner, who has over-whelming emotional needs of their own. Sometimes this causes the carer to become angry and withdraw from the child rather than leading them to respond and to care. For some it may be experiences in their own childhood which make it difficult for them to relate to the baby (Hobson 2002), for others it may be that the baby's temperament poses a challenge that they find hard to meet (Sutter et al. 2003), while some mothers may experience postnatal depression (Morrell and Murray 2003). Some carers find it difficult to be consistent in their care, and respond erratically, sometimes giving the infant what they need and sometimes not. If these more negative responses are repeated then the infant learns that the adult is not reliable and the infant has to live with an unhealthy level of uncertainty (Cairns 2002; Schofield and Beck 2006). This can cause the infant's brain to become flooded with cortisol, a stress hormone, which often leads to the infant becoming even more agitated and demanding.

When babies do not attach securely to their parent or Key Person, then different behaviours emerge instinctively or are developed by the young child to cope. Some babies and young children become withdrawn and do not attempt to engage with the carer. At the other end of the spectrum, some become so anxious that they constantly demand attention to ensure they are not 'forgotten' again (Schofield and Beck 2006). These behaviours place a great strain on the parent and also on any practitioners who seek to build a healthy relationship with that child in the future.

A securely attached child is building up an image of themselves 'as someone who is lovable and well-loved' (O'Connor 2013: 5). Because of this they are able to cope when things do not go well and when they become emotional about events or relationships. The securely attached child 'may well get upset, angry, sad or anxious, (but) they trust others to help them and they do not stay agitated for too long. They are building that all-important "emotional resilience" that is essential for good mental health.'

How carers can respond to the infant from birth to age 2 months:

- Be alert to, and interpret, what the baby is trying to communicate.
- Talk to the baby about what you are doing and what you are thinking.
- Use a sing-song, high-pitched tone of voice, exaggerated facial expressions and wide-opened eyes when interacting (motherese). These types of behaviour capture the baby's attention and help them to keep focused on interacting (Gable 2010).
- Because the baby is not attending to the meaning of specific words, make your sentences longer and less repetitive than they will be later on.
- Make eye contact as you talk to the baby, smiling, singing and interacting all the time.
- Mirror the baby's sounds, expressions and gestures, and see if they imitate yours.
- When the baby vocalizes, listen and respond, taking turns in the beginnings of a 'conversation'.

The development of interactions

From 2 months to 6 months

Primary intersubjectivity

Research suggests that as babies, humans are biologically wired to 'coordinate their actions with others' (Stone et al. 2012). The reciprocal relationship between mother (usually) and infant, often referred to as intersubjectivity, facilitates all manner of social, emotional and cognitive learning for the infant. Intersubjectivity emphasizes that personal relations are about sharing experiences with others, about connecting with someone else and making reciprocal emotional contact (Hobson 2002: 61). Through their interactions, both parent and child are concerned with developing and co-creating shared understanding, each contributing to a place of 'harmonious interpenetrating mix up' (Balint 1992: 66). Intersubjectivity is not only concerned with communicating messages, feelings and intentions but, as the infant becomes older, also involves a growing awareness of the perspectives of the other person.

From around the second month, babies clearly begin to communicate for social reasons. Rather than gazing neutrally at his parent, the infant becomes far more attentive and can concentrate for longer periods of time. He actively seeks eye-contact and will match his parent's expressions and increasingly follow his looks to them with 'smiles, vocalisation and hand gestures, as well as the more deliberate and well-formed mouth and tongue movements that are described as 'pre-speech' (Murray 2014: 11). This period of increased social engagement is termed 'Primary Intersubjectivity'. Trevarthen (1993; 1998) describes primary intersubjectivity as the active and imme-diate response by an infant to an adult's communicative intentions. Trevarthen and Aitken (2001) suggest that:

> In measured and predictable cycles of response to regular time patterns in the adult's behaviour, the infant moves its face, hands and vocal system to modified patterns of adult vocal expression. (p.6)

Trevarthen and Aitken believe that in appropriate conditions – if a newborn is alert, rested, free of stress and with a sensitive caregiver – then primary intersubjectivity is discernible from birth. Not everyone accepts these conclusions, which rely on the interpretation of detailed video records (Smith et al. 2010), but certainly by the time the infant reaches its second month, sociability accelerates and their relationship with their primary carer reflects the baby's 'striking drive towards and capacity for social communication' (Murray 2014: 11).

At around three to four months babies' visual acuity improves dramatically. Whereas previously they were able to see objects in focus around 22–30 cm away, a baby's vision by this time is approximately the same as an adult's (Murray 2014). The baby's increased capacity to see further afield stimulates their curiosity to engage with objects and other people in the world around them. Babies cease, for example, to engage in the same high level of eye-contact with their parent, and will enjoy look-ing around, perhaps becoming absorbed exploring something within easy reach. The baby's interests and motives during social engagements change, and spurred on by these developments, parents find different ways of communicating with them. For example, parents can introduce body games such as 'Pat-a-cake Pat-a-cake' or 'Round and round the garden'. These rhymes often have a musical, rhythmic structure because it is known that babies of this age show an increasing sensitivity to melodic contours and to rhythmic changes (Robinson 2008) and the rhymes often have a climatic end that focus on a part of the baby's body or end with a noise or a clap or explosive sound.

Mirroring and marking

Inevitably, as a baby's expressiveness during face-to-face interactions develops, par-ents become more interested in and engaged in supporting their baby's social behav-iour. Parents will often mirror their baby's sounds, gestures or actions, thereby sending positive signals demonstrating their interest and attentiveness. Parents also show facial 'marking' of their baby's signals which, 'unlike mirroring, are not imitative but… highlight particular baby actions and affirm them' (Murray 2014: 11). By responding with particular enthusiasm to particular gestures, sounds or expressions, the parent emphasizes that these are of significance and, over time, their responses signal to the baby that certain actions bring about certain (desirable) reactions (Weitzman and Greenberg 2002). Marking is significant in the development of interactions because it 'demonstrates similar features to those between conversational partners, where the baby is given time to express himself and where the parent then makes comments such as 'Oh I see' or 'Is that right?', 'as though highlighting his behaviour as significant and a real contribution to a two-way conversation' (Murray 2014: 13). Both mirroring and marking create a connectedness between the parent and the infant. They help to sustain the baby's involvement and enjoyment and are the foundations of all future communicative exchanges.

Social sensitivity

During this period of two to four months, babies become increasingly sensitive to the nature of face-to-face interactions. Experimental studies show that babies are affected by abnormal or unexpected behaviour on the part of their social partner. The seminal 'still face experiment' (Tronick et al. 1978) demonstrates that there is an 'expectation' in even very young infants that there will be some kind of similarity between the way that they are behaving and their carers' response. This experimental procedure, used with infants from 2 months to 9 months, involves three phases: (1) the mother interacts normally with her baby, face-to-face; (2) she follows an instruction to assume a still or poker face and to remain unresponsive to her infant; (3) she returns to a natural social interaction. Even at 2 months the outcomes are dramatic. Two-month-olds faced with an unresponsive mother become sober and look away. After repeated attempts to bring the mother out of immobility the infant eventually withdraws. Kogan and Carter (1996) studied the ways in which infants differ in the final recovery phase of the procedure. Four-month-olds of sensitive mothers re-engaged smoothly following the stiff face. By contrast, infants of less sensitive mothers tended to turn away from or seemingly reject their mothers when the still face phase had ended.

Babies of this age also fail to show their normal smiles if the sequence of steps in a familiar game, like 'Peek-a-boo', is changed, or if the adult ends the game with an inappropriate emotion (for example, looking sad, angry or fearful). By contrast, when more natural changes occur – as, for example, when the adult simply turns away to talk to someone or to look at something nearby – the baby is unperturbed and generally watches with quiet, positive interest. So it seems that infants' attempts to regulate their own emotions depend on the emotional availability of their parents or carers (Murray 2014).

How carers can respond to the infant aged 2 months to 6 months:

- Talk to the baby about what is happening, what they might be looking at, what you are doing.
- Give meaning to the baby's efforts to communicate – 'Oh, you don't look happy, it must be time for your bottle'; 'That's such a big smile. You like this book, don't you?'
- Make the most of the times when you and the baby are facing each other – e.g. changing nappies, mealtimes or singing. Babies are fascinated by adult faces and love to look at them when they are close.
- Pay attention to the baby's unique way of expressing emotions, preferred level of activity and tendency to be social (Gable 2010).

- Follow the baby's focus of interest and comment on it.
- Establish eye contact, raise your eyebrows and smile and communicate in enthu-siastic 'motherese' in order to signal that something interesting is happening.
- Laugh and have fun with the baby – the more you smile, the more they will smile in return.
- Give the baby plenty of time to respond and to take the initiative in communicating.
- Be responsive to the baby's emotional signals and interpret what they are trying to tell you.
- Sing songs and nursery rhymes, especially those with repetition and actions; use body games to create a shared focus of fun.

From 6 months to 9 months

Spoken language and communication

By this stage in their development infants are communicating intentionally and most have become very sociable (Weitzman and Greenberg 2002). The 9- to 12-month-old begins to babble, producing a string of consonants such as 'dadadadadada'. He begins to understand his first words and responds to the naming of objects, showing recogni-tion if an adult says 'car' or 'teddy'. The infant at this stage also begins to use gestures in association with simple words, such as waving and saying 'bye-bye'. He can relate some gestures to the appropriate context, such as raising his arms when he wants to be picked up. There is evidence that the infant can now remember the location of hid-den objects, widening the possibilities for parents and carers to play games of hide and seek, especially with favourite toys. Imitation becomes much more proactive and the infant picks up and repeats words in the way that previously he imitated expressions, sounds and gestures.

Secondary Intersubjectivity

During this stage the baby shifts from making his needs known (to be fed, changed, touched, loved) to making his desires known. To begin with, if the infant wants a favourite toy, he will simply look towards it, possibly lean in its direction, and make noises to express the desire to have it in his hands. The parent or carer is left to inter-pret what these gestures and sounds might mean as the infant is not yet ready to look at his parent or carer to signal that what he wants is help in getting his toy.

Towards the end of this stage, the infant's social development takes another shift. He moves from Primary Intersubjectivity (the active and immediate response to another's communicative intentions) to Secondary Intersubjectivity, when an object or event become a focus between the parent or carer and the infant. This means that the infant becomes aware that the adult is connected not only to himself, but to objects and events in the world around. The infant is becoming 'conscious of the other's con-sciousness' (Hobson 2002: 63). Stern (1985) proposes the emergence of the 'intersubjec-tive self' around 9 months of age, in which the infant is thought to notice that others are affected by his agency just as he is affected by the agency of others. In this way, suggests Stern (2004), 'Two minds create intersubjectivity. But equally, intersubjectivity shapes the two minds.' Trevarthen (1993; 1998) and Hubley (Trevarthen and Hubley 1978) define secondary intersubjectivity as coordinating and sharing with another person one's attention, feelings and intentions toward an object, event, or action. There are many experimental studies (e.g. Phillips et al. 2002; Behne et al. 2005; Sommerville and Woodward 2005) showing a developmental transition at 9 months in self-awareness, emotional communication, attachment behaviour and cognition. These studies are fundamental in establishing that particular forms of infant behaviour reveal developmental changes in self- and other-awareness.

Within the first 6 to 9 months, babies begin to anticipate the actions of their parent or carer (Robinson 2008) and their gaze will dart ahead in anticipation of what is about to take place – for example, looking to the fridge when their parent goes into the kitchen for a snack. Babies can even seem surprised if they see someone showing an interest in one object (looking at it or pointing to it) and then apparently changing their goal by picking up and holding a different object (Murray 2014). Importantly, says Murray, much of the baby's understanding of the intentions behind what other people do develops in line with his ability to do the same things himself. Thus, 'once babies start to grab hold of things or begin pointing, they become able to see the goal of others' grasping and pointing; when they can crawl themselves, they can anticipate another crawling baby's path of movement' (p.26).

The baby develops other behaviours too that support his growing awareness of himself as a focus of others' interest. The 6- to 7-month-old baby begins to develop a repertoire of his own 'party tricks' and uses them in increasingly complex ways to negotiate his social interactions. These party tricks often begin unintentionally, with an action or a noise that cause his parent to laugh or respond positively to what he has done. When the baby experiences this positive response, he then begins to do the same action or noise deliberately to provoke the positive response over and over again. Humour, teasing and jokes tell us a great deal about children's level of development and what is on their minds (Kutner 2013). As they mature, young children learn to use humour, not only for its intrinsic value but also for what it does for relationships and interactions (Cunningham 2004).

How carers can respond to the infant aged 6 months to 9 months:
- Take every opportunity to interact with the baby.
- Talk to the baby and then pause to allow the baby to respond.
- Take the baby's gestures, sounds and expressions as serious attempts to communicate and respond accordingly – talking, smiling and responding to show you are trying to interpret what the baby has communicated to you.
- At this stage make your sentences shorter and more repetitive.
- Use words consciously to start to broaden the baby's vocabulary; name objects while your gaze and the baby's gaze are in the appropriate direction.
- Match your comments to the baby's focus.

- Be aware of how much the baby is beginning to imitate what you say and what you do... and be a good role model.
- Use the proper names of objects – e.g. 'the ball', rather than 'it', 'that' or 'them'.
- Use actions with words, such as waving when you say 'bye-bye' or holding up your hands out to the baby and saying 'up'.
- Respond positively to all the baby's attempts to link words and actions together: 'Oh I can see you want me to pick you up!'

From 9 months to 12 months

Spoken language and communication

As children approach one year of age their capacity for language increases dramatically. While babies may only be able to produce a few words at this point, it is important to remember that they can comprehend far more. In fact researchers have found that babies begin to understand language about twice as fast as they learn to actually speak. Communication by this stage is intentional; babies have become very sociable and have moved to a phase where communication is connected up – both with others and with objects. This means that the baby has begun to develop a greater understanding of other people's experiences of the world, and to connect others' experience of the world with his own. By nine to ten months, most children understand the names of many of the important people in their lives, including their own, and know the names of many significant objects e.g. 'ball'; 'bed'; 'car'. Even if they cannot yet pronounce words accurately, they are beginning to use sounds consistently that have a specific meaning – for example, 'uck' might mean 'look'. Some children at this stage may be saying a few simple words and certainly they will increasingly be attempting to imitate adult speech. Their increasing ability to establish 'joint attention' with their parent or carer means that the focus of an interaction can be jointly maintained. One pleasurable development at this stage is the baby's ability to take turns during games and songs such as 'Row, row, row your boat'. This turn taking is crucial as babies move towards competence in being true conversational partners.

Increased mobility

As babies reach their first year, many will become increasingly mobile. The mobile baby can crawl, pull to standing, and some may be taking their first steps. This combines with the emergence of simple depth perception in most children by age 12 months (Robinson 2008). This increasing capacity to explore the world, and improved visual coordination, leads to an increase in curiosity as more of the world is within the baby's reach. With more to reach and see and grasp there are greater opportunities for adults to comment on, to name and to describe what the child sees and feels and hears. As the infant develops still further the concept of shared interactions, he responds to any conversational responses to his own exclamations and initiations. These exchanges with an interested and attentive adult provide many opportunities for the young child to express his feelings through facial expressions, bodily movements and vocalisations (Robinson 2008).

Social referencing

From around the age of 10 months infants become generally more aware of other people's responses, particularly those of their primary carer. They begin to use the reactions of others to guide their own behaviour, looking towards their parent or carer for a response to help them deal with a new experience. They need the adult to assess the situation and give them a positive or negative reaction, so that they know how to proceed (O'Connor 2008). It might be that the young child looks for guidance before acting – is it safe to walk through this gate; touch this fire; pick up this paper? Or it might also be that they are looking to see their adult's emotional reaction – does mum like this person; is it safe to be with this dog? Social referencing relies on a child's ability to read facial expressions (which is why children on the autistic spectrum fail to use it as a cue) and once a child has reached this stage of development they are likely to copy the reaction they see on the face of their carer. Infants not only use social referencing to establish boundaries – it can also lead to establishing how they will react in similar situations. For example, a mother's horrified scream and subsequent fuss when her child falls over may establish a similar pattern of behaviour on the part of the child whenever this occurs again. It is interesting that, as the infant's social acumen develops, there comes a point when the child looks for the adult's reaction, grins, and does the complete opposite, seeing how far his behavioural boundaries can be pushed.

Social referencing is frequently considered to be primarily a visual phenomenon (Recchia 1997). In one of the first experiments to show how an infant's behaviour is guided and regulated by his parent's responses, known as the 'Visual Cliff', the infant crawls over an acrylic surface providing invisible support over an apparent drop. The infant's mother is looking across at him from the other side. At first she is asked to display expressions of fear and anxiety, and then expressions of confidence and cheerfulness (Sorce et al. 1985). Most infants crossed the 'cliff' if their mother's expression was confident or cheerful, but not when fearful or anxious. Interestingly, in replicating the visual cliff scenario with 12-month-olds (Vaish and Striano 2004), the babies received different cues from their mothers about how to respond, and the infants who responded fastest were those who received facial *plus* vocal cues, rather than just vocal or just facial. In a further study by Moses et al. (2001) they found that 12- to 18-month-old infants would use vocalisations of an adult (positive, such as 'nice!'; 'wow!'; or negative such as 'liuu!' or 'yeech!') to modulate their behaviour with a strange toy. These findings suggest that vocal cues, even without a visual reference, are more potent than facial clues in guiding infants' behaviour.

Stranger anxiety

This increased awareness of others leads babies around this stage of development to demonstrate a clear distinction between the people with whom they feel safe and secure, and unfamiliar adults of whom they they are wary or fearful (Murray 2014). As we have seen, throughout their first eight months or so, infants develop a special attachment to their parents, the basis of which impacts on the quality of all future relationships. But around 9 to 12 months, the infant who was happy to be close to unfamiliar people suddenly becomes far more cautious and apprehensive. If left in the company of an unfamiliar person the previously contented baby now shows anxiety and will often fret until the familiar figure of their parent or carer returns. In the 1970s, the psychologist Mary Ainsworth and her colleagues (Ainsworth et al. 1978) developed a research technique to assess the quality of attachment in 12- to 18-month-old children. Known as the 'Stranger Situation Test', it allowed researchers to observe children's reactions and patterns of behaviour when left in an unfamiliar place with an unfamiliar adult. The way that the child responded to being separated and united with their parent was seen as an indicator of the security of the attachment. As O'Connor (2013) explains, because a securely attached child has built up a memory of the parent as someone who keeps them safe, at this age they will likely cry when the parent leaves and generally be happy when they return. An insecurely attached child might either be ambivalent about the parent leaving or even distressed at their return. As the young child develops socially and emotionally, it is important that parents and carers understand the significance of the attachments that children develop in their earliest months and how this ultimately leads to the child becoming both confident and independent of those in their immediate circle.

How carers can respond to infants age 9 months to 12 months:

- Copy the baby when he is babbling, take turns, and 'have a conversation'.
- Use language all the time to talk, describe and explain things to the baby.
- Repeat the words the baby says and enhance them – the baby says 'car', you say 'Here's the red car.'
- Respond to the baby's pointing, making every effort to understand the messages they are trying to give.
- In conversation with the baby, always pause to let him/her have a chance to 'speak'.
- Be thoughtful about the 'messages' you give the baby, especially when they are looking at you to see how you react to situations or people.
- Remember that the baby relies on you for their security and turns to you for reassurance in unfamiliar situations and with unfamiliar people.
- Continue to expand the baby's repertoire of songs, rhymes and stories that allow the child to 'have a turn'.
- Sing action rhymes such as 'Incy wincy spider' and 'Round and round the garden' that use the body to tell a story.

From 12 months to 18 months

Spoken language and communication

By the end of this stage most children will be able to say around 20 familiar words such as 'milk', 'car', 'more'. Words are often used in a baby way – 'wa-wa', for a favourite blanket, for example – so that strangers or relatives might not be able to understand, but the parent or carer usually does (Lee 2008). It is often the case that the toddler uses one word for a whole range of different purposes. 'Dadda', for instance, could mean 'dadda's gone', 'dadda's coat', 'pick me up dadda' – or it could mean 'all men'. The toddler at this stage of development usually understands some simple phrases, often the ones they hear a lot during the day such as 'coat on', 'lunchtime' or 'all gone'. The toddler will persevere if not responded to, finding better ways to express himself until he gets the response he wants. It is at this stage that the toddler really enjoys action songs like 'I had a little turtle' or 'Miss Polly had a dolly'.

Social connections and interaction

As the toddler matures, he displays further evidence of his awareness of others as they relate to him as a person and to objects in the world. There emerges an appreciation that others have feelings and a growing understanding of the intentions of the goal-directed actions of others (Robinson 2008). At this stage the toddler begins wanting to give things to others. For example, he may hand a cup to his dad who, in turn, hands it back to him, only to have it returned by the toddler who gets great pleasure in repeating this activity many times.

This secondary intersubjectivity is further demonstrated as the toddler takes a more reciprocal part in playing. Before this stage it is normally the parents who set the scene for a game and orchestrate the moves, but now the toddler begins to take on the same roles as his parents have previously done. One of the video sequences illustrating Murray's book (2014) shows Ben (age 12 months) hiding his face with the cloth used to wipe his hands after lunch (a game his mother has instigated many times before). His mother supports the game structure by saying a big, anticipatory 'ahhhh…', before sharing the 'boo' with the delighted Ben as he removes the cloth from his face.

Pointing

It is at this time that toddlers demonstrate their new-found skill of pointing. The toddler realizes that there is an association between themselves, an object, and the other person, and uses this knowledge to draw the adult's attention to the object of interest. An infant points in one of two ways:

- *imperative* **pointing**: which really means 'I want' – such as pointing at a cup, book or toy
- *declarative* **pointing**: when the child points to something of interest in order to draw another's attention to it… such as a tractor, balloon or bird.

What is crucial about this ability to point is that it demonstrates an understanding, on the part of the very young child, of shared interests and joint attention. The baby has its first inklings of 'you', 'me', 'we', and realizes that he can draw someone's attention to something he is interested in. This is the first major step towards the development of a 'theory of mind', which is basically an understanding of other people's mental states and that they, too, have beliefs, desires and intentions that underpin their behaviour (see '18 months to 24 months' below).

How carers can respond to the child aged 12 months to 18 months:

- Respond to any conversational opener from the toddler – modelling two-way communication is crucial.
- If the toddler is pointing at something, tell them what it is – 'It's a baby!' – and enhance this where possible – 'I wonder if she's going to the shops like us?'
- If the child says a two-word sentence, respond with a longer sentence – e.g. 'Dadda's coat'… 'I think dadda's coat is in the cupboard.'
- Tune in to the toddler, even when they are hard to understand. They are trying to get across a message and will be frustrated if your response does not attempt to understand what this is.
- Share books together, as stories are an excellent way into conversations.
- Look at photos together, another great way of starting a conversation.
- When having these 'conversations', make sure you are responding to what the *toddler* finds interesting rather than asking a lot of questions about what *you* think is interesting.
- Spend lots of time outside together talking, listening and exploring – there's so much to talk about in the outside world.

From 18 to 24 months

Spoken language and communication

Around their second year, most children will undergo a vocabulary spurt, increasing their word knowledge to around 200 words (although as we have seen in Chapter 1, the number of words used by a child is influenced by the number of words spoken to the child). By this stage, the young child will probably be using two-word sentences. These 'sentences' frequently refer to a number of possible scenarios – for example, 'Mummy's hat' might refer to 'There's mummy's hat'; 'I want mummy's hat'; 'Mummy's putting her hat on". Many parents and carers will be familiar with the fact that it is at that this stage that children learn the word 'No'. They often use strong negatives – 'No' or 'Not' – at the beginning of sentences to emphasize their feelings or ideas. It is also around this stage that children start asking questions, especially 'What?' and 'Where?' and, in return, they understand simple questions e.g. 'Where's your book?' If they are using language alongside an attentive and responsive adult, this means that the child begins to engage in brief spoken conversations.

Theory of Mind

Through their increasingly sophisticated interactions with parents, carers and siblings, the young child learns to coordinate different perspectives on the world, and learns to view situations more objectively. Having an understanding of other people as people who have desires, beliefs and their own interpretations of the world is often referred to as having a 'Theory of Mind' (Smith et al. 2010). The term 'theory' reminds us that we cannot see or touch the mind and can only infer (or theorize) about the mental state of another from what they say or how they behave. Because it involves emotions, desires, deceptions, beliefs and differing perspectives, it is also virtually impossible to define with any precision, which is why psychologists disagree about when a child is capable of this mental state. Until relatively recently, many psychologists considered that the child's ability to appreciate that another person could hold a belief about the world that differs from what the child himself knows to be true (that is, that the other person holds a 'false belief') was achieved only around 4 years of age – the age when, given certain tests, children gave correct answers to questions about other people's 'false beliefs' (Wimmer and Perner 1983). However, Murray (2014: 35) claims that this view is changing, and studies now show that within the first two years the young child not only becomes able to grasp important elements of others' experience but, towards the end of this period, has an intuitive sense of the fact that others may have different experiences from his own, including having 'false beliefs' about the world.

Playing games

Around the age of 12 months children's pretend play develops, giving many opportunities for interactions to become playful as well as meaningful. To begin with, the child plays at being himself – for example, pretending to curl up and go to sleep. He performs pretend actions, on himself using real-life objects or realistic looking toys, such as pretending to drink from a cup or eat with a spoon. Nearer 18 months the child is able to perform pretend actions on others, such as brushing a doll's hair or offering a toy phone to his parent or carer. He is also able to perform the same action on two different people, dolls or toys – for example, feeding himself with a spoon and then feeding the dinosaur with a spoon. Some children at this stage are able to substitute a toy object for the real object, but the toy has to look similar to the 'real thing' or the child won't be able to pretend with it.

In their second year the young child's sense of humour really develops (Cunningham 2004) and he engages happily in teasing those he feels secure with. Teasing shows the child's awareness that the other person's experience is something that can be manipulated. The child offers the parent something – such as a toy – and then, at the last minute, withdraws their hand and hides it behind their back so the book cannot be 'seen'. The responsive adult reacts with a look of exaggerated shock and disappointment which results in much pleasure and laughter on the part of them both. Essential to teasing is the collaboration between the child and his parent or carer, with the adult 'typically giving clear signals in the form of pretend shock expressions, that their disappointment is not serious' (Murray 2014: 35).

As these social and interactive skills become all the more developed, babies show their awareness of the links between their own experience and that of other people through deception. This can be playful, as when the child hides from a parent or carer, but it also occurs when the child wants to do something or have something that the adult may not want. Murray (2014) reports that one technique commonly reported by parents is when the child tries to distract them while attempting to get something he is not meant to have. This often takes the form of him establishing eye contact with the parent, and actively holding their gaze so that they do not look at what his hands are doing in the meantime. Such strategies reflect quite sophisticated social understanding since they involve children's deliberate efforts to manipulate other people's perspectives on their own behaviour.

How carers can respond to a child aged 12 months to 24 months:

- Respond quickly and predictably to toddlers' communicative efforts – e.g. 'You're pointing at the fridge. Is it time for some juice?'; 'Bah-bah? I'll go and find your blanket.' (Gable 2010)
- Continue to expand on and enhance toddlers' one- and two-word communications and build sentences round their words – e.g. 'Hot. That's right. The soup is hot. It's been on top of the oven.'; 'Bubbles. Yes, there are lots of bubbles in your bath. They've made your legs disappear!'
- Give toddlers one direction at a time and provide warnings before transitions – e.g. 'We're going to leave for the shops soon.'; 'OK, it's time to get ready for the shops now.' 'Go and get your coat from the cupboard.'; 'Oh good – you've got your coat on. Off we go the shops.'
- Label toddlers' emotions – e.g. 'When you fall and get hurt, you feel sad.'; 'Playing with Pepa (the dog) makes you feel happy – doesn't it.'
- Make the most of daily routines and talk toddlers through routines in the sequence in which they happen – e.g. 'First we put some water in the paddling

pool.'; 'Now you need to take your clothes off.'; 'Get into the pool and I'll splash you with the water!'
- Engage in pretend play with the toddler, following their lead and letting them remain in control of the play – e.g. 'Oh, you're taking the pram to the shops. Can you get me some eggs?"; 'Here comes the truck to take the car to the garage.'
- Engage in songs and rhymes to do with body parts as children can now name around six to eight body parts of their own.

Summary

Interactions with babies and toddlers rely on skilled and sensitive interpretation by carers – both parents and practitioners – of the meanings and intention of young children's gestures, facial expressions and emerging language. The quality of those interactions are determined by the attachments that babies make in their earliest days as they turn to their parent expecting to have their most basic needs met. If babies find that their parent is unresponsive or unreliable, then all future interactions will be based on uncertainty and insecurity. This may make relationships with other adults, and with other children, difficult to form.

The capacity of babies and toddlers to develop strengths in speech and language depends on the linguistic responses of parents and practitioners to the infant's overtures to communicate, and also to their emotional responses. What matters is that practitioners working with babies and toddlers see them as effective communicators, constantly seeking a warm and sensitive adult to engage with. In each of the remaining chapters in this book, the specific viewpoint of babies and toddlers is represented in separate paragraphs that reflect their particular needs as non-verbal communicators. However, it is important to note that the attributes of effective practitioners working with babies and toddlers are the same as those for practitioners working with children of all age groups within the Oxfordshire Project (see Chapter 10).

Ask yourself

1 Do I see babies and toddlers as effective communicators?

2 Do I take the time it takes to interpret a baby's signals?

3 Do I take turns with the baby so they learn the language of communication?

4 Do I understand my role as educator in the development of children's speech, communication and language?

3

Knowing the child well

> Knowing a child well improves the starting points for quality interactions

Introduction

We have seen in Chapters 1 and 2 how vital it is that children's attempts at communication, be they verbal or non-verbal, are reciprocated by an attentive and responsive adult. The study *Researching Effective Pedagogy in the Early Years (REPEY)* (DfES 2002b) shows that the more knowledge the adult has of the child, the better matched their support and the more effective the child's subsequent learning and development. Early childhood educators need to understand the cognitive, cultural and social perspective of each child in order, in Stremmel's words, to 'build bridges' between what the child knows and what he is capable of knowing (1993, quoted in DfES 2002b: 47). Rogoff (1990) also uses this analogy when she describes the role of the adult in interactions with the child as 'guided participation', actively building bridges between what the child knows and new information to be learned.

So much of learning is dependent on meeting new situations which are then assimilated into what the child already knows, understands and can do. The more the practitioner knows about the child, including knowing them as a learner, the more effectively the practitioner will be able to help the child make connections between what is known and what is new. Knowing the child well allows the practitioner to initiate or respond to interactions at the right time and in the right way, finding just the right 'hooks' on which to attach a conversational exchange. In this chapter, we explore why and how practitioners come to know their children sufficiently well to interact with them in positive and constructive ways, and the difference it makes to the young child to be 'held in mind' (Winnicott 1960 – see Chapter 2).

Focus on babies and toddlers

Practitioners who care for the needs of very young babies often have the opportunity to get to know their children well because they are with them for so much of each day. Those who are childminders or who work in day nurseries may well be the primary carer for a very young child from early in the morning until a parent comes at the end of a working day. The more a practitioner knows a baby, the more they are able to understand what the baby is trying to communicate. The attentive practitioner becomes skilled at differentiating the type of cry or the gestures that the baby uses to convey a particular need. Manning-Morton (1994) reminds us that although a baby's crying makes us tense, this discomfort makes us act, which is just what the baby needs.

Babies have a variety of different ways of telling practitioners that they are hungry, uncomfortable or lonely. Crying is the primary means, however, by which they communicate their needs and, as we saw in Chapter 2, it is important that babies learn quickly that they will be soothed and comforted (O'Connor 2013). Robinson (2008) suggests that this does not mean a slight delay is harmful, but a baby needs to learn with confidence that someone will come and that his feelings of distress will go away. Babies give messages about how they feel, not just through crying but also through the sounds and actions they make. They might wave their arms, or kick or make sounds of pleasure. They express their interest in communicating by gazing at practitioners' faces, searching with their eyes, smiling, babbling, reaching, laughing and shouting (Manning-Morton 1994).

Research shows us that these kinds of interactions usually take place with people they know, when the baby is most likely to be calm and relaxed. When a baby is settled, he is in the most receptive state to take advantage of the care and the learning opportunities that the carer provides. With strangers, or if they want to stop an interaction, babies show their displeasure by looking away, tilting their heads away, grimacing, whining and pushing away with their arms and legs (Manning-Morton and Thorp 2001). In these many and varied ways, babies communicate and 'entice adults into a two-way communication' (Sure Start 2002).

Practitioners who know their babies well can identify their different signals and are more likely to respond appropriately. Taking action is not always possible, but responding to babies, understanding and paying them attention, is important. When practitioners are not with babies consistently, then knowing them well and being able to tune in to their needs becomes a far greater challenge. Within the Oxfordshire ACI project team there were practitioners who were with babies from 8.30am to 6pm in the evening, whilst another worked in a crèche where parents were casual users of the facilities and where babies were left, often anxious and confused, to make a relationship with practitioners in a very short space of time. The interactions with the practitioner who did not know her children well were far more tentative and less likely to lead to sustained communication.

What practitioners need to learn about children

About children's families and histories

> " 'Children are members of families and communities. They come to us with a past, a unique package of experience, understanding and emotion.' (Reggio Emilia UK Tour, 1997)"

A child who believes that not just they, but their family and their histories are of interest to another person is more likely to feel that they themselves matter. When another person shows interest in a young child he begins to acquire feelings of empathy so that, in turn, he learns to be interested in others. Why would you want to show interest in someone else if no one has ever shown an interest in you?

Many young children live lives that are far removed from the experiences of those who work with them. It is so important that every practitioner comes to understand each of their children as individuals who have their own personal histories and their own unique personalities that are formed, influentially, by their parents and the circumstances into which they are born. If judgements are made about children and their families, based on the yardstick of practitioners' own lives, then any child who falls outside of those narrow parameters may sense feelings of alienation or disapproval from the very practitioner with whom they are meant to forge a close relationship. If expectations are set that do not take account of family circumstances or a child's life story then practitioners will not have at their fingertips those intimate details about the child which can bolster relationships and lead to easy and natural interactions.

> "Vulnerable children are often more concerned with self-preservation than learning."

By showing an interest in children and their families and getting to know them well, a practitioner can gain a greater understanding of where sensitivities lie, when stress is likely to be triggered, and how relationships are forged within that particular family unit. The child who does not experience the give and take of conversation at home will struggle to answer the questions or to offer a point of view in discussions that are a familiar feature of an English school classroom. The child who arrives at nursery or school tired, undernourished or stressed will not be ready to learn but will, more likely, be more concerned with self-preservation.

Knowing a child well means taking the time to understand what has influenced their personalities, their interests, their attitudes to school or nursery, and their ability to relate to others. Understanding takes time, effort and commitment. It means that a practitioner genuinely wants to stand in the shoes of the child in an attempt to understand why concentration, perseverance and learning might be a challenge.

About children's cultures and communities

The cultures and communities within many English nurseries and classrooms are rich and varied. Once again, many of these cultures will not be familiar to practitioners if they are not similar to their own. If early childhood educators want to get to know children well they need to learn as much as possible about the cultures of their children and the communities in which they live and are brought up.

Culture affects every aspect of daily life. What we eat, what we wear, how we experience rules and sanctions, whether we worship, are all determined by culture and by the communities in which we daily interact. Some families are relatively insular, living in a street where they only know others to nod to as they pass on the pavement and where the nearest family members live many miles away. Other families are surrounded by an extended family, all of whom have a hand in bringing up the children and who share a communal responsibility for each other's welfare. This experience of community – be it through family, place of worship, hobbies or social circles – influences how the child manages social situations in nursery and in school, and will determine a child's approach to making relationships with adults and their peers.

The home environment is, as Brooker describes, a 'learning culture' all of its own. It 'consists of all the ways of living, and systems of meaning, which prevail in each child's family' (Brooker 2002: 1). To understand how children will respond and react to the learning culture of the school, practitioners first need to appreciate the learning culture of the home. What are parental attitudes to schooling? Are parents ambivalent? Are they keen, but demand formality? Are they overanxious and pressurizing? Whatever experiences the child has had at home will manifest themselves in some way in the nursery or classroom. So to understand the child well, practitioners need to understand the influences of the home.

Practitioners also need to understand that, unless they learn about and respect these different cultural influences it can be all too easy to make judgements about child-rearing practices and parental expectations in relation to children's attainment. Parents bring up their children according to their own cultural rules, and these rules only become disadvantageous when they conflict with the culture of the nursery or school, which may promote quite different expectations, language and behaviours. Rogoff (2003: 11) says that 'Cultural processes surround all of us and often involve subtle, tacit, taken-for-granted events and ways of doing things that require open eyes, ears, and minds to notice and understand.' The task of the early childhood educator is to become more familiar with those cultures and communities with which they are not familiar through their own life experiences. In this way, practitioners will come to understand and respect what is different, and appreciate the strengths that come from the diversity of cultures and communities that make up our educational settings.

About children's prior experiences and knowledge

Knowing children well means knowing about the prior experiences they have had which shape them as learners and which impact on their knowledge and understanding. Meadows (1993: 70) writes that 'Having no starting-point, or an unnecessarily distant one, or a starting point from which one sets off in the wrong direction, will hamper learning.'

When children first start in nursery or at school, their previous experiences are usually, though not always, the ones they have had in the home. Practitioners who understand the impact of those prior experiences on each child's attitudes and capacity to learn and, therefore, on their role as educator, are better placed to understand the most effective starting points for learning and to make strong connections between what is being learned at home and what is planned in the nursery or classroom.

Home visits can give early years practitioners crucial awareness of attitudes to learning in the home, the way in which family time is valued, and how it is spent. Bronfenbrenner (1979) describes individuals and environments as 'mutually-shaping systems', each reacting to changes in the other. His model of the ecology of human development describes how the individual impacts on the environment in which he lives, while the environment influences the individual, requiring a process of mutual accommodation. So each individual child impacts on his or her own environment – parents, siblings, experiences – while, at the same time, all of these features of the child's environment impact on the individual child. This is why knowing about the child's prior experiences and knowledge gives practitioners vital information for responding to and scaffolding their attempts to learn while planning appropriately and meaningfully for the next stages of their learning.

There are certain experiences that children will have had, and will continue to have, that the practitioner cannot share first-hand – experiences that children have had before they arrive at nursery or school, and those they have at the weekends, in the evenings and on holidays. The closer the relationship with parents and carers, the more the practitioner comes to understand the world of the child away from the setting and how much this contributes to or works against the experiences they will receive in nursery or school. Such relationships are built on trust, and the more that families appreciate that conversations about their child's life away from nursery and school are to do with the child's well-being and the quality of their educational experiences, the more open parents are likely to be about their home and their family experiences. When families are resistant to such conversations it is usually because they feel judged. By getting to knowing families, cultures and communities well, the sensitive practitioner is more likely to send the signal that all children – and their families – are welcomed and respected.

Close relationships with families, and with children, also mean that practitioners are often party to intimate information about families and the lives they lead. Here again it is crucial that practitioners remain sensitive to and respectful of this information and do not abuse it in any way. Knowing about family life, about a child's pets or the names of family members, about what children do in their spare time and where the family goes shopping, all mean that a practitioner is given details of family life that sometimes parents are shocked to discover are known! But these intimate details also give the practitioner valuable starting points for teaching and learning. Most children love to talk about themselves and their families, and once a conversation is centred on the child it often blossoms into something broader and more wide-ranging if the practitioner has the sensitivity to follow the threads of the child's thinking.

It is the role of the practitioner to create shared experiences with the children in the settings in which they work. Practitioners cannot replicate the shared experiences of the home, but as relationships are being forged with children day in, day out in the educational setting, then the caring, responsive practitioner has numerous opportunities to create, share and reflect on current and prior experiences with their children. While researching longitudinal ethnographic case studies of four 3-year-old children at home and in playgroups, Flewitt (2005) discovered many of the longest home

> "In the home, parental responses are contingent upon the competence of their child."

exchanges concerned past shared experiences (similar to the findings reported by Wells and others in Chapter 1), jointly reconstructed by the mother and the child, with mothers acting as communicative prompts for their children, encouraging them to continue talking by reminding them of past events, supplying elusive vocabulary, and understanding the idiosyncrasies of their child's speech. Compared with being at home, the observed children spoke little in playgroups, partly because they were no longer supported by the shared understandings present in their homes. Though it is clearly more challenging to share significant moments and understandings with a group of children in a setting such as a playgroup, as opposed to the more intimate setting of the home, practitioners still need to recognise the importance of building up their own learning history with each child and see themselves as part of each child's ongoing educational story.

The importance of the Key Persons Approach

If practitioners are to know their children well, then no one is better placed to do so than the child's 'Key Person'. The Key Persons Approach was introduced to all Early Years Foundation Stage (EYFS) settings in England in 2008 when the *Statutory Framework for the Early Years Foundation Stage* (DfES 2008a) made it mandatory for every child to have assigned to them a named member of staff to support their development and act as the key point of contact with that child's parents. While the *Practice Guidance Cards* accompanying the Statutory Framework (DfES 2008a) have been superseded (DFE 2012), they still offer practitioners valuable reminders of the importance of having a special someone who is known to the child and their family and who the child and family knows well. Figure 3.1 reminds us of the underlying principles behind Key Persons in an early years setting:

The Key Persons Approach was established through the research of Elfer, Goldschmied and Selleck (2012; see also Selleck 2006) who were concerned about the 'serial care' of many young children, particularly babies, and who believed that these babies and young children would only thrive with consistent care from a familiar adult. They championed care for these very young children by 'someone not everyone'. While acknowledging that monomatry (infants being cared for by one mother figure) is not a precondition for healthy human development, research has clearly shown that children thrive on consistency of care from an adult who shows sensitivity and responsiveness to their needs (McGurk et al. 1993). Elfer et al. (2012: 5) suggest that some of the key features which a nursery should provide for a baby or child replicate those provided by a parent in the home, including 'coming to know the child very well, showing the child spontaneity, immediacy and delight in interactions, and the ability to be involved in an intense relationship without being overwhelmed by it'.

Being given the immense responsibility of being a Key Person potentially gives every practitioner access to the knowledge about that child – their family, culture and

---

Secure attachment
- A Key Person will help the baby or child to become familiar with the setting and to feel confident or safe within it.
- A Key Person develops a genuine bond with children and offers a settled, close relationship.
- When children feel happy and secure in this way they are confident to explore and to try out new things.

Shared care
- A Key Person meets the needs of each child in their care and responds sensitively to their feelings, ideas and behaviour.
- A Key Person talks to parents to make sure that the child is being cared for appropriately for each family.

Independence
- Babies and children become independent by being able to depend on adults for reassurance and comfort.
- Children's independence is most obvious when they feel confident and self-assured, such as when they are in their own home with family, or with friends and familiar carers such as a key person.
- Babies and children are likely to be much less independent when they are in new situations, such as a new group, or when they feel unwell or anxious.

DFES (2008a)

Figure 3.1 EYFS Practice Guidance Card 2.4: Key Person

community – that we have seen in this chapter is so crucial to efficacy in supporting that child's learning. The Oxfordshire ACI Project showed repeatedly that conversations were most effective when they were held one-to-one between a child and a responsive adult and, frequently, that adult was the child's Key Person. This chimes with the findings of another small scale project undertaken in Oxfordshire between 2005–8, led by Dorothy Selleck, that examined the role of the Key Person in a range of early years settings. These young children gave the researcher a clear message that interactions with their Key Person were more attuned, and more likely to have positive outcomes for them, than interactions with adults who were unfamiliar. Some of the poignant messages from the babies in this project, published by Oxfordshire County Council (2006), illustrate the importance of intimate, participative exchanges between a practitioner and each child in their care:

- 'Please really talk to me, please be less busy – stay and play with me, and get to know me and my folks.'
- 'I need a Key Person in the nursery to be close to, who will listen to me and understand me and keep me safe and included.'
- 'You need to understand what I am interested in and the 'project' I am working on. Please try not to interrupt me when I am busy. I want you to give me the materials or attention that will nourish my schema.'
- 'I have lots of ways of communicating – please listen and watch the ways that I do it.'

('Main messages' from 'Are You Listening to Me: Oxfordshire babies speak up for themselves': OCC 2006)

The impact of knowing children well

DVD footage from the Oxfordshire ACI Project repeatedly showed that the quality of an interaction, and whether or not it was sustained, resulted from the child being relaxed. Where the child was not relaxed, it was most often because the practitioner was not relaxed either. Discussion and analysis of the DVD footage, by the practitioners involved in the project, led to some interesting findings about the impact of knowing a child well on the relaxation of both the child and the practitioner during an interaction.

When children are most relaxed

Children are most relaxed when they know the adult well
According to Csikszentmihalyi (1990; Nakamura and Csikszentmihalyi 2002), flow is 'the state in which people are so involved in an activity that nothing else seems to matter; the experience itself is so enjoyable that people will do it... for the sheer sake of doing it'. Knowing the adult well means there is trust and reassurance within the relationship and that children feel confident in bringing their ideas and thoughts and feelings to the adult without fear of being patronized or dismissed. Conversations 'flow' because they are natural and genuine and because both parties are

engaged in and find pleasure in the exchange. The Oxfordshire project DVD footage shows that when a child knows a practitioner well, they are comfortable in each others' personal space and there is a closeness in the relationship that is emotional as well as physical.

Children are most relaxed when following their own agenda and not an adult's

The project footage shows that even babies are alert to the mood of their practitioner and that when the practitioner is feeling rushed – either because there are nappies to change or when there is an adult-led activity to manage – then the tension in the adult passes to the child. Young children, of whatever age, are most relaxed when the agenda is theirs and not the practitioner's. In such situations the child knows that both activity and outcomes lie within their control and, therefore, there is no pressure to meet someone else's expectations. In these circumstances, when a conversation begins, it arises from something the child is choosing to do or think about, and consequently has meaning and relevance for the child.

Children are most relaxed when they chose to speak to an adult rather than when made to respond to an adult's conversation

Sometimes as children play, experiment or investigate they are so utterly absorbed in the activity they have no need to talk at all. In reporting on his famous study on being 'Under Five in Britain', Bruner says, 'When a child is thinking hard about what he's doing, elaborating his play, he is not *talking* about it but *doing* it.' (1980: 63). What disrupts the child, and sets them on edge, are the constant efforts of some practitioners to start a conversation when the child neither wants nor needs one. When a conversation arises naturally from an activity – either because the child wants to make a comment to someone or wants to ask a question – then the practitioner becomes part of the thinking process and their response contributes to the child's understanding. When the adult tries to force an agenda, to ask leading questions, to check whether a child knows something, or to steer their thinking in a direction that has an adult purpose, then the child more often than not fails to respond. Answering a practitioner's persistent questions interrupts thinking, distracts attention, and halts conversation (more of this in Chapter 9).

When practitioners are most relaxed

Practitioners are most relaxed when they do not have an adult-led agenda to follow

Almost every practitioner in the Oxfordshire project spoke at one time or another about the tension that comes from having to get something 'else' done, rather than focusing on the child and their conversation. For practitioners in the baby room it was nappies, feeds and rotas. For the teachers in Year 2 it was adult-led teaching, assessments and SATs (national assessments at age 6–7 years). The increased emphasis in recent years on outcomes (be they welfare requirements or educational goals) has created tension for all early years practitioners as they attempt to achieve the targets set by adults, rather than those preferred by children. When a practitioner has an objective in mind, then it is harder to find space for the objectives of the child, and there were many examples in the Oxfordshire DVD footage where the two sets of desired outcomes – the practitioner's and the child's – were in conflict.

Practitioners are most relaxed when they aren't interrupted by other children

In the majority of the project filmed sequences, the conversation between an adult and a child was interrupted by another child or children. Real life in busy nurseries and classrooms means that it is rare for a practitioner to have the opportunity to talk to one child without others coming along and wanting the practitioner's attention. What the DVD footage revealed was that if the child who was interrupting was ignored, then he or she became more and more persistent about interrupting! So it was clear that ignoring an interruption was not an option. If the practitioner turned away from an interaction to begin a conversation with the child who was interrupting, then the child who was left got fed up and, on many occasions, turned away and left. If the first child stayed and the conversation was resumed, it was apparent more often than not that the flow of the original interaction was lost. On some occasions the practitioner started a conversation that was in no way connected to the one they were having before the interruption, and sometimes the child's thinking had moved on and they themselves started a different conversation often to win back the attention of the adult. This meant that allowing an interruption to become more important than the original interaction was not a good option either.

Through trial and error, the most efficient way to deal with interruptions seems to be to acknowledge the child who interrupts, but to let them know that they will be seen when the interaction with the original child is concluded:

'Yes Sam… I'll come and see it when I've finished here with Myra.'
'Just one minute Giti. I'm just reading this with Bethan and I'll be with you.'

Such acknowledgments keep the interrupter satisfied, but are not so long that the practitioner and child involved in the original interaction lose the flow and thread of their conversation. The Project practitioners felt it was important to have a whole school or setting policy about interruptions, so that all children understood they sometimes have to wait their turn. What the practitioners also said was that they had to remember to go back to the child who had interrupted, so they kept their promise to talk to them in the end.

Practitioners are most relaxed when they don't feel compelled to speak

There has been an increasing focus in recent years in the English education system on the role of the adult. Quite properly, the role has been defined and redefined in order to bring about improved standards in the quality of learning and teaching. As we shall see in Chapter 9, this has resulted in an increase in practitioner intervention in children's learning. Yet, very often, the practitioners in the Oxfordshire project reported that when they intervened – to ask a question or make a comment – it had a negative or, at best, neutral impact on the learning of these very young children. The child or children were more likely to clam up than open up and have a conversation. As part of our research we trialled 'Don't Speak Until You're Spoken To'. This was not relevant in adult-led situations, of course (see Chapter 6) but, in child-led situations the results

> "Interactions flow when both practitioner and child are relaxed."

were overwhelmingly positive. When practitioners sat attentively, but quietly, and waited for a conversation to come to them (rather than initiate or force a conversation with a child), the resulting interaction was richer and more sustained because it started from the child's own thinking or the connections they were making, rather than from what the practitioner presumed or wanted them to be thinking about. Because the role of the practitioner then became to respond rather than initiate, the conversation had more relevance and meaning to the child, and the conversation was more genuine and natural. Ironically, by being comfortable with silence, the practitioners actually encouraged better quality and more sustained conversations.

Talking to someone and not everyone

One of the most interesting features of effective interactions, revealed by the Oxfordshire material, is that in order for interactions of quality to take place, practitioners need to talk to *someone* and not *everyone*. Rojas-Drummond and colleagues describe this as employing a strategy of 'extension' rather than 'rotation' (2013: 14). Such a strategy can seem to conflict with early years principles of equality, where every child is asked what they think, encouraged to join in, and contribute to a conversation. Yet the Oxfordshire research quite clearly shows that the deepest and most meaningful interactions – the ones where children's thinking is most frequently challenged and extended – take place between a practitioner and a child, to the exclusion of others.

This chimes with the findings of the influential government-funded project *Researching Effective Pedagogy in the Early Years* (REPEY) which reported that 'sustained shared thinking occurs most successfully in a 1:1 or 1:2 situation'. The researchers go on to say that 'if a child was alone, 1:1 with a practitioner, or in a child pair (with or without a practitioner) they were more likely to experience more high challenge episodes than they would if they were in a larger group' (DfES 2002b: 60). Sustained shared thinking (SST) is the term used by the researchers to describe the interactions between practitioners and children that led, by the REPEY project's definition, to the most effective pedagogy in early years settings. More recently, Siraj and her colleagues (2015) have developed this concept of SST, concerned that some people have considered 'extended periods of exchanges or long conversations as a requirement and essential', a concern I recognize as I have frequently been asked on training courses how many exchanges have to pass between an adult and a child for the interaction to be 'sustained'. Siraj and her colleagues explain in their new publication that this is not the point of SST, and have now helpfully placed the emphasis of practitioner involvement on 'a contribution to thinking' which can, of course, be brief or extended. They also note that this may include 'standing back' and allowing the child to 'explore, familiarize, solve problems, and think by themselves' (2015: 7).

To make a valid contribution to a child's thinking remains challenging when more than one child is involved. It is too hard to follow the idiosyncratic and complex threads of a child's thinking while simultaneously trying to orchestrate the contribution of other children. When practitioners attempt to do this, interactions inevitably remain somewhat superficial. Small group conversations do have value, of course, when children are more socially mature. They encourage children to become more familiar with listening to others, to build on ideas others have put forward, and to be motivated and inspired by someone else's thinking. However, if 'sustained shared thinking' is dependent on co-construction, such interactions will inevitably be of deeper quality when two are sharing their thoughts and ideas, rather than a whole group. Talking to someone and not everyone allows the practitioner to follow the twists and turns of one child's thinking and to respond in ways that are relevant and appropriate to that child at that moment.

Analysing your own practice

By the conclusion of the Oxfordshire ACI Project, the project team developed a series of prompts to support the analysis of their practice (and the practice of others). In relation to 'Knowing the Child Well', the criteria are as follows:

Features of interactions where the child is known well

- Both the child and the adult are relaxed in each other's company.
- Both the child and the adult are happy in each other's space.
- Both child and adult are comfortable with silences.
- The conversation connects to previous shared experiences and knowledge about each other.
- The conversation is relaxed, genuine and natural.
- The conversation often takes a humorous turn.

Features of interactions where the child is not known well

- The child and the adult frequently look uncomfortable.
- The child and the adult do not want their personal space invaded.
- The child frequently looks around or somewhere other than at the adult.

- Considerable time is spent finding a way to tune in to the child.
- There are often misunderstandings on both sides, but particularly on the side of the adult, about what the child is doing or thinking.
- The adult resorts to questioning the child excessively as a way of extracting a response, rather than engaging in a more natural two-way conversation.

Transcripts: knowing the child well

It is not easy to transcribe DVD footage of young children learning. So much of what transpires between a practitioner and a child is visual rather than verbal. As we shall see in later chapters, much depends on body language, tone of voice and gesture. However, there are some transcripts which do usefully exemplify the points raised in each chapter, and the following two transcripts are clear exemplification of the difference between one interaction where the child is known well, and one where they are not.

Transcript 3:1 'Andy, Alice and Jack's train'

Alice is 18-months-old, and Andy is her Key Person. Alice has been with Andy since she was 6-months-old. Her older brother Jack was also in Andy's group, so the family are well known to him. In this clip, Andy is kneeling beside Alice as she looks into a cupboard and finds a train – a train that her brother Jack used to play with in the baby room.

A: A train. You like trains! Your brother Jack's got trains hasn't he?

C: Jack.

A: Jack – that's right!

C: *(Alice points towards the door leading to where the older children play at the nursery.)*

A: Jack's out the door as well? *(He laughs.)* He does go that way. *(Alice taps him on the head with the train.)* Ooh! *(Alice laughs.)* Oohh! On my head.

C: Yeh. *(Alice puts the train on top of the cupboard and Andy watches. She then turns to him with a big grin and puts the train on her own head.)*

A: On *your* head! *(Andy points at the train.)* James the train.

C: Jack.

A: Jack. Where's Jack? *(Alice turns away and puts the train into the cupboard. She then shuts the door of the cupboard with a big bang.)* Oohh! *(Alice laughs. Andy laughs.)* Oohh!

C: *(Alice points to the top of the cupboard.)* Train.

A: Train. Shall we put the train up on the top? *(He does so and Alice picks it up.)* On the top.

C: Jack *(And points to the 'big nursery' doors.)*

A: Jack. I think he's in big nursery isn't he, playing with the trains in big nursery. *(Andy moves from his knees to settle down sitting on his bottom.)*
C: Daddy.
A: Daddy's at work.
C: Mummy.
A: Mummy's at work. And where's Alice? *(She doesn't answer but turns away; he taps her shoulder.)* Here's Alice. Alice is at nursery – like Jack.
C: Train.

Analysis

The practitioner and child are completely at ease in each other's company. This is apparent from the body language, which shows them very close together, with Alice happy to invade Andy's personal space, and Andy happy to let her do so. His tone of voice is consistently warm and relaxed, even when she taps him on the head with the train and makes a loud bang with the cupboard door. When Andy shifts from his knees down onto his bottom, he is letting Alice know that he will stay with her for as long as the interaction lasts and that he is giving her his full attention. Because he knows her well, he is able to interpret her gestures (especially the pointing) and also make connections between her words 'train'; 'daddy'; mummy' and the meaning that might lie behind them. He is constantly reassuring her about her place in the nursery, but also her connections to the world of her family. He knows enough about the family to reassure her that mummy and daddy are 'at work', but that brother Jack is close by 'in big nursery'. He also reassures her of Jack's closeness to her (physically as well as emotionally) by saying, 'You like trains! Your brother Jack's got trains hasn't he?'; '[he's] playing with the trains in big nursery', and 'Alice is at nursery... like Jack.' Almost all Andy's questions are clarifying what Alice has said, but the two which are direct and require an answer are ignored – 'Where's Jack?' (Alice turns away and puts the train into the cupboard) and 'Where's Alice?' (she doesn't answer but turns away). There are several periods of silence while Alice explores and thinks. Andy does not attempt to fill these, but waits, in most cases, until Alice turns back to communicate with him.

If we return to the Oxfordshire project's 'key question' to use when evaluating an interaction (see Chapter 1), we can now usefully ask: 'Did the child gain something positive from this interaction that s/he would not otherwise have had?

What does the child gain?

1   This practitioner likes me.
2   This practitioner is interested in what I say and the ideas I have.
3   This practitioner listens to me and tunes in to my thinking.

4   This practitioner has fun with me and enjoys my company.
5   This practitioner knows about my family and remembers important things about me and my life.
6   This adult is ready to help me learn things.

Note: After reading the transcripts in the following chapters, you might want to ask yourself: **What does the child gain from this interaction?** (both positive and negative)

Now we move to an interaction between a practitioner and a child who do not know each other well. Giti usually teaches in the nursery school (children aged 3–4 years). Today she is in the day nursery because they are short-staffed. The staff have put out resources on one table to stimulate activity around the theme of birthdays (candles, cards, Play-Doh, etc). Giti comes to sit alongside Ellie (19 months) who is playing with Play-Doh with one hand, and holding her toy 'Mousey' in the other.

Transcript 3:2 'Giti, Ellie and the birthday cake'

A: Ellie, Ellie... I'm going to make a birthday cake here. *(Ellie sticks a candle into the Play-Doh Giti is using.)* Oh, have you got a candle for my birthday cake? *(Ellie sticks a candle into her own Play-Doh.)* Oh thank you. That's lovely isn't it? Is it for this? *(Touching Ellie's toy mouse.)* Who's it for this birthday cake?

C: You.

A: Is it? What do you want to sing? *(Ellie doesn't respond.)* Shall we sing Happy Birthday? *(Giti sings.)* Happy birthday to you, happy birthday to you, happy birthday dear... Who's this?

C: Mousey.

A: *(Giti continues to sing)* Mr Mouse... Happy birthday to you. *(Ellie looks away at another child.)* Ellie. Ellie. *(Ellie looks back.)* Shall we blow the candle out? Shall we blow it out? *(She lifts it towards Ellie.)*

C: With my fingers.

A: You do it. *(Ellie 'snuffs' the candle with her fingers. She then picks up another candle and puts it into the cake.)* Two candles. *(Turning to another child.)* Have you got a card for me? Thank you Sara *(She shows the card to Ellie.)* Ellie, would you like a card? *(Ellie nods. Giti puts the card down on the table. Ellie continues to put candles into the Play-Doh cake.)* I can see you're putting lots of candles in now. Oh my goodness... lots and lots. You're putting them in really carefully. Good girl, that looks really lovely doesn't it? And another one. Wow.

C: When's my mummy coming?

A: Is that... is that for your mummy? *(Ellie looks down but nods.)* Is this for your mummy?

C: It's for Mousey.

A: It's for Mousey. Mousey looks really pleased. *(Ellie leans Mousey towards the cake so he can nibble some.)* Is it Mousey's birthday? How old is Mousey?

C: Blow it.

A: What darling?

C: Blow it.

A: Blow it? Can Mousey blow it? Shall we blow it together with Mousey? *(Giti goes to move Mousey towards the cake, but Ellie puts the toy high up behind her back.)*

Analysis

Ellie and the practitioner do not know each other. When the adult sits down at the table she starts to speak about the activity that has been planned, rather than tuning in to what the child is actually doing. The practitioner is thinking about 'birthdays', whereas Ellie is exploring the Play-Doh and not interested at all, at first, in birthdays as a focus. The practitioner's tension in this situation causes a number of things to happen. Firstly, she fills the uncomfortable silence with questions. Most of the questions are rhetorical... at least the child is not interested in answering them. When the child does speak, the practitioner is not sufficiently listening to respond appropriately. The first time when the child says the toy's name is 'Mousey' the teacher then sings Happy Birthday to 'Mr Mouse'. Then, when Ellie asks when her mummy is coming, the practitioner deliberately mishears and turns the child's question into a question of her own – 'Is that for mummy?' – in order to deflect Ellie away from a question she is uncomfortable in answering. The practitioner asks questions and then answers them herself. She takes the birthday card from one child and then gives it to Ellie, thereby not seeming to value the interaction with the second child. As a result of the practitioner's tension in this situation, Ellie shows that she, in turn, is not relaxed. She often ignores the adult, does not usually answer her questions, interrupts the exchange with the query about her mummy, and finally removes Mousey at the end from the practitioner's grasp.

What does the child gain?

1 This practitioner doesn't know me or know about my life.
2 This practitioner interrupts what I am trying to do.
3 This practitioner asks me too many questions.
4 This practitioner isn't listening to the answers I give.
5 This practitioner seems tense and isn't enjoying my company.
6 This practitioner seems more interested in her own ideas than in mine.

Note: After reading the transcripts in the following chapters, you might want to ask yourself: **What does the child gain from this interaction?** (both positive and negative)

It can be seen that children almost always gain something from an interaction, but it may not be something positive. Interactions with practitioners who are not well known or who are not sensitive to the child who is unknown, can lead to 'gains' that are undesirable and which, if perpetuated, will make conversation and interaction increasingly difficult to achieve.

Summary

Knowing children well enables practitioners to make fine-tuned judgements about what will be the right thing to say, in the right way and at the right time. But knowing a child well takes time and commitment. It means forging a strong relationship with the family and knowing about the community in which the family lives. It means appreciating that the life the child lives away from their early years setting will have a profound influence on the child's ability to take advantage of what the setting offers. It means understanding that the more that is known about the child, the easier it is to find a conversational hook on which to hang an interaction that has meaning and relevance for the child. In the next chapter we consider how practitioners can develop environments that are conducive to conversation and how an ethos is created that enables both practitioners and children to be sufficiently relaxed to enjoy shared, pleasurable and purposeful interactions.

Self-reflection

1 How well do I know each individual child in my group/class?

2 Do I build on children's interests and ideas when I interact with them?

3 Do I fully understand the role of the Key Person – emotionally, socially and cognitively – for the child?

4 Do I take the time to talk to 'someone' and not always 'everyone' – what impact does this have?

4

Environments conducive to conversation

'Young children learn from those they trust and with those who foster enthusiasm for learning.' (Trevarthen 2002)

Introduction

In 2006, the Basic Skills Agency commissioned research to consider how the physical environment impacts specifically on speaking and listening skills. Contributing to this research, Roskos and Neuman (2002) suggest that certain features within the physical environment and learning context provide an important infrastructure to enable the quality and quantity of children's oral language experiences to develop. Alongside their findings, the Basic Skills Agency published a 'communication supporting classrooms observation tool' which highlights the physical environment as crucial in facilitating children's exposure to diverse aspects of language and the organization of space and provision of materials as important for maximizing language richness (DfE 2012a). However, research shows that an environment conducive to talk and interaction is as much concerned with emotional space as it is with physical space. This chapter will examine both of these elements in analysing the environment that practitioners create.

Focus on babies and toddlers

The quality of the emotional environment in an early years setting becomes all the more important the younger the child. Manning-Morton (1994) says that for the youngest children, the most important resource for learning to communicate is the 'consistent, continuous care of responsive, familiar adults'. Sally Thomas (2002) suggests that in the early weeks and months of life the adult's face is the child's first Treasure Basket, revealing all manner of expressions, emotions and feelings in response to the child's efforts to communicate. In the absence of their parent(s), babies need to build secondary attachments with the Key Person in their setting who will offer them consistent, continuous care. Without these secondary attachments, O'Connor (2008) suggests that very young children will 'not be able to trust the responses of the adults to whom they look for reassurance and to make sense of new situations'. Practitioners working with babies and toddlers need to be aware of how watchful very young children are of adult reactions and responses to people and events. Smiles and expressions of surprise, happiness or warmth will be met with reciprocal expressions on the part of the child. An expression of disapproval or fear is likely to be registered by the child and possibly mirrored by them, whether it is what the child is feeling or not. Any tension in the practitioner's body, their face or their voice will give off signals that the adult is feeling stressed, that perhaps they lack time or energy or inclination to be a communicative partner, and that this interaction is not pleasurable. If a young child experiences these negative vibes too often then they will learn to keep their emotions to themselves and not attempt to interact with their practitioner for fear of being rebuffed. Young children, like all human beings, are affected by the mood of those around them. Cross, grumpy or impatient practitioners will affect the mood of young children, and impact on their confidence and well-being, in just the same way as being surrounded by those who are happy and relaxed. The baby who is subjected to the mood swings of an adult will not be secure in their relationship with that person, and will tend to withdraw rather than be drawn to the very person on whom they are supposed to rely. A positive emotional environment is created by practitioners who are consistent in their responses. The everyday tasks of nappy-changing, mealtimes, or going for a walk can all be reasons to get stressed (on the part of practitioner *and* child), or they can be opportunities for bonding, sharing experiences, and communicating feelings.

Physical environments that are conducive to conversations with babies and toddlers contain many features that are common to all young children (see below). However, there are certain particular considerations for those working with the youngest children:

- Young babies can be overstimulated by too many toys or people around them, and may cry to register their feelings. If the noise level in a setting rises it can make babies and toddlers fractious. If toddlers share spaces with older children they should have areas where they can retreat and not compete for space, resources or adult attention.
- Settings for babies and toddlers should be 'home-like', with sofas, cushions, pictures and small cosy spaces, rather than the larger more commercial spaces created for children 3-years-old and over. Use fabric drapes, for example, to 'lower' ceilings and make sleeping areas secure and welcoming.

Emotional space

An emotional space for the child

Trevarthen (2002) writes that children are born with motives to learn, not just *from* other people, but in companionship *with* them. In our nurseries and classrooms, what children continue to need is Manning-Morton's (1994) consistent, continuous care of responsive, familiar adults. This interpersonal relationship between practitioner and child is referred to by Rose and Rogers (2012) as 'interactional synchrony', which they describe as the relationship between practitioner and child in which the practitioner 'sensitively *tunes into* the child in a way that is 'in sync' with the child's needs and interests' (2012: 34). Tuning into children is the subject of the next chapter of this book but, in relation to creating emotional environments that are conducive to effective interactions, the prime message is that practitioners need to be 'in sync' with their children, leading to an empathetic responsiveness between adult and child, which conveys their shared emotions (Stern 1985).

The practitioners who are often best placed to create this shared emotion are those who have a role as a 'Key Person'. In Chapter 3, we saw the importance of the Key Person in creating close and trusting relationships with specific children and their families. The Key Persons Approach (Elfer et al. 2012) offers a valuable contribution to a setting's ethos in creating an emotional space where relaxed interactions can thrive. Having 'someone and not everyone' to talk to is more likely to result in a child being relaxed and trusting, both of which will inevitably contribute to more positive interactions.

As children move through nursery and into school there is an increasing pressure on practitioners to neglect the emotional environment in which children are educated in favour of an environment promoting targets, outcomes and goals. Yet one of the three Prime Areas of the Early Years Foundation Stage requires practitioners to help children 'develop a positive sense of themselves and others; form positive relationships and develop respect for others; develop social skills and learn how to manage their feelings; to have confidence in their own abilities' (DfE 2012b: para 1.6). Children cannot be expected to develop these personal, social and emotional attributes unless they experience an environment that promotes such attributes, and are alongside practitioners who model them. The uniqueness of young children means that their needs – emotional, social, cognitive and physical – will only be met by practitioners who know them well, who are alongside them and their developmental journey day in, day out, and who remain 'in sync' with their individual needs.

An emotional space for parents and carers

Being relaxed and being trusted is important, not just for children but also for their parents and carers. The Key Persons Approach, that is so important to the well-being of the young child, can be equally important to their parent or carer. O'Connor (2014) suggests that parents need to feel that the practitioners looking after their children are 'not only tuned in to their children, but are also tuned into them, how they feel about being apart from their children and the experiences they want for them' (2014: 44). Elfer et al. (2012) claim that the benefits of a Key Persons Approach for parents (particularly mothers) is that it ensures that parents, like their children, have the opportunity to build a personal relationship with 'someone' rather than 'all of them' working in the nursery. They suggest that 'the benefits are likely to be peace of mind and the possibility of building a partnership with professional staff who may share with them the pleasures and stresses of child-rearing' (p.23). Elfer et al. describe this special relationship with parents as the third element in a 'triangle of trust' between children, parents and practitioners. They remind practitioners that relinquishing part of the care and teaching of a baby or child to the staff in an early childhood setting is a big step, leaving some parents anxious that their child may not be cared for and given the attention that they would themselves give or, on the other hand, having concerns that their child will transfer their love and affection to the caregivers, thus leaving the parent feeling abandoned themselves. So, in creating an environment that is conducive to interactions, practitioners must be concerned for the interactions they have with parents and carers. By creating a 'triangle of trust', Key Persons in the nursery or classroom can 'provide a means through which (their) concerns may be taken into account' (p.35).

An environment that is emotionally conducive to relationships and interactions also takes account of all parents, and practitioners should always be sensitive to the warmth of the welcome that any parent or carer receives as they walk through the doors of the setting. Have parents received a home visit so that a relationship is established with the practitioner on secure and familiar territory? What signs and requests do parents see written on the walls and noticeboards of a setting as they arrive? Do those messages say 'Welcome' or do they say 'Don't'? Are messages, notices and newsletters written in languages that include all the parent community, or do they exclude some families? The physical environment can be highly significant in giving messages about the quality of the emotional environment to the whole family.

An emotional space for the practitioner

In order for practitioners to create a safe, emotional space in which children and their parents can thrive, they also need to ensure that their working environment is emotionally supportive of them as individuals. We can see that the 'triangle of trust' must involve the Key Person as one critical component of the relationship between the child, the parent and the setting. Elfer et al. remind us, however, that this relationship 'makes very real physical, intellectual and emotional demands upon the key person' and that these need to be 'understood, planned for and supported by… management' (Elfer et al. 2012: 23). O'Connor (2014) suggests that if the quality of the Key Person relationship has the biggest impact on the well-being of children attending an early years setting, then we must always consider the welfare of the Key Person. This means that every Key Person has the right to private discussion time with a mentor, manager or senior teacher to talk about every aspect of the role in order to 'offload'… the emotional challenges of working in such a close relationship with children and their families' (p.44).

Every early years practitioner knows that working with very young children brings emotional challenges. Tuning in to a young child's personal, social and emotional needs can touch on or sometimes expose a practitioner's own feelings, fears and vulnerability, and it takes professional integrity to sustain the necessary feelings of warmth and intimacy crucial to the role of the early childhood educator while keeping an appropriate professional distance. When practitioners feel good about themselves they are in the best place to support others, in turn, to feel good. I like O'Connor's (2014) analogy with the oxygen masks in an aeroplane: adults who do not put their own mask on first are not in a position to help those more vulnerable people who are relying upon them. The warm, attentive and relaxed practitioner encourages both children and their parents to have conversations that are of value. It is the everyday relaxed nature of intimate conversations that lead to a deeper knowledge and understanding of each child and how members of a family relate one to the other. As we saw in Chapter 3, it is knowing the child and the family well that opens up endless possibilities for interactions that deepen the emotional bonds between a practitioner and a child, and lead, in turn, to educational opportunities to support and extend learning.

Physical space

There are a number of key features of the physical environment that appear time and again in any review of the literature on environments that are conducive to talk and high-quality interactions. A significant contribution to this field has been made by Elizabeth Jarman, whose 'Communication Friendly Spaces Approach' *(www. elizabethjarmanltd.co.uk)* has pioneered many radical rethinks about the use of space in both nurseries and early years classrooms. Jarman says that her approach 'focuses on the role of the environment in supporting speaking and listening skills, emotional well-being, physical development and general engagement'. Much of her work has influenced the thinking of practitioners in the paragraphs below.

Key features of physical spaces conducive to high-quality interaction

Place

The first feature is, quite literally, the space that is provided – both indoors and out. It is clear that cramped, noisy spaces are not conducive to sustained conversations. We saw in Chapter 3 that both young children and the practitioners who work with them need to feel relaxed in order to tune in to each others' messages and signals, and the environment plays a big part in enabling this to happen. As part of their ongoing research for the Oxfordshire ACI Project, the participants explored what the national project *Every Child a Talker (ECAT)* (DCSF 2008) identified as 'communication hot spots' for conversation: places where young children seemed more willing to hold an extended conversation with an adult. When the Oxfordshire project participants were asked: 'Where, in your setting, are children most likely to talk to adults?', the answers were many and varied. In one setting it was outdoors, in another the home corner, in another at the snack table. Many of the practitioners agreed that it was in an enclosed area that had been created either indoors or out, such as a den or a willow tunnel.

In time, it became clear that it was not the actual place that mattered but, once again, where children felt most relaxed. So in answering this question, practitioners were able to identify the balance between those areas where their children felt at ease and were ready and willing to interact, and those where – for one reason or another – they were more reticent. In one setting, for example, practitioners agreed that their children were most relaxed outdoors, which led them to realize that all the child-led activities were outdoors and all the adult-led activities were indoors, and that this imbalance in their provision needed to change.

While discussing 'hot-spots' for children, it became apparent that it is not only children who have places in a setting where they feel more relaxed than others – practitioners have them too. On returning to film for the third and fourth time in a classroom or nursery I found some of the project participants in exactly the same area of the setting they were on previous occasions. When I asked why this was the case, the practitioners said something along the lines of : 'It's where I'm most relaxed.' This led to further discussions about spaces and places in the nursery or classroom where *practitioners* feel at ease, or are less confident about supporting learning. For some it was the block area, for some it was outdoors (because children did not stop to have conversations), for some it was in child-led learning rather than adult-led. The places where practitioners felt less relaxed varied, but until their existence was acknowledged, nothing could be done to address the insecurities. In one setting I worked in, all the staff admitted that they 'walked around' the block area uncertain as to how to support and extend the learning taking place there. So, in that setting, the children who most liked the block area and wanted an interested and attentive adult to be alongside them, found they were not there.

> **"The emotional as well as the physical environment impact significantly on a child's willingness to relax and share their thinking and ideas"**

Noise

Jarman (2009) reminds us that being in a noisy atmosphere makes it difficult for children – and indeed adults – to concentrate, which can have a negative impact on speaking and listening skills. It is easy for early years settings to become very 'busy', and the hustle and bustle means that noise levels impinge on the opportunity to have relaxed conversations. As adults we only have to think how hard it can be to have a decent conversation in a noisy club or pub, or when loud music is playing, to realize that noise can reduce a conversation to single word exchanges.

An environment that is conducive to interactions is designed with quiet areas that allow speaking and listening to take place with ease. Most young children love being in a den, under a table, in a willow gazebo – anywhere, in fact, where there is space for just one or two, and where conversations seem special and private. For many children speaking in public – on the carpet or in a group – is difficult, and can inhibit those who do not yet have the courage or confidence to speak in a more public space (see Transcript 8:2). This is not to say that such children should not be encouraged to speak in such situations, but if these more public occasions are the sole opportunity to speak with an adult, then many children will withdraw and many learning opportunities will be lost.

There has been an increase, of late, in the use of (particularly) recorded music in settings. Music is, of course, wonderful for creating mood and for accompanying some activities, but there is a danger in leaving it on continuously. It then becomes 'muzak', the kind of noise that happens in supermarkets or at the other end of a telephone call when you are put on hold, when the only awareness you have of the music is when it stops. Music must have a clear purpose and not just be a way of filling the space with noise. Too many of our children come from homes where a TV or radio is playing incessantly and where the television, in particular, is used as a 'babysitter' rather than as a source of shared attention between parent and child (Karmiloff-Smith 2012). They do not know the concentration that can come from a quiet and more peaceful environment. Too many of our young people have had their heads so permanently filled by noise that when asked to concentrate in an exam, when no earphones are permitted, they find it immensely difficult. The research of Mark Andrews (2013) shows not only does too much continuous background noise 'disrupt people's concentration', it also 'affects people's health by increasing general stress levels and aggravating stress-related conditions', and that 'Continued exposure does not lead to habituation; in fact, the effects worsen.'

> **"** A noisy environment is not conducive to speaking, listening or thinking. We must ensure we do not create learning spaces that make interactions difficult **"**

Light

Another feature of the environment emphasized by Jarman is the use of light. All the evidence points to the fact that human beings prosper more in natural sunlight than in artificial light. Jarman (2009) quotes research in California by the Heschong Mahone

Group (Heschong et al. 2002) which found that learners with lots of daylight in their classrooms progressed 20 per cent faster in mathematics and 26 per cent faster in reading in one year than those with the least exposure to daylight. This research was followed up by Mott et al. (2012) who reported the tendency of artificial light to be associated with more headaches and the exacerbation of some visual impairments (Winterbottom and Wilkins 2008); that artificial light can impact on mood and response to different learning situations (Knez 1995); and that mood may also determine the sharpness of cognitive abilities such as concentration and memory (McColl and Veitch 2001). While these research studies were not always conclusive, it does point to the fact that we need to ask important questions about how lighting is selected and used in our early years settings. Mood and concentration are inextricably linked with the desire and capacity to hold a conversation, and practitioners need to ensure that the lighting in their setting is not causing as much of a distraction for some children as noise levels might be.

Wherever possible, settings benefit from as much natural light as possible (with the facility to use blinds to negate glare). In the preschools in Reggio Emilia, light is created through the design of spaces which interconnect visually if not literally, so that 'if the body cannot get there then eyes and ears can' (Bishop 2001: 78). This is perhaps a reminder not to cover windows and the glass in doors with so many pictures or notices that children's sightlines are destroyed and natural light is unnecessarily reduced. Where artificial light is essential, Jarman recommends using transparent fabric or light-diffusing panels to reduce the harshness. But it is important to remember that artificial light can be used judiciously to create atmosphere, focus attention on something, create mood, and spark a conversation. Mark Dudek, in his inspirational book on kindergarten architecture (1996), suggests that 'total uniformity' is undesirable, and that certain walls be highlighted to focus attention while other spaces are less bright, creating calmer and 'quieter' places to be.

> **"Creative practitioners use light, just as they use sound, to provoke different responses from children, leading to animated and absorbing interactions"**

Position

The positioning of equipment and furniture has a significant effect on the quality of interactions in early years settings and classrooms. There has been interesting research in primary classrooms (e.g. Hastings and Schwieso 1995) showing that although teachers group tables and chairs to encourage children to talk, children are rarely given tasks that encourage them to collaborate, so talk is generally not about work and children are frequently told off for talking and not getting on with their (individual) tasks. The environment must support the pedagogy that practitioners want to promote. If interactions are seen as key to children's learning and development, then the environment must be evaluated for the opportunities it provides for interactions to flourish, and scrutinized for any situations where the positioning of furniture or resources impedes the likelihood of interactions taking place.

If a setting has both quiet and noisier areas for communication it is best that they are not side by side. I have seen beautifully organized and arranged book corners never used because they are placed alongside the home corner with all its busy comings and goings, and children who want to be quiet are constantly distracted by the home corner's hustle and bustle. Likewise with small world play. I watched a group of reception age girls (4-year-olds) attempting to create a complex and imaginative tale of dragons and princesses continually disturbed by boys making their exuberant way to the outside area and knocking against the small world table, overturning the characters which the girls had so carefully arranged. Practitioners need to look for the opportunities for talk they have created in their settings and then check that these are not disturbed by the activity going on next door or nearby which might well undermine the quality of interactions between peers and between children and practitioners.

It is really important to plan some spaces for reflective interaction in the outdoor area. A den made from a blanket over tree branches, a willow tunnel, a seat under a tree or a gazebo, all give children a sense of intimacy and focus that enables both parties involved to be able to concentrate on the other person and the subject in hand. We have seen how often interruptions disturb the rhythm and flow of an interaction, so being away from others, where interruptions are less likely to occur, gives children the opportunity to open up a conversation and move from the mundane, of-the-moment remarks to deeper, more meaningful interactions that offer practitioners the opportunity to support their children's social, emotional, linguistic and cognitive development.

> "Practitioners need to plan for their environments to have interaction-friendly spaces"

Stimulation

It is a common fault to think that early years environments should always be 'stimulating'. Indeed, it is a word too frequently used when people refer to the quality of environments for early learning. Like all environments, the early years setting needs variety. Settings need places that are quiet and places that can be noisier; places that are darker and subdued and places that are airy and bright. Likewise they need places that are stimulating and places that are calmer and more tranquil. If young children are to talk to practitioners, they need opportunities to be in both kinds of space – which can lead to very different conversations. Conversations in quiet places are often more contemplative and can frequently be personal and revealing. When children feel safe and confident that they will not be interrupted they will often reveal deeper thoughts about issues that are troubling them, which are important to them, or which they are struggling to understand. They will have the opportunity to think reflectively and maybe talk through solving a problem, without being too distracted by others around them. Conversations in stimulating spaces are often energetic and quick-fire. They ricochet from one person to another in a succession of co-constructed suggestions and ideas. Such conversations often accompany action and experimentation and demand a highly attentive practitioner to follow the threads of the children's thinking.

When I review the environments in settings and schools, I sometimes find an over-emphasis on one kind of environment. Sometimes the environment is kept too quiet, with children suppressed by the practitioner's desire to control everything that takes place within it. This kind of repressed quiet does not bring about the conversations that take place in a den or shady arbour where a safe haven for interaction has been created and both children and practitioners are relaxed. Repressed quiet makes children – and practitioners – tense and, as we have seen in Chapter 3, this frequently foils the flow of an interaction. Equally an environment can be overstimulating. If everything is new and different and exciting then children ricochet from one activity to another without any sense of settling calmly to something familiar. In these environments the quality of learning remains superficial because children are always looking for something 'else' and never develop the concentration and perseverance that comes from playing with resources and materials that are known and with which children can build on their previous experiences.

> "The most effective early years settings encourage interactions in places that are familiar, calm and reassuring as well as novel, stimulating and provoking"

Time

Children need to know that adults have time for them and will take time to listen to them. It is all too easy to walk past a child with a brief 'A-hah' which, however friendly, hardly gives a child the sense that what they have said matters. If a child starts a conversation, or is to be encouraged to sustain that conversation, then a practitioner's body language has to send the message that they have all the time in the world to listen.

It is easy to imagine that the longer the time a practitioner spends with a child then the more opportunities there are for shared thinking and contributions to learning. But this is not always the case. A practitioner can be alongside a child for a considerable length of time but, as we have seen in Transcript 3:2, because there has been little attempt or success in tuning in to the child and their thinking, the practitioner may simply be interrupting the child's learning rather than enhancing it.

> "Effective practitioners are alert to every conversation that comes their way and realize that valuable interactions do not only arise at planned and predictable times"

It is the *quality* of time spent with children rather than the *quantity* of time that convinces children that a practitioner is interested in them, their ideas and their conversation, and that will encourage them to interact another time. The practitioner whose body language shows they are attentive and interested will encourage a conversation to continue, and the response of the practitioner will determine whether the child feels that speaking to that practitioner is worthwhile or not and something they would choose to do again.

Experiences

Many of the most effective interactions recorded as part of the Oxfordshire ACI Project came 'out of nothing'. They began as a result of a chance remark about a new coat, a sick hamster, a squashed worm or the class lists on the wall. The effective practitioner is alert to every opportunity for a conversation and conscious of the fact that nothing matters more to the confidence and linguistic and cognitive development of a child than to stop, get down and listen to what the child wants to say. Most children have a whole sackful of things that they want to say and to share. Chilvers says children have a 'built-in urge to tell you, in some way, what they are thinking, feeling, seeing, hearing, smelling, touching. They are powerful communicators.' (2006: 5). More often than not all children need is an attentive audience and they will open up a conversation. All practitioners need to do is to be that attentive audience.

Though many valuable interactions arise spontaneously, this does not mean practitioners do not plan for them. As we have seen in this chapter already, practitioners plan environments and resources and experiences that provide optimum opportunities for interactions to be initiated and sustained. But practitioners also plan experiences that will engage children's interest in order to stimulate their verbal contributions – for example, hiding characters from a favourite book in a sack and predicting who will come out next to tell their part of the story. These kind of planned experiences have immense value, but practitioners need to guard against forcing or manipulating interactions that suit their purposes as the educator rather than bringing the richest communicative contributions from the child. In the Oxfordshire DVD footage, when we asked or expected children to talk, they often did not. Put children into a 'circle time' situation, or ask them to explain an idea or to tell everyone about something they have done, and their replies become more limited and inhibited than when they have chosen to interact spontaneously. They often said something they thought the practitioner wanted to hear rather than necessarily what they were thinking or feeling. In addition, because in these planned situations children were frequently competing for the practitioner's time and attention, there was less time for an interaction to develop in depth. There are times, of course, when we want slightly older children to have the experience of speaking confidently to a group, to show they can express their thoughts and feelings to others, and to show awareness of the needs of listeners. However, speaking in public, answering questions in a large group and listening to others, develops a set of skills as separate from interaction for thinking, as handwriting is different from creative writing. Both are important, but the skill set and objectives are different. If we want talk for learning (Mercer and Hodgkinson 2008), then we must create opportunities without stress, without expecting answers on the spot, and without always defining the agenda – the very strategies that so often characterize interactions 'on the carpet'.

If educators appreciate the importance of talk to the young child as outlined in Chapter 1, then nothing is more important than responding to that conversational opener from the child. Many of the richest conversations come out of nothing and out of nowhere. They are topics that come into a child's head as they remember something or see something that triggers a memory or a connection. Their topics can sometimes seem random, but the attentive adult usually finds a thread to their thinking which shows that what they are saying is a result of a memory, some previous experience, or a current concern.

Analysing your own practice

These are the features of effective practice that the Oxfordshire practitioners identified in analysing the learning environment in relation to the quality of adult – child interactions:

Features of interactions where **environments are conducive**

- Children and their parents and carers feel valued and believe that what they have to say matters.
- Practitioners prioritize interactions with children over anything else.
- There are spaces to talk quietly and places that stimulate talk during action.
- Practitioners give children 'all the time in the world' by stopping, getting down to their level, and listening.
- Experiences provide many reasons to talk, to discuss, and to raise questions.
- Light and noise levels and resources all support the quality of interactions.

Features of interactions where **environments are not conducive**

- Children and/or their parents and carers do not feel that what they say is valued.
- Practitioners pass by children's conversational openers, rather than stopping, getting down and listening to what they have to say.
- Too many places are noisy and not conducive to interaction.
- Children who enjoy very active, outdoor learning never get a chance to talk with attentive practitioners.
- Practitioners do not give children the time they need to think things through and to raise their own questions.
- Bright lights, noise levels and overstimulation detract from the quality of conversations.

Transcripts: environments conducive to conversation

Transcript 4:1 'Nina and Charlotte in the sandpit'

Charlotte (18 months) is in the sandpit outdoors with her Key Person Nina. Charlotte is saying 'crumble sand', a phrase she has used a lot in the sandpit recently.

C: This be the crumble sand, crumble sand.

A: *(Smiles, mirroring what Charlotte is doing.)* Crumble sand.

C: The crumble sand *(Sits back to look at her efforts.)* Ha-ha! *(Returns to moulding the sand.)* Need crumble sand.

A: You like that don't you? Are you going to do it again?

C: Me do some.

A: *(Still mirroring what Charlotte is doing.)* You like doing that one.

C: *(Sits back.)* There's a chair.

A: *(Smiles at her.)*

C: Shall I make another one?

A: Yes.

C: Then I can make a house.

A: That seems like a nice idea.

C: Make... a house.

A: Do you need me to move round? Shall I move round a little bit?

C: Yes.

A: To give you some space.

C: Yes... give me some space!

A: Yes... that's it, you need space don't you?

C: Yes.

A: And you're going to build another... is it a wall for the house? *(Charlotte doesn't answer.)* Is it a wall?

C: There.

A: Is that where you want to build it? So, what do we do... do we just scoop the sand like this with our hands... but over there. Is that what you want to do?

C: Yeh. I need to be over there then.

A: You're going over there then, OK.

C: *(Charlotte moves.)* I've made two spaces there *(She carefully moulds the sand.)* There you go!

A: There you go! That was really well done.

C: Can you move out the way?

A: Of course. *(They laugh. Charlotte moves back to where she was before.)* Now, what's next? What else do we need to put into our house?

C: We need to... crumble sand, crumble sand, crumble sand, crumble. *(She sits back.)* There you go! It's a house.

A: Is that your house? Who lives in your... *(Charlotte bashes the 'house' down.)* Oh! All gone.

C: Crumble sand! *(They look at each other and grin.)*

A: Is that all crumbly? All crumble and gone now.

C: (*Stands up and stamps all over the sand.*) Crunch, crunch, squash, squash, squash.

A: Squash, squash, squash.

C: (*Picks up spade and holds it in front of her, looking at adult.*)

A: You've got your spade. I've got my spade. What shall we do with our spades? (*Charlotte doesn't answer.*) I think I'll dig a hole.

C: I think I'll dig a hole too.

Analysis

This transcript is characterized by how relaxed the practitioner and child are in each other's company. There is a lot of smiling and some lovely humorous exchanges between the two. They are outdoors, which Charlotte loves, and Nina is happy to be there too. The sandpit is big enough for creative play (not a small sand tray), and is covered by a canopy so there is a feeling of it being enclosed and intimate. Charlotte is enjoying the physical sensation of moulding the sand. In Nina, she has a warmly attentive practitioner who is following her lead. Charlotte is not really interested in making the 'house'. In fact the only time that Nina asks a direct question, 'Who lives in your...?', Charlotte's response is to bash the house down.

Ask yourself: *What does the child gain?*

See the end of the transcripts in Chapter 3 for ideas.

Transcript 4:2 'Debbie and Star Wars'

Debbie teaches in Year 1. The school has a terrific outdoor area: trees, logs, a mud kitchen, rope swings, places to dig and places to plant. A group of boys are playing Star Wars. Their leader, Harry, is one of a handful of boys who sit at the back of a carpet session unable to pay attention, and adults find difficult to 'engage'.

C: Mrs B. (*Hands her a small log.*) Do you want a laser to keep you safe?

A: Yeh... can I use it, yeh?

C: Yeh (*He turns away.*)

A: Harry... sorry... what do I do?

C: You keep your hand there (*Pointing to a specific place on the log.*)

A: OK. And where do I put it? On my shoulder or under my arm?

C: No, look, you hold it here.

A: You show me. (*He does so.*) Right, OK. And what... if I see any droids?

C: If you see droids. And there's that...

C2: Battle droids.

A: OK. What do they look like? What colour are they?

C: They look like...

C2: They're metal.

C: (*Very emphatically.*) No, they're not little... they're *big*... the same size as me.

C2: I said they're *metal*.

A: Metal... he said they were metal.

C: Yes (*Nods.*) And there's some, there's some other stormtroopers who are baddies.

A: *(Brandishing her 'laser'.)* Coo, I feel like a real soldier... it's good *(Grins at C2.)*

C2: And Mrs B., if you see any white guys with guns and they're kind of turquoise-ish, and there are robots and there's a gun and they're in space, shoot them cos they're baddies.

C: Mrs B., Mrs B. – you know that pan there? *(Pointing to the mud kitchen.)* You know all them pans?

A: Yeh.

C: That's the baddies' camp.

A: Oh.

C: If you see white guys with helmets on... they're goodies.

A: Hang on... I'm getting confused... I'm going to be shooting the wrong ones Harry. The ones that are goodies, what colour are they?

C: White.

A: White.

C: Yeh – they got helmets on.

A: Helmets on... right. So anyone without a helmet on, or metal, I shot? Yeh?

C: Yeh.

A: Am I on my own, or is anyone else going to help me?

C: We'll help you.

A: OK . So do I stay here or can I, like, go off and...?

C: This is the laser beam. You put it there and then you put your shield over it and then it kills all them droids.

A: Oh right.

C: It's a laser beam.

A: Thanks for arming me Harry. I feel a bit safer now *(She settles down holding her laser ready.)*

C3: There's one there!

A: Oh, where?

C: *(Looking up.)* Oh yeh, and there's big ships like them ones.

A: OK, alright, I'm gonna get it *(Aims her laser.)* Ready Kiran... you going to help me?

C3: Liam put your head down!

C: *(To teacher.)* You press this button there *(Pointing to a specific point on the log.)*

A: Oh not, I pressed it wrong!

C: You pressed the shield. You sent the shield grenade at me. They got a shield an' it kills...

C2: Mrs B., this one's got a...

C: *(Whispering to C2.)* Mrs. B pointed the shield grenade at me.

A: I did it wrong! I gotta press this bit.

C: Yeh, 'cos they got to explode, 'cos they got to explode this and then the shield comes off and they didn't even know that.

A: Oh right.

C: And they can't hear us now.

A: Oh well, that's all right isn't it. OK... so I'm gonna press this if I see anyone, yeh?

C: Yeh *(Runs off towards the 'baddies' camp.)*

A: Cool.

C: Hey – you almost got that tree down!

A: Oh, oh sorry. I'm not very good. I'm new. *(C2 grins at her.)* I'm not as expert as you. I'm not very good at shooting. Right, help me out Guy (C2).

C2: You know… the place where… when you have to keep looking at me… but when I put my thumbs up that means it's good to shoot.

A: All right, OK. I'm relying on you.

C2: *(Runs off.)* O-ohh.

A: *(Watches where he goes closely.)* Oh! *(Stands up and shoots.)* Pshhew! He put his thumbs up!

Analysis

The children involved in this play do not respond to an indoor, more static environment. They prefer the freedom of the outdoors and the opportunity to develop their own self-initiated play. By inviting the teacher into the play they are showing a great deal of respect and affection. They know, from previous experience, that she will join in and enhance their play, not condemn it (because it is 'gun play') or try and take it over (because it doesn't have her objectives). The teacher remains absolutely engaged in the storytelling throughout. By joining in and following their lead, the teacher creates a strong relationship with the boys that will spill over into more formal, perhaps more sedentary, learning situations when the need arises. She will know more about the boys' interests and will use them as a 'hook' for the learning that she leads. The freedom of the environment in which the boys are playing allows them to be creative and imaginative and helps them improve their social skills as they negotiate and act out their story.

Ask yourself: *What does the child gain?*
See the end of the transcripts in Chapter 3 for ideas.

Summary

This chapter analysed the various factors of an environment that is conducive to high-quality interactions. It emphasized the importance of the emotional environment as much as the physical environment, and suggested that, as with most aspects of early education, a balance is required between environments that stimulate and excite and those that calm and consolidate. The quality of adult–child interactions is profoundly affected by the environment in which they take place, and practitioners need to be familiar with all the different features of their nursery or classroom that could impact on whether children chose to engage in sustained exchanges, or not. In the next chapter we consider more closely how practitioners tune in to children's thinking, and how effective practitioners make judgements about when and whether to intervene in children's learning.

Self-reflection

1   Do I value interactions? Do children and their parents believe they are listened to and responded to?

2   Where are children most relaxed in my setting? Where am I most relaxed?

3   Does our environment encourage – both emotionally and physically – high-quality interactions to take place?

4   Am I alert to every conversation that comes my way?

5

Tuning in to the child

The effective practitioner tunes in to the child rather than expecting the child to tune in to them

Introduction

In Chapters 3 and 4 we saw how practitioners prepare for effective interactions by getting to know their children and families really well and by creating a learning environment that is conducive to conversations and interactions. But for interactions to be effective, they are dependent on the sensitivity of the practitioner in tuning in to the needs of the child at any moment in time. Knowing what a child is thinking, how they might be feeling, the help they might be seeking, all impact on what the practitioner chooses to say and whether what they say is helpful. In this chapter we consider the moment when an interaction presents itself, and just how tricky it can be to say the right thing in the right way and at the right time. Every day, practitioners make a thousand split-second decisions about when to interact, how to interact and, indeed, whether to interact at all. So what is it that influences this decision-making process and what factors are taken into account when deciding whether an interaction might turn to interference?

Focus on babies and toddlers

Tuning in to babies and toddlers is achieved when practitioners see them as capable communicators and are sensitive to the different ways these very young children are seeking to be heard. Babies and toddlers use gestures, cries, sounds and facial expressions to tell adults what they are thinking and how they are feeling. The attentive practitioner has to interpret these various communicative signals in order to tune in to the child and respond in appropriate ways. Practitioners firstly need to spend as much time with a baby as possible. The more familiar a practitioner becomes with each individual baby's repertoire of gestures and sounds, the more successful the practitioner is likely to be in interpreting what the baby is trying to convey. It helps to follow the baby's lead. This might be pointing at a toy, energetically kicking his legs, a turn of the head in the direction of an aeroplane. When practitioners are alert to these gestures and what they might mean, they have a starting point for an interaction.

With very young children it helps enormously to be down at their physical level. If the baby is in a pram or on the floor he will respond more readily if the practitioner's face is close by and he can see the practitioner's expressions of interest and concern. When the practitioner responds appropriately, the baby senses that the practitioner is really interested in him. It may be that the practitioner repeats what the baby has done or the sounds he has made. It may be that the practitioner comments on what the baby has done or mirrors his actions. But by interpreting the gestures, sounds or expressions of the young child, the practitioner is seeing the baby's behaviour as intentional. Even though the baby may not understand what the practitioner is saying, in time he will come to realize that his behaviour can make things happen and that his sounds and cries and gestures communicate meaning to someone else. With toddlers who can communicate but are not yet using words it is helpful to interpret their messages 'as she would if she could' (Weitzman 1992) – e.g. the child says 'dah' when asking for juice. Instead of saying 'OK just a minute I'll get some...', Weitzman suggests 'translating' the child's message, and repeating it back to him, saying it as he would if he could: 'More juice. You want more juice?'

Young children seem to be remarkably adept at sensing whether there is synchrony between their actions and the reactions of adults. Murray and Trevarthen (1985) sat 2- and 3-month-old infants in front of a television which showed an image of their mother seated in another room. A disruption was introduced that delayed the response of the mother to the child by 30 seconds. When the baby watched the monitor, what he saw was the mother responding to his actions of 30 seconds before. So the mother's responses were not 'in sync' with what the baby was expressing at the time and the babies became agitated and distressed because their mothers did not seem to be tuned in to how they were feeling. Tuning in to babies and toddlers is the foundation of all effective interactions. When practitioners make every effort to interpret the messages that a child without verbal communication is trying to convey, then not only does the practitioner acknowledge that the baby has intentions, but the baby comes to believe in themselves as someone worthy of attention. Young children come to see themselves as others see them, and when practitioners demonstrate that these very youngest children are to be respected then the babies, in time, come to respect themselves.

The child as a learner

As children become older, whether or not an interaction is seen as interference depends to a considerable extent upon practitioners' views of children as learners. If children are seen as passive recipients of adult instruction, then the role of the practitioner will be interventionist: deciding upon and planning for the learning

> ❝'To have discovered a quarter of the answer to his question is of more value to the child than to hear the whole answer, half-understood from another.' (Frederich Froebel 1887)❞

experiences of the child, for the child. In that case, the practitioner will lead the child's learning, she will explain and demonstrate and inform and instruct and then ask questions to see what has been learned and understood. There will be little room for the thoughts and ideas of the child and even less room for following a child's individual interests. If, on the other hand, practitioners view children as active participants in their own learning, then the adult's role shifts to being a supporter and facilitator of those child-initiated experiences. When practitioners view children as 'rich in potential, strong, powerful (and) competent' (Malaguzzi 1993), then the responsibility for an effective interaction lies in practitioners' attunement to children and their needs.

Attunement revisited

As we saw in Chapter 2, 'attunement' is a term used when a child's carer 'lets the child know his or her emotions are met with empathy, are accepted and (if appropriate) reciprocated' (Rose and Rogers 2012: 41). Underdown (2007) describes the complex and multifaceted process of attunement as one when, through 'empathetic responsiveness', the practitioner looks closely for verbal and non-verbal signals from the child that suggest how the child is feeling and what their current needs, interests and fascinations might be. Rose and Rogers (2012) remind us that these signs and signals are not always obvious and 'may be expressed differently by different children'. The developmental differences between children are greater the younger the age of the child, which is why the first principle of the Early Years Foundation Stage is 'The Unique Child', reminding us that children are 'constantly learning… in different ways and at different rates' (DfE 2012b: 3).

Attunement not only involves tuning in to the child, but doing something as a result. Rose and Rogers say that practitioners need to be 'fully aware of the child in every way *in the moment* (and) adapting our interactions to suit the child's receptivity to them' (2012: 54). This latter point is crucial. The Unique Child does not only mean that the child's needs and interests are highly individual, but that the response of early childhood practitioners should be contingent upon this individuality. Each child has put together their own personal cognitive jigsaw of the world (Fisher 2013) where what is new is assimilated into what is already in place. The ways in which children do this are many and various. Some children 'jump straight in' to new experiences, embracing them, trying them out, rejecting and refining as they go along. Others stand and watch, closely observing what others are doing before trying something for themselves, evaluating and assessing risk and possible outcomes before taking action. Some children have had the advantage of a running commentary on life, when significant others have explained, described, demonstrated and exposed them to a variety of new and stimulating experiences that have caused them to be ever more curious about the world and its possibilities. Others have been contained and constrained and denied a wider view of the world, experiencing only limited possibilities and opportunities. As we saw in Chapter 1, some children have heard language constantly, have had their vocabulary

broadened, and have experienced ongoing positive interactions with a range of people. Others have limited exposure to such interactions, experiencing verbal exchanges that are one-sided and, all too often, negative and inhibiting. In order to offer effective support to each of these differing individuals, practitioners must be able to offer personalized opportunities that come from knowing each of their children well and knowing how and in what ways they can best progress their learning and development.

Strategies for tuning in to children

There are certain strategies that can be used by all practitioners to help ensure they say the right thing, in the right way, at the right time. Drawing on analysis from the Oxfordshire ACI Project, the following are the key strategies that project participants used to tune in to their children.

Observation

Young children show us what they are interested in, what they know, and what they can do by their actions. Early learning is active learning, and whether a baby is exploring their immediate surroundings on an activity mat, or a three-year-old is tearing around the outside area fuelled by surges of testosterone, their movements, their focus, their intent, their engagement, tells the attentive practitioner much about what they are fascinated by and what they are trying to achieve. The early years practitioner cannot take home a pile of books to mark that show a child's level of understanding or competence in a particular subject. The role of the early years educator is more complex than that.

Young children demonstrate language, mathematics, science, creativity, physicality – sometimes all within one activity – and the task of the practitioner is to make sense of what is seen, to recognize any significant steps in learning that may have taken place, and to identify where help and support are needed to make further progress (Dubiel 2014). Before practitioners make any decision to intervene in learning, they must have evaluated all of the above and have carried out an internal dialogue with themselves to decide what, when, and whether help is needed.

'What, when and whether' is a helpful mantra for enabling the practitioner to tune in to the child.

What help is needed prompts us to consider:

- Is the child managing well on their own? *If so, I won't interfere.*
- If the child is not managing, could I say something or do something that would help? *What might that be?*

When help is needed prompts us to consider:

- Is the child grappling, but not yet struggling? *Grappling is good, having to work hard to understand or achieve something is good, but becoming so frustrated that they give up is not.*
- If I step in now, will I support the child's efforts or will they feel disempowered? *I'll wait to see whether the grappling becomes struggling and be ready with some ideas to help the child over their learning hurdle.*

Whether help is needed prompts us to consider:

- Would it be best to do or say nothing? *Early childhood educators feel increasingly pressurized to step in and do something – to ask questions, to comment, to make suggestions. All of these strategies have their place (see Chapter 9 in particular), but sometimes the best thing to do is to do nothing.*
- Maybe the answer to *'whether'* is… 'not yet'.

It is easy for early years practitioners to feel that if they are not directly engaging with children then they are not doing their job properly. I would argue that observation *is* direct engagement with children. The practitioner is engaging with the child's thinking. Although the practitioner's body may be still and their mouth may be closed, the practitioner's mind should be working hard asking, internally, all the questions that might otherwise pour out and drown the child: 'What is she trying to do?' 'I wonder what sparked that play episode?' 'Would some dinosaurs in the garden reignite their interest?' – and so on.

To be directly engaged with young children's thinking is the highest form of interaction – and sometimes it does not involve talking. Unless practitioners observe children with care and attentiveness, how can they possibly know what the child is interested in, what he can do, and what help he needs? Practitioners who do not invest time in observing young children are those who are clumsy in their support and guidance because they are making assumptions about what their children need or are learning, rather than basing their interactions on evidence. Effective interactions are based on effective observation of children's learning.

Clipboards

Often when practitioners are observing children they want to take note of any significant points in their development. This is good early practice. However, it is imperative that clipboards (and Post-its, sticky labels, tick sheets) do not get in the way of interactions. Effective interactions rely on the practitioner giving the child eye contact and close attention. The minute the practitioner breaks away to write something down, then the child may be left feeling as though what they are saying is no longer of interest. If practitioners want to sustain interactions with young children they must give them sustained attention. Anything of note said by a young child (and written observations should only be of something 'significant') can be remembered and written down once the interaction has ended. The main focus of practitioner attention should always be the child, not the clipboard. If young children feel that everything they say is being recorded and judged in some way then they are likely to become reluctant to talk whenever the practitioner is around. In some settings I visit children must feel as though they are being pursued by the paparazzi, as cameras, video cameras and iPads are pushed into their faces at every turn. It is essential to use these devices only when it will not interrupt learning, and certainly not in the middle of an interaction.

Active listening

Observation must involve active listening. Sometimes practitioners observe from a distance (a perfectly reasonable strategy at times), but this means they cannot always hear what children are talking about. The problem here is that what a child is doing is not necessarily what they are thinking about, talking about, or learning about. This is particularly true with child-led activities using tactile resources that do not demand maximum attention: the sand, the water, the craft table, the Play-Doh, for example, can all be explored and experienced, often without the child being completely involved. Very often children use these activities to watch others, to 'hide behind' because they feel safe and familiar and because from there the child can observe what others are doing. Sometimes, because the activity is so familiar and the child is so skilled – building a Lego model that has been built many times before, for example – then the child's mind is free to think about whatever else is at the forefront of their consciousness – something that is happening at home, their pet who is poorly, their forthcoming birthday party. Practitioners who do not tune in to children's conversations often intervene in their learning with an inappropriate or irrelevant comment or question (see Transcripts 9:5 and 9:6). Too often children's thinking is interrupted in order to try and make sense of the question a practitioner has asked. Because the question does not suit the child, and the answer does not suit the adult, both become frustrated by an interaction that serves no one's purpose.

> **"** 'Listening is a time of long pauses.' (Reggio Children 2001)**"**

Even when practitioners observe and listen to children it is still all too easy to ignore what is seen and heard in order to march on with an agenda that meets the adult's interests rather than the child's. If the practitioner approaches a learning situation, whether initiated by them or initiated by the child, with a predetermined outcome in mind, then this often makes the practitioner deaf to the child's responses, especially if they do not match the practitioner's thinking (see Transcripts 6:4 and 9:1).

> "The practitioner who approaches an activity with learning objectives in mind is less likely to tune in successfully to what a child is actually thinking."

Listening to children is respectful (Lancaster and Kirby 2010); it shows that the practitioner is concerned with the child's feelings as well as his thinking. It ensures that practitioners have the right starting points for an interaction because the practitioner builds on what the child has said, rather than leaving his thinking by the wayside.

The educators in Reggio Emilia have developed a principled 'pedagogy of listening' in which they view listening as:

- Sensitivity to the patterns that… connect us to others; abandoning ourselves to the conviction that our understanding and our own being are but small parts of a broader, integrated knowledge that holds the universe together.
- A metaphor for having the openness and sensitivity to listen and be listened to… not just with our ears, but with all our senses.
- A time full of silences, of long pauses, an interior time.
- An act… behind which is often a curiosity, a desire, a doubt, an interest.
- Welcoming and open to differences, recognizing the value of other's point of view and interpretation.
- An active verb that involves interpretation, giving meaning to the message and value to those who offer it.
- Requiring openness to change… it demands we have clearly in mind the value of the unknown.
- The premise for any learning relationship – learning that is determined by the 'learning subject' and takes shape in his or her mind through action and reflection, that become knowledge and skill through representation and exchange.

(Reggio Children 2001: 80–1)

Co-construction

Tuning in to the child is made easier if the practitioner has shared the child's learning journey with them. The practitioner who has been alongside the child day in, day out is more likely to understand what has stimulated a play episode, or what has led to an investigation or exploration. It will help the practitioner know why the child has met a learning hurdle and how to help them over it. However, this continues to presuppose that the role of the practitioner is to tune in to and come to understand the child, rather than the other way around. If our view of the child as a learner is that they are competent and self-motivated and that they are constantly involved in the active construction of meanings through first-hand experience, then the role of the adult becomes cast as equally active in the construction of understandings of the child and their thinking.

Expanding their concept of sustained shared thinking, Siraj-Blatchford et al. (2002) say that it is a necessary condition that 'both parties are involved' and that the cognitive construction between practitioner and child is mutual, 'where each party engages with the understanding of the other and learning is achieved through a process of reflexive co-construction' (p.34). In her book Children's Minds (1987), Margaret Donaldson writes, 'For a conversation to go smoothly, each participant needs to try to understand what the other knows, does not know, needs to know for his purpose, wants to know for his pleasure.' (p.18). However, when an interaction or conversation takes place between a practitioner and a child who may be only 18 months or even four years of age, then child development tells us that the child may well be too egocentric to know, or care, what the other knows, wants to know, or needs to know. So the onus is on the practitioner to get alongside the child and to skilfully sustain a conversation through their attentive listening and judicious commenting in order to maintain the momentum of the child's thinking. We have already seen that it is very easy at times to halt the child's learning momentum and replace it with the practitioner's objectives and goals. In these circumstances there are two likely outcomes. The practitioner takes the conversation on a detour that suits them rather than the child and disconnects the child from the threads of their own thinking (see Transcript 6:4). This results in the child disengaging from the interaction and from any possible learning that may have taken place as a result. Alternately, the practitioner may not have spent sufficient time waiting, watching and wondering, before intervening, resulting in a mismatch between what the practitioner says to the child and the thoughts going through the child's mind at the time (see Transcript 5:2), leaving the child bemused and possibly frustrated by an intervention that disturbs their learning momentum.

The co-construction of understanding presupposes that there is a mutual desire to achieve similar goals, but that, particularly in child-initiated learning (see Chapter 6), the role of the practitioner is to remain in step with the intentions of the child and, as Marion Dowling neatly puts it, 'to go with the grain of their learning' (2013: 15). The co-construction of understanding presupposes that there is no one right answer (the adult's), and that both practitioner and child can actively engage in exploring a range of solutions and a number of possibilities. Co-construction suggests an equal partnership which, although the practitioner may have more experience, relies equally on the participation of both adult and child to achieve a mutually satisfying learning outcome. Even when life has given one partner greater expertise, the role of that person is still to tune in to the perspective and understanding and feelings of the other in order to know how best to support and scaffold their development. Co-construction does not mean that both partners are equal in knowledge, experience or skill; rather it suggests that the relationship between the partners is sufficiently reciprocal that they build on each other's thinking and develop each other's ideas.

Being fascinated

Finally, in order to tune in to the child, the practitioner must be fascinated by children. This may seem obvious, yet I have observed episodes between practitioners and children where the interactions show all too clearly that the practitioner isn't fascinated *enough* by the child they are interacting with. It is clear that the practitioner's attention is not sufficiently focused on the child to achieve the attunement that an effective interaction demands. At times, it appears that the practitioner is too anxious to get on with whatever they were going to do before the child engaged them in conversation. It appears that the practitioner makes no attempt to forge a connection between what they want to talk about with the child and what the child apparently wants to talk about with them. Waiting and watching and wondering (see Chapter 6) about children is a time-consuming business. It requires practitioners who are willing and able to decentre (Donaldson 1987), to put the child at the heart of what is said, done and achieved, rather than the practitioner and their goals, outcomes or targets.

Some of the DVD evidence from the Oxfordshire Project shows instances where achieving the adult's objectives is given greater priority than achieving the child's. It shows practitioners who are more interested in ticking something off an assessment sheet than following up on a conversational opener from a child. It shows practitioners who ignore the baby's cries in order to get all the babies fed and their nappies changed by a certain time. Being fascinated by children means finding them, their conversation (both verbal and non-verbal) and their ideas more rewarding than anything else. When practitioners are not fascinated by children they will not take the time it takes to understand them or their feelings or their ideas. There will always be 'something else' to do in a busy nursery or classroom, but the practitioner who is fascinated by children is the one who will want to stop, get down, listen and tune in to the child's comments or questions and will find their thought processes too interesting to ignore.

The hundred languages of children

Loris Malaguzzi, the founder and driving force behind the preschools and toddler centres in Reggio Emilia, believed that children try and tell us what they know, are interested in, and can do in a myriad of different ways. He says they have 'a hundred languages and a hundred hundred hundred more', but that all too often 'they (adults) steal ninety-nine… they tell the child the hundred is not there'. If you are not familiar with Malaguzzi's poem, The Hundred Languages of Children, take the time to read it and reflect on whether you are receptive to all of children's one hundred 'languages'.

The hundred languages of children

The child is made of one hundred.
The child has
A hundred languages
A hundred hands
A hundred thoughts
A hundred ways of thinking
Of playing, of speaking.
A hundred always a hundred
Ways of listening of marvelling

Of loving
A hundred joys
For singing and understanding
A hundred worlds
To discover
A hundred worlds
To invent
A hundred worlds
To dream
The child has
A hundred languages (and a hundred hundred hundred more)

But they steal ninety-nine.
The school and the culture
Separate the head from the body.
They tell the child;
To think without hands
To do without head
To listen and not to speak
To understand without joy
To love and to marvel
Only at Easter and Christmas
They tell the child:
To discover the world already there
And of the hundred
They steal ninety-nine.
They tell the child:
That work and play
Reality and fantasy
Science and imagination
Sky and earth
Reason and dream
Are things
That do not belong together
And thus they tell the child
That the hundred is not there
The child says: NO WAY the hundred is there

Loris Malaguzzi

Working out what a child is thinking is more valuable than looking at what they are doing

When we watch children, listen to their ideas and respond to their conversations, we become increasingly sensitive to the connections they make, to what ignites their

interest, and what leads to their misunderstandings. When tuning in to children in the ways described above – through observation, active listening and co-construction – the practitioners in the Oxfordshire ACI Project found it really valuable to redirect the focus of their attention away from a child's *activity* and towards their *thinking*. The project participants adopted a simple prompt to 'look at the face not at the hands'. In this way, focus is directed away from the activity and towards the child's mind: whether they are engaged, where the focus of their attention lies, whether they are holding a conversation (with themselves or with others), what their conversation is about. Now this may seem too simplistic. Indeed it is clear that no human can ever truly know what another is thinking. But surely that is at the core of effective interaction and communication: to make the best guess possible about what is in the hearts and minds of another. Whether we are interacting with a partner, a work colleague or a child, we can only do the best we can do to work out what they are thinking and why. 'Look at the face not at the hands' reminds practitioners that the child's activity is not necessarily related to the child's thinking. There are some activities, where children are so competent and familiar that their minds are set free to think about other things. Consequently, if a practitioner starts a conversation on the premise that the child is thinking about what they are doing then the result is often a blank look from the child as the practitioner talks about something that is far removed from the child's own thoughts at the time (see Transcript 9:4). By tuning in to the child's thinking, the practitioner is helped to focus on

> **"Look at the child's face, not only at their hands!"**

the right subject matter, to follow the connections that the child is making in their thinking, and to respond appropriately with conversational turns that maintain the child's learning momentum.

Deciding when and whether to interact can be the difference between interacting and interfering

By focusing on what the child is thinking, a practitioner is able to make judgements about when and whether the child needs support at that particular moment in time. I have suggested in the previous section that by paying attention to a child's thoughts, rather than merely their actions, a practitioner is helped to make decisions about the child's level of engagement, which seems to have a significant impact on the effectiveness of any subsequent intervention. As we explored this issue further it became clear to the participants in the Oxfordshire Project that the level of a child's involvement in an activity has a significant impact on when and whether a practitioner should interact with the child, and whether that interaction will enhance the child's learning or simply interfere with it.

These deliberations inevitably brought us to the seminal work of Ferre Laevers, the Director of the Research Centre for Experiential Education in Belgium, whose study of the importance of children's involvement in their learning led to the development of the *Leuven Involvement Scale (LIS) for Young Children* (Laevers 1994). The LIS is a 5-point rating scale where at Level 1 there is 'no activity' and at level 5 there is 'sustained intense activity'. Laevers maintains that involvement stems from one source, and that is 'the exploratory drive… the intrinsic interest in how things and people are, the urge to experience and figure out' (Laevers 2005: 5). When children are most involved in their learning, when practitioners see 'sustained intense activity', it can be easy to think that by intervening we can somehow enhance the child's experience and make it more effective or rewarding. When a child is concentrating intently on trying to achieve a goal, it can be natural to want to join in the excitement of their learning. However, as Bruner (1980) reminds us, when a child is thinking intently about what they are doing, they do not always have the headspace to hold a conversation at the same time. Intense concentration sometimes means that all of the child's energy is focused on thinking about and wrestling with whatever they are trying to figure out or explore. Consequently any intervention from an adult becomes interference. In order to respond to a practitioner's comment or question the child has to stop what they are doing, to 'surface' from the deep-level thinking in which they are immersed, and to engage with the questions or comments of the practitioner. Even the most innocuous query – 'What are you doing?' – can cause a child to have to stop what they are doing in order to answer the question! However, there are also times, when the child's intense involvement makes them eager to share what they are doing or discovering. On these occasions, when the child brings the conversation to the practitioner, then it is more likely that any subsequent interaction will be relevant and helpful to the child and will enhance rather than interfere with their concentration and thought process.

> "When a child is deeply involved in their learning they do not always have the head space to talk to us."

Analysing your own practice

These are the features of effective practice that the Oxfordshire practitioners identi-fied in analysing the quality of their attempts to tune in to children:

Features of an interaction where the practitioner has tuned in to the child

- The practitioner is watching and listening with 'warm attentiveness'.
- The practitioner is waiting to decide how, when and whether to intervene.
- The adult's conversation (when/if it comes) builds on what the child is thinking and not (necessarily) what they are doing.
- The child is interested in what the adult says, rather than surprised or annoyed by it.
- The practitioner follows the threads of the child's thinking even when it goes off on unpredictable tangents.
- Both the child and the adult are clearly gaining something positive from the interaction.

*Features of an interaction where the practitioner has **not** tuned in to the child*

- The child's thinking and/or activity is interrupted by the practitioner's conversation.
- The child is bemused by the practitioner's questions or comments.
- The child is distressed or frustrated by the practitioner's intervention.
- The practitioner asks questions that are beyond the comprehension of the child or irrelevant to him/her.
- The conversation does not serve the purpose of the adult or the child.
- The child (and maybe the adult) want the interaction to end as soon as possible.

Transcripts: tuning in to the child

Transcript 5:1 'Paula, and Hugh's wheelbarrow'
Hugh is an articulate child of 2:11 years of age. He is in the outdoor area of his nurs-ery playing with a wheelbarrow when he turns it over on its side and runs indoors to fetch his Key Person, Paula, telling her that his wheelbarrow won't go. Paula follows him outside.

C: The wheel... the wheel at the front didn't go.
A: Pardon.
C: The wheel at the front didn't go.
A: The wheel at the front didn't go? Shall we have a look and see what the prob-lem is?
C: Mmm. *(Ted nods and leads Paula to where he has left the wheelbarrow. He crouches down beside it and Paula gets down on her knees alongside him.)*
A: Would you try and push it so we can see? *(Ted pushes the wheelbarrow along. He looks at Paula expectantly.)*

A: Ah. Is it going now?

C: *(Putting his head right down to peer underneath the wheelbarrow)* Yeh... isn't.

A: Ahh. I tell you what we could do. Could you turn it over *(She uses her hands to demonstrate a 'turning over' movement. Ted does so too.)* And sometimes, when mechanics look at things...

C: Yeh.

A: ...they crawl underneath *(using hand gestures again)* or they have a special pit so they can get underneath them and they will have a look to see if it's working OK. *(She turns the wheel of the wheelbarrow to see if it is running freely.)* What do you think Ted? Does that look OK?

C: No.

A: No? What's the problem?

C: There's something inside making it not go.

A: Hmm.

C: When you push it it goes and when you tow it it doesn't go...

A: Ahh. So...

C: ...and it doesn't go in there an' an' it comes and turns again and those wheels go round and then I turn this and it didn't go round.

A: So when you push it *(hand gestures)* it goes, and if you tow it it doesn't?

C: Yes.

A: Ohhh. Shall we test it?

C: Yes *(Jumps up.)*

A: Shall we try? Ooh, so... will you push it for me? *(Ted does so.)* Let's watch that wheel. Yep – that's going around beautifully. So it works when you push it... *(Ted turns the wheelbarrow over again.)* Yep, still OK?

C: Nope.

A: No? It's still got a problem?

C: Yes. *(He tries to turn the wheel that is now jammed against the ground.)*

A: Ahh.

C: See... don't go.

A: Now I wonder why? What's stopping it from going?

C: Underneath.

A: Ahhh – it was touching the floor *(hand gestures)* wasn't it, and that stopped it from going. 'cos look, now there's a gap... *(hand gestures)*

C: Easy! *(Ted turns the wheelbarrow right over so the wheels are in the air.)*

A: Whoo! Will it go... will it go when it's like that?

C: No.

A: No? Have a try. See if that wheel will go round. *(Ted goes to push the wheelbarrow which is still upside down. Paula laughs.)* Oh, the wheelbarrow won't go will it! Why is that?

C: Upside down!

Analysis

This transcript shows the importance of practitioner and child being relaxed in each other's company, as well as the skill of the practitioner in tuning in to the thinking of such a young child. Ted is confident that his thoughts and ideas will be listened to respectfully. Through her body language and her tone of voice, Paula conveys warm attentiveness and sends the message that she will give Ted all the time he needs. Paula uses every opportunity to comment on what Ted is doing and saying, repeating back his words to ensure she has understood. Paula uses many strategies to tune in to Ted's thinking successfully. She listens with great care and looks at him intently throughout the interaction so that Ted knows he has Paula's full attention and she, in turn, notices the many clues he gives as to why he is thinking and saying what he is (e.g. 'So when you push it goes *(hand gestures)*, and if you tow it it doesn't?'). Paula reflects Ted's ideas back to him, encourages him to test his theories, and supports him to understand her side of the conversation by using gestures to exemplify her words. She does not get frustrated by his repeated answer of 'No', but rather is fascinated by his response, persevering until they both reach a mutually satisfying conclusion to Ted's problem.

Ask yourself: *What does the child gain?*
See the end of the transcripts in Chapter 3 for ideas.

Transcript 5:2 'Martha, Lewis, and the circuit'
In a reception class, one group has been experimenting with different ways to light a Halloween pumpkin, including circuits with batteries. They have left the table now, but Lewis, a much younger (summer born) boy has been drawn to the bulbs going on and off. He goes over to the table where the teacher is still sitting.

A: Lewis did you want to see this?

C: Yes.

A: *(Picking up the connecting wire.)* Look, look. There we are. There's a bulb… and we're connecting it to the batteries, look. If you turn it up the other way… look… here… if you touch here. Touch this one. And look what happens to the bulb *(he looks)*. And when you take it off…

C: It turns off.

A: It turns off. When you take it off it…

C: Turns off.

A: Now I wonder why that is?

C: *(He looks at her and nods.)*

A: I wonder why it turns off, Lewis, when you take the wire off? *(He doesn't answer.)* Why does that happen?

C: Umm… It gets really sad.

A: Because, oh, it's really sad. *(Lewis continues to make the bulb go on and off.)* What happens when you turn off the light switch at home?

C: *(Looks at her.)* Umm… it's poorly. *(They laugh.)*

A: When you have… you put on your light switch at home, the light goes…

C: *(He watches her mouth and his mouth makes an 'o' shape like hers.)* O-o.

A: On.

C: On.

A: And when you switch it again *(Lewis looks down at the battery in his hand)* the light goes o-o- *(he looks back at her mouth again)*.

C: Off.

A: It's a little bit like this *(she takes the battery and connecting wire to show him)*. So it's on and then it's off. On... and... off. Can you make it go on and off?

C: Yeh.

A: Go on then.

C: *(He takes the battery and connecting wire back, smiling.)*

A: On... off. On... off. On... off. On... off. See? What do you think?

C: It's tricks!

A: Mmm. I wonder, I wonder what makes it... I know when you're touching the battery it lights up, but how does that happens? What makes it work?

C: *(Not looking up.)* Yeh – it does. *(He puts the battery down.)*

A: What are you going to do now Lewis? *(He leaves.)*

Analysis

Lewis is drawn to the batteries and bulbs because he wants to play. He wants to make the bulb go on and off. He would probably have needed adult help to do that, but instead the teacher tries to give him a lesson on circuits. The questions he is asked are far too complex for him to understand or to answer (e.g. 'I know when you're touching the battery it lights up, but how does that happen? What makes it work?'). He does his best to make sense of what the teacher is asking, but she misses some interesting answers (e.g. 'It gets really sad.') because she already knows in her head the answers she wants. He also watches her face intently for clues as to what she wants him to say. For example:

A: When you... put on your light switch at home, the light goes...

C: *(He watches her mouth and his mouth makes an 'o' shape like hers.)* O-o.

He knows that whichever answer is correct they both begin with 'o'. The questions and level of understanding she expects show that she has not tuned in to what Lewis is really interested in, or his level of comprehension.

Ask yourself: *What does the child gain?*

See the end of the transcripts in Chapter 3 for ideas.

Summary

This chapter has been concerned with how effectively a practitioner tunes in to the baby or young child in their setting. The time and energy taken to do so can make the difference between interacting and interfering. Choosing the right moment, the right way, and the right time is a matter of fine judgement on the part of the practitioner, and learning is impeded when practitioners do not take the time it takes to work out what a child is thinking and where their attention is focused. In the next chapter we consider the difference between interactions that are led by the adult and those that are initiated by the child.

Self-reflection

1 Do I always take the time it takes to observe, listen to, and tune in to each child?

2 What can I learn by focusing on 'thinking' rather than 'doing'?

3 Are the quality of interactions improved by *waiting* to interact until a child is less intensely involved in their learning?

4 Do I usually choose the right moment to interact, or do I sometimes interrupt children's learning?

6

Who leads the learning?

There is no contest between child-led and adult-led learning. It is the one without the other that gives young children an impoverished educational experience

Introduction

The Early Years Foundation Stage (DfE 2012b: para 1.9) states that each area of learning and development must be implemented 'through a mix of adult-led and child–initiated activity'. Yet what that 'mix' should be has rarely been clarified. Indeed, it would be very difficult to do so, as what is an appropriate mix depends on many factors, including the age of the children and the objectives of the practitioner. However, what seems to matter most is that practitioners are clear about the different purposes of adult-led and child-led activity. It is important, therefore, to establish what is meant when these terms are used, and this chapter seeks to clarify the difference between learning that is led by an adult, and learning that is led by the child, and to examine the benefits of both.

The Oxfordshire ACI research revealed that the nature of an interaction, particularly when involving children over 3 years of age, is affected significantly by who is leading the learning. If a child has initiated the activity and is in control of the outcomes of that activity, then the ways in which the practitioner interacts should support the momentum of the child's learning. If the practitioner has initiated the activity, then she has reason to steer and guide the learning towards her own planned outcomes, which impacts on the way in which she engages with the child. Both have value for the child and contribute in significant ways to learning and development.

Focus on babies and toddlers

From birth, the new baby explores the world within his grasp. He uses all his senses to start constructing an internal model of how the world works, from all that he sees and hears and touches. Piece by meticulous piece he investigates what is new and matches it with what he already thinks he knows and understands. The young infant's interactions with his environment create the conditions for learning to thrive. But the fortunate baby is also picked up. A warm and attentive adult says, 'Look at this! See what you might miss if I don't show this to you.' The personal and social worlds of the child cannot be separated. Children inhabit a world that is shaped by the significant people in their lives – parents, siblings and the wider community – and so, the personal experiences of the child are mediated by social experiences that enrich and enhance all that is possible in terms of learning and development

Babies are born with a tremendous capacity for learning. They are excited by what, to adults, may be the most ordinary objects and events in life. They are driven by exploration and by discovery, and are rarely daunted by difficulties they encounter. These very young children are busy formulating their own hypotheses and trying them out through physical manipulation and social interaction, through asking questions and working out answers, through testing ideas and refining their own thought processes. When objects, events and other people challenge the working model the baby is constructing then he is forced to adjust the model to account for the new information. Throughout the early months of life, the baby is processing a myriad of these new experiences, reshaping, expanding and reorganizing his internal view of his world.

The task for the practitioner, in this never-ending quest for new skills and understandings, is to encourage and support the baby's innate drive to be a learner. Usually this means following the baby's lead, being interested in what the baby is interested in, mirroring what the baby is doing or the sounds he is making, commenting on what the baby is looking at and showing concern for the feelings he is expressing. But, the role of the practitioner is also to introduce the baby to experiences that he might not otherwise have because they are beyond the limits of his current personal capacity. Without warm and attentive adults, the baby might not know what they do not know and might miss many things about the world that another, more experienced person already knows and can show them. The successful development of babies demands both sets of experiences: time and opportunity to explore their own world in their own way and in their own time, and being shown new and different aspects of the world by knowledgeable and experienced others.

The benefits of learning alongside an adult and learning independently

In making decisions about 'Who leads the learning?' it is helpful to consider the differing benefits of learning alongside an adult and learning independently. Too many people still believe that children who are learning alone are somehow missing out and that their experiences are in some way deficient. Nothing could be further from the truth. There are times when learning alongside an adult is the most effective way to learn and times when an adult inhibits what needs to be learned. The benefits of learning in these two different scenarios can be summarized as follows:

Learning alongside an adult

- Learning is focused – the practitioner narrows down the range of possibilities so children concentrate on one or two specific objectives.
- Learning is modelled – the practitioner uses language, demonstrates behaviours (e.g. listening, taking turns) which the child will hopefully come to emulate.
- Learning is scaffolded – by being alongside the child, the practitioner can give just the right level of support at the right time, to move the child on or help the child consolidate.
- Learning is encouraged – the practitioner gives reassurance and affirmation that sustains a child's concentration, perseverance and motivation.

Learning independently

- Children talk more than when they are in a group with a practitioner.
- Children use their initiative and solve problems for themselves because the practitioner isn't on hand to help.
- Children take more risks and resort to trial and error more than when a practitioner is watching or helping.
- Children collaborate and learn the cut and thrust of cooperation.
- Children sustain learning for longer if they are following through their own ideas.
- Children's learning often crosses subject boundaries and draws on all they know, rather than being focused and (sometimes) disconnected.

Both these learning situations clearly have benefits for the child. When a practitioner is there, support is very specific and focused and children are introduced to new concepts or skills by a more experienced person. When children learn independently, they test out what they know and what has been modelled by adults, making these their own. Learning without an adult is not a deficit model. When learning independently, children rehearse valuable life skills which will support their development socially and emotionally, and enable them to function effectively in families, at school, in future relationships and at work.

Learning alongside an adult and learning independently are not just valuable for the child. They are also valuable for the adult. When working alongside a child, the practitioner has first hand evidence of how that child learns and where any struggles or misunderstandings may be occurring. When the child is learning independently, the practitioner has time to observe and to see what the child can manage alone, without scaffolding, and where they still need support or encouragement. It is crucial that practitioners observe and assess children in both contexts. If children are only ever assessed in an adult-led situation, then the same children will be 'successful' and other children may repeatedly be seen as problematic. But the very children who respond best to learning alongside an adult – often those with better language and more advanced social skills – do not necessarily manage as well when learning independently. They may have become too dependent on the practitioner's reassurance and praise to have the intrinsic motivation to achieve something under their own steam. Similarly, the child who presents problems in a group situation alongside a practitioner may flourish when left to their own devices without feeling the pressure to deliver something they believe the practitioner wants. The same child who finds it hard to concentrate and respond in the adult-led group may be the very one who leads and organizes and inspires the more independent learning that takes place at another point in the day. Learning alongside an adult and learning independently have something to teach both the child and the practitioner.

Independent learning is not abandoned learning

While independent learning allows the child to develop and demonstrate many different skills than those shown in an adult-led context, it must never be assumed that the practitioner has no role in these contexts. Independent learning is not abandoned learning. If children are learning independently – whether on an activity initiated by the practitioner or one initiated by the child – then at some point or other the practitioner needs to be seen

❝Independent learning is not abandoned learning.❞

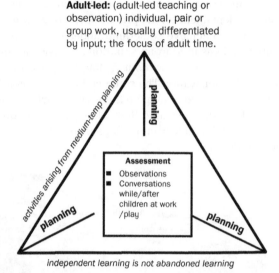

Adult-led: (adult-led teaching or observation) individual, pair or group work, usually differentiated by input; the focus of adult time.

Assessment
- Observations
- Conversations while/after children at work /play

activities arising from medium-temp planning

planning

planning

planning

independent learning is not abandoned learning

Adult-initiated: activities that arise from adult planning; sufficiently open-ended for children to work on independently until the adult is ready to support.

Child-led: experiences that children control in terms of experience, time and resources.

Figure 6.1

to pay attention to the learning taking place. Children need to know that everything that happens in the nursery or classroom is of value to the practitioner – and to them. If children's independent learning is constantly ignored by the practitioner in favour of adult-led learning, then children will quickly lose focus or interest and the independent learning will lack depth and commitment. Certainly, young children can remain involved in play episodes, irrespective of the practitioner's engagement, for long periods of time. But most young children love an audience, and will respond with pleasure to the practitioner who shows an interest in what they are doing and possibly joins in with the action (see Transcript 4:2).

The difference between adult-led, adult-initiated and child-led learning

I have outlined in previous work (Fisher 2013) that I believe there to be three main contexts in which children learn in any high-quality early years setting (see Figure 6.1). The names given to these contexts may vary, but what matters is to make explicit the difference between learning and teaching in these different situations–for the child and for the practitioner.

Adult-led learning
The practitioner has planned objectives and stays with the child or group of children while the learning takes place.

Adult-initiated learning

The practitioner sets up resources or experiences with planned intentions, which children then engage in independently until the practitioner is ready to come and observe or interact.

Child-led learning

Resources, experiences and outcomes are freely chosen by the child and are under the control of the child (see DCSF 2009). This may or may not have the direct involvement of the practitioner.

Interactions in adult-led, adult-initiated and child-led contexts

The Oxfordshire ACI Project analysis of adult-child interactions within these three different learning contexts shows, quite clearly, how the role of the practitioner needs to change in response to the needs of the children and, in particular, how the role changes as a result of who has (or should have) control over the learning.

Adult-led learning

When supporting adult-led learning, the practitioner knows exactly what outcomes they want to achieve. They have planned them with care, using prior knowledge of the child's learning experiences and guidance from the EYFS. In these scenarios, the practitioner steers and guides children towards those outcomes. They make suggestions, ask questions, tell children the names of things or how things work. In adult-led scenarios, however responsive and sensitive they may be to children's ideas and thought processes, practitioners ultimately remain in control of the direction and the outcomes of learning (see Transcript 6:1).

Adult-initiated

In adult-initiated scenarios, a practitioner also has a clear purpose for planning an activity or experience. Knowledge of the child or children, and of their previous learning, gives the practitioner evidence to plan either for consolidation of that learning, or to explore its next steps. The practitioner sets up an activity – such as putting bubbles or capacity containers in the water tray – with the express intention of promoting certain kinds of knowledge or understanding. However, once the practitioner has set up the activity, they leave the children for a while so that they can get on with their learning independently. The practitioner will return to the child or group later, but the child or children have the opportunity to take the planned learning in different directions and arrive at different end points because the practitioner is not there all the time. When the practitioner does return, their role is to be intrigued and to try and fathom what learning has taken place. Practitioners need to ask themselves (not the children):

'Did you learn about or practise the things I thought you would?'

'If not, what were you interested in and what learning did take place?'

'Would an intervention move things on here or would it just interfere?' (see Transcript 6:2)

Through watching what the children have been doing and clarifying what the children have been thinking, the practitioner can then make a decision about whether to steer the learning back to their original objectives or go with the new learning that has emerged. The practitioner also makes a decision about whether to interact or whether the learning has a momentum that will be interrupted if she intervenes. Just being nearby and showing warm attentiveness lets children know the practitioner is interested, and the sensitive practitioner will then judge whether an interaction will enhance the learning at this juncture or interfere with it. In adult-initiated situations, the control of the learning is shared: initiated by the practitioner, and then taken on by the child(ren).

Child-led

In child-led situations that have evolved independently, the practitioner approaches not knowing what it is that the child or children are trying to do or what scenario they have been creating. Child-led learning is often spontaneous and frequently unpredictable. So in this situation, the practitioner must wait and watch before deciding whether and when to intervene. In supporting practitioners to be sensitive in their approach to children's play, I like the alliterative phrase **'Wait, Watch and Wonder'**.

'Wait' reminds practitioners to start by doing nothing. 'Wait' says the practitioner is being respectful of the activity and learning already taking place. 'Wait' means the practitioner is not going to trample over the child(ren)'s ideas and interrupt their activity with unhelpful questions. 'Wait' means that a child has the opportunity to include the practitioner in their play if they choose: 'You can be the customer.'; 'Can you hold this tower?' (whether verbally or by gesture). 'Wait' often means a conversation is more likely to come to the practitioner, sparked by their close attentiveness, opening up a natural, genuine opportunity to respond to the child's thinking.

'Watch' (which includes active listening as we have saw in Chapter 5) reminds the practitioner that what a child is doing is not necessarily what they are thinking about. 'Watch' means that the practitioner sees the interplay between different children and whether this needs support. 'Watch' means the practitioner sees who is leading and who is following. 'Watch' means the practitioner is more likely to understand the intent and purpose of children's activity and also the level of involvement in that activity, which can help the practitioner decide whether now is the right time to intervene.

'Wonder' reminds the practitioner to ponder on what exactly the child is trying to achieve, or what it is that the child might need to stimulate them further. 'Wonder' means that the practitioner is fascinated by the focus of the child's learning and is asking herself, 'I wonder what...?', 'I wonder why...?', in order to understand the purpose and direction of the child's activity, which may be quite different from what the practitioner had anticipated. 'Wonder' suggests that the practitioner will think about when and whether an intervention will enhance the learning, or whether it is flowing sufficiently well without her and is best left alone.

To 'Wait, Watch and Wonder' means that the sensitive early years practitioner uses their time to learn *about* the child. In child-led situations it is the child who is in control of the learning and the role of the practitioner is to be what the child needs them to be to support that learning. However, just because the practitioner is *focusing* children's thinking does not mean that they adopt a didactic style. Just because the practitioner is *following* a child's thinking does not mean that sometimes they cannot tell a child something or demonstrate something. Effective practitioners use a whole range of strategies in every situation. What determines the effectiveness of an interaction is whether the practitioner is clear about the purpose of that interaction and whose agenda is being met.

> **"**When approaching activities that have been taking place independently it is helpful to Wait, Watch and Wonder!**"**

The purpose of an interaction

As we have seen, both adult-led and child-led learning have value both for children and their practitioners. But, by their very definition, one is serving the purposes of the child (child-led learning), while the other is serving the purposes of the practitioner (adult-led learning) – even though, of course, the adult's purpose is to benefit the child. Interactions are affected by whether they take place in the course of activities led by the child or those that are led by the adult, because they give or remove the right to steer the interaction in a certain direction. It is the purpose and intention and direction of an interaction that alters the role of the practitioner and affects whether she is focusing the child on specific learning intentions or following the learning intentions set by the child.

If a practitioner approaches an interaction during child-led activity in exactly the same way she approaches one that is adult-led, then there is a danger that neither will be truly effective. In the adult-led scenario, the practitioner may meander too far from the purpose of the activity and never achieve the objectives that have been planned (and, after all, there is no point in planning an adult-led activity if there is little attempt to meet the adult's objectives). In a child-led scenario, the practitioner may be overly tempted to steer the child away from his own intentions and towards outcomes that suit the practitioner more. Making a distinction about whose purpose an interaction is serving means that practitioners can be clearer about the direction an interaction should take and how much they can and should intervene in its outcomes.

Adult-led learning:	Practitioners **focus** children's thinking.
Adult-initiated learning:	Practitioners **fathom** children's thinking.
Child-led learning:	Practitioners **follow** children's thinking.

The balance between adult-led and child-led learning

While both adult-led and child-led learning have value, it is finding the appropriate balance between them that has taxed practitioners recently in this country. The nursery school tradition, on which so much of Great Britain's finest educational practice is founded, is rooted in principles of child-centeredness (see, for example, Froebel 1908; Isaacs 1929; Steiner 1965; Montessori 1967). These early pioneers valued 'child-initiated' and 'self-directed' activity resulting in an 'intrinsic motivation' to learn. Froebel, in particular, distinguished very clearly between the activity of the child in carrying out its own impulses or desires, and the activity of the child in response to the suggestion or instruction of its parents or teachers (Hughes 1923). In a preface to her book, *The Discovery of the Child*, Maria Montessori (1967) says, 'The education of even a very small child does not aim at preparing him for school but for life.' This statement is in stark contrast to the government's recent rationale for the statutory Early Years Foundation Stage (DfE 2012) which, they say, 'promotes teaching and learning to ensure children's 'school readiness' (p.2).

Government ministers have been increasingly persuaded of the importance of early education, initially because it seemed to lead to economic savings over time (Schweinhart et al. 1993), and also because of evidence from their own longitudinal studies (Sylva et al. 2004) of the importance of early learning for later educational success. Regrettably, those responsible for political decisions have had little faith in the value of play and of children exploring and discovering the world for themselves, and early childhood settings are under increasing pressure to introduce more adult-led aspects of learning, particularly in literacy, to children many practitioners claim are too young to cope (House 2011). Many children in this country believe themselves to be failures because they cannot achieve the targets set by others when, in fact, they are of an age when they should be setting most of the targets for themselves. The failure of many of our children to reach these externally imposed, and often unrealistic goals, is resulting in a loss of confidence and self-esteem, the bedrock dispositions on which so much of early learning is constructed (Fisher 2002; Roberts 2002; Dowling 2010). The failure of our children is not because they cannot achieve, or that their practitioners have been ineffectual in teaching them; the failure of many of our children is a result of the fact that they simply have not been alive long enough to manage the conceptual agenda thrust upon their practitioners, who in turn thrust it on them.

In 2007, the National Assessment Agency issued guidance about the completion of the Foundation Stage Profile (FSP) assessments (required of all children in the last term of their reception year at age four/five) which stated:

> When making a judgment for the FSP, practitioners should draw on at least 80% of evidence from knowledge of the child, observations and anecdotal assessments, and no more than 20% of evidence from adult-directed or focused assessments (NAA 2007)

By stating that the vast majority of children's assessments should be undertaken during child-led learning, there lay a supposition that the vast majority of a reception child's time would be being spent on child-led learning, rather than that which was adult-led. However, it is clear that in the intervening years the balance has swung in the other direction. From the anecdotal evidence of countless practitioners on training courses, the balance in classroom practice in schools, in particular, is being affected by the school monitoring agenda. Teachers say that when senior leaders come to monitor the quality of teaching in classrooms that it is adult-led learning that they focus on. And when Ofsted come to observe lessons, they frequently want to see learning objectives for the activities taking place which, of course (by the government's own definition below) precludes any play activity which is:

> 'freely chosen by the child, and is under the control of the child. The child decides how to play, how long to sustain the play, what the play is about, and who to play with. There are many forms of play, but it is usually highly creative, open-ended and imaginative. It requires active engagement of the players, and can be deeply satisfying.'

> *'Learning, Playing and Interacting'* (DCSF 2009: 10)

So practitioners are left unclear. Guidance still suggests that both adult-led and child-led learning matter. The recently reduced EYFS (DfE 2012), for example, states that:

> each area of learning must be implemented through planned purposeful play and through a mix of adult-led and child-initiated activity (para 1.9)

It goes on to say:

> There is an ongoing judgement to be made by practitioners about the balance between activities led by children, and activities led or guided by adults. Practitioners must respond to each child's merging needs and interests (para 1.9)

However, the document then says:

> As children grow older, and as their development allows, it is expected that the balance will gradually shift towards more activities led by adults (para 1.9)

This latter statement is profoundly misleading on two levels. Firstly, it implies that adult-led learning is somehow preferable to child-led learning and something that older and more able children aspire to be doing all the time. Yet, as we have seen, adult-led learning and child-led learning often lead to two very different skill sets and are appropriate for quite different, although complementary, outcomes. Secondly, it suggests that somehow child-led learning is a precursor to adult-led learning, that the one leads to the other, and that once more adult-led learning can be undertaken (because the child is more developmentally mature) that child-led learning is then redundant. Neither of these is true. Knowledgeable practitioners appreciate that adult-led learning offers a child something different from, but complementary to, child-led learning and it is one without the other that leads to an impoverished educational experience.

So practitioners are (rightly) left to make decisions (to use their 'ongoing judgement') about the mix of adult-led and child-led learning for themselves. I am often asked to put figures to the balance between adult-led and child-led learning. Regrettably there is no formula (although I think the NAA guidance that 80 per cent of observations be of child-led learning was immensely helpful). Finding the appropriate balance depends on many factors that feed into a practitioner's autonomous judgement about how the organisation of the learning day best meets their children's needs.

On any one occasion, the balance between adult-led and child-led learning may depend on:

- the experience and confidence of the practitioner
- the learning needs of the child on that day
- the learning needs of a particular group
- the day of the week
- whether it's afternoon or evening
- where children are in the cycle of learning (exploring or playing or consolidating, etc)
- whether it's early in the school year or later
- whether it's raining/windy.

Given that decisions about an 'appropriate' balance are so context-specific, the following prompts may help in the decision-making process:

- From birth to age seven, young children benefit from a balance between adult-led learning and child-led learning that favours child-led learning.
- Young children have an innate drive to follow their own interests until age seven (Bredekamp 1987) when they become more ready to learn from the provocation of others (this does not mean that they cannot learn from others before then, but that they prefer to follow their own interests, drawing on others when they choose rather than when the adult dictates).
- Until age three/four, all learning should be child-led or adult-initiated (see definitions earlier in this chapter). Very little adult-led learning (other than stories/songs/rhymes/sharing time) should be introduced before the age of four unless it is specific to the needs of an individual child–e.g. how to hold a saw correctly, how to count in a game of skittles. Even small group adult-led cognitive (as opposed to social) learning is simply too abstract and too challenging physically (Goddard Blythe 2005) and mentally (Rojas and Chan 2005) for younger children
- When adult-led learning is introduced, children will respond to it far more readily, and with greater concentration, if they still have sufficient opportunities during the day to follow their own interests for substantial periods of time.
- Adult-led learning still needs the respectful and responsive practitioner who follows children's threads of thinking and builds on their ideas and observations, even if they bring the focus of attention back to the adult objectives in the end.

Who leads the learning?

In deciding how to respond to and interact with children it is crucial to determine who is leading the learning. While many of the strategies used in adult-led, adult-initiated and child-led situations are similar, the contribution of the practitioner in an interaction is hugely determined by whether they are aiming to meet their own objectives for the child, or whether they are supporting the child to meet objectives of their own. If it is the adult who leads the learning, then any interruption or deviation by the child must be responded to appropriately but, in the end, the practitioner needs to bring the child back if possible to the planned learning objectives. If the practitioner does not do that then there is little point in having planned an activity or experience in the first place. It is all too easy to get deflected by a child's interest to the point that both practitioner and child forget the purpose of the interaction, the objectives become lost because of too many sidetracks, and the goals of the activity are never achieved. The Oxfordshire DVD material showed that adult-led learning often forgot its purpose, lost its focus, and ended up confusing rather than illuminating learning. This was partly because early years practitioners often like to wrap up learning in exciting packages that say 'This is fun'! Now this has many advantages when teaching young children, but it is possible that the 'packaging' sometimes masks the package (see Transcript 6:1) that the attempt to make an activity palatable and exciting overrides the learning objectives and confuses what it is that the child is meant to achieve.

If the child is to lead the learning, then the practitioner must resist any temptation to hijack that learning for their own purposes (see Transcripts 5:2 and 6:4). The purpose of child-led learning is for children to follow their own interests, to use their initiative, and to see their ideas through. If the practitioner muddles the purposes of such learning then they run the risk of taking the leadership of the learning away from the child and manipulating it for their own ends. When practitioners interfere in the purposes children have for their own learning then they run the risk of children ceasing to use their initiative and putting forward their ideas because they know the practitioner will end up taking both from their grasp. It will also mean that all those attitudes and dispositions to learning brought about by child-led, independent learning will never get the opportunity to flourish.

Analysing your own practice

These are the features of effective practice that the Oxfordshire practitioners identified according to who leads the learning:

Features of an interaction where the practitioner is leading the learning

- The practitioner has a clear purpose for the activity/interaction which the child(ren) understand (if this is age appropriate).
- The practitioner identifies what children already know/can do and does not make assumptions.
- The practitioner scaffolds each child in different ways to bring about the intended learning.
- The practitioner focuses children's attention on what is to be learned.
- If children's thinking goes off on a tangent the practitioners brings it back after a suitable length of time so the learning intentions are not lost.
- The practitioner does not muddle children's thinking by setting up fake challenges or problems.
- The practitioner ensures that children's original ideas and thoughts are listened to, respected, and acted upon.

Features of an interaction where the child is leading the learning

- The child's purpose for the activity/experience is not hijacked by the practitioner.
- If the child initiates an interaction the practitioner listens to hear what the child is thinking about (rather than doing).
- The practitioner responds to the child's conversational opener sensitively and with relevance to the child.
- The practitioner follows the child's thinking and does not try to lead their thinking in a different direction.
- If the child does not speak, the practitioner does not feel compelled to fill the silence.

Transcripts: who leads the learning?

In order to track the changes in the behaviour of the practitioner, Transcripts 6:1, 6:2 and 6:3 are of the same teacher in the same reception class.

Transcript 6:1 'Sandy's water'
The reception group have received a challenge. The class bear (Sandy) needs to be fed and watered when the children aren't at school. The teacher has set up a bucket of water, guttering and plastic tubing for the children to find a way of getting the water from the bucket (at the top of some steps) to Sandy (sitting on a chair below). Currently one boy is pouring water into the tubing from the top of the steps, and a group of girls are standing by Sandy at the other end.

A: Oh look, look what's happened when you've lifted it *(the tubing)* up.

C: *It's (the water)* coming out!

A: It's coming out.

C1: Hey. Don't cut it *(the tubing)*! It's getting wet!

C2: He's happy.

C1: He's drinking.

C3: Please can we...?

C4: It's wet.

C1: Miss M–it won't work when it's night-time 'cos no one'll be pouring anything in there.

A: Ahh, Bethany's just said it won't work at night-time because no one is going to be pouring anything in.

C5: I'll stay here all night.

C6: I'll stay here all night.

A: And if you're not allowed to stay here all night?

C7: *(who stood thinking very hard)* You can stay here too!

A: I could? I don't think I'd like to, I think I'd be too cold.

C8: But you could be wrapped up with thermals.

A: Every night, for ever and ever? No, I don't want to do this every night.

C4: Would you hold this *(some guttering)* Miss T?

C1: It's not coming... it's not going, not going *(they wait some more by Sandy)* It's coming!

A: It worked when you lifted it up and it worked when Ben lifted it up.

C3: Let's go and pour more water in.

C1: He's getting wetter! He's getting wetter!

C8: We need more water here.

C1: Put some more water in

A: Have we run out of water?

C1: Yes.

C5: Yes.

A: OK, do you want to take the bucket in and get some more water so we can carry on?

C8: But the challenge says we can't get any more water.

A: Why not?

C8: 'Cos the challenge says you can't... put it... take it down

A: OK... let's read the *challenge* to see if we think we're allowed to get some more water *(she goes to fetch it)*. It says, you can't carry the bucket down to give him water, but it doesn't say you can't carry it down to get some more water.

C1: Oh.

A: So that's OK.

Analysis

This is a fun, active, outdoor activity. It is, however, clearly adult-led. The challenge belongs to the teacher (i.e. she has 'designed it') and she has provided a limited range of resources to achieve it. Whenever something is said that will reinforce her learning objectives, she repeats them: e.g.

C: Miss M – it won't work when it's night time 'cos no one'll be pouring anything in there.

A: Ahh, Bethany's just said it won't work at night-time because no one is going to be pouring anything in.

The teacher has a preferred solution in mind. At the very start of the explorations, she says:

A: Oh look, look what's happened when you've lifted it *(the tubing)* up.

[Then a minute later...]

A: It worked when you lifted it up and it worked when Ben lifted it up.

Despite this being a 'challenge' for the children there is only one desirable outcome in the teacher's mind. It belongs to the teacher and it is concerned with pouring water successfully down tubing and guttering. All other solutions are dismissed. Very creatively, the children actually solve the challenge, as it has been presented to them, in the first 25 seconds of the clip:

C5:   I'll stay here all night.

The teacher rejects this because it is not the solution she wants.

A: And if you're not allowed to stay here all night?

To which the next creative thinker replies:

C7:   You can stay here too!

Again the 'solution' is rejected:

A: I could? I don't think I'd like to, I think I'd be too cold.

Undeterred another child replies:

C8:   But you could be wrapped up with thermals.

Again the teacher rejects the solution:

A: Every night, for ever and ever? No, I don't want to do this every night.

Because the challenge belongs to the teacher and the activity is adult-led, the practitioner is not sufficiently 'listening' to the children's creative and imaginative solutions. Many opportunities for testing and trialling hypotheses are missed. In addition, the children are left unclear as to why their ideas are squashed and the rather more mundane 'let's keep pouring water down this guttering' is being encouraged. It is all too easy, when a practitioner has learning objectives in mind, to miss the creative contributions that children make.

By the end of the clip, the children have understood the 'rules'. They have to do what the challenge says, not solve the problem. Child 8 says:

C8:   But the challenge says we can't get any more water.

A: Why not?

C8:   'Cos the challenge says you can't... put it... take it down.

The adult then shows that the challenge can be manipulated to suit her objectives:

A: It says, you can't carry the bucket down to give him water, but it doesn't say you can't carry it down to get some more water.

The role of the practitioner in adult-led learning is to focus children's thinking. However, it is important that this does not mean that practitioners ignore the ideas children bring to any resulting interactions.

Ask yourself: *What does the child gain?*
See the end of the transcripts in Chapter 3 for ideas.

Transcript 6:2 'Matt's water tray'
The reception class has a new water feature consisting of three black 'builders' trays of varying heights. Because the equipment is new the teacher has set it up in descending height order. In the trays is some guttering of varying lengths. Alongside the trays are some tall skittles. There is an outside tap. Matt has been experimenting with pouring water down the guttering using a watering can. When the teacher comes over to see what he is doing he tells her he is trying to make the water go up. The teacher is crouched down by the water trays.
Matt has placed some skittles inside the water trays and is trying to balance the guttering between the skittles. One piece of guttering falls off and knocks the others.

A: Ooph! *(they both laugh)*. It's like a catapult *(she picks it up)*. I can't remember which one you had it on. Was it this one?

C: I think it was yeh, like this *(he moves to another piece and moves it)* and that was like this... I think. Like... that *(another child goes to move a piece of guttering)*. No Maggie don't put it down there!

A: Maggie if you hold it up.

C: And I can do this *(balancing one piece)*... This one's slipped down *(he lifts another piece)*.

A: *(who has been watching intently)* Shall I hold onto this one?

C: Yeh.

C2: My arm is aching *(the adult holds her piece also)*.

A: Oh that's quite heavy that piece, isn't it?

C: *(balances his final piece of guttering then says)* But I think I need to move that one.

A: This one?

C: Mmm-hmm *(the adult stands to hold the piece he has indicated)* Just... mmm... knock this off *(she crouches down again)*... Under there.

A: Ahhh–that might help 'cos that's going down now.

C: Hmm... I can get that bit then.

A: So... we've got to link this bit to this bit?

C: *(looks for a while, then walks up and down looking at each piece of guttering)* Hmm... *(looks at her, she is looking attentive)*... I think we'll do it... I need to move this a bit closer *(moves a skittle that is still on the ground)*.

A: Yeh, or you could lift it into the tray?

C: *(he looks for a while)* Yeh! *(he lifts up the guttering and the teacher lifts up the skittle and puts it in the tray)*... right... and since we put that through there... and if it balances... there...

A: Ohh, that's looking good, because that's sloping down now

C: Yeh... *(another boy carries over another piece of guttering)* No Rick—we don't need any more! *(he carries the watering can to the bottom of the water feature and pours water into the guttering)*

A: Ohh, it's coming out! You did it!

Analysis

In this transcript the control over the outcomes of the activity shifts to the child. Although the practitioner set up the resources with certain intentions in mind (an adult-initiated activity), she has left the children to explore and find their own challenges. When she returns to see what Matt is doing, she spends a lot of time watching and tuning in to his investigation. The child talks far more because he is in control. The teacher is far quieter because she is watching and wondering. There is a considerable amount of silence while the child is thinking, and the practitioner does not fill this with pointless questions. She watches his face to see what he is thinking and trying to do. When he has a solution, she listens to it and tries to help him achieve it because she doesn't have preconceived solutions in mind (as in Transcript 6:1). The child sees the adult as a useful resource, happy that she holds and moves things to help him out, because she is not trying to take over. The practitioner plants one or two helpful ideas – e.g. 'So we've got to link this bit to this bit'; 'You could lift it into the tray?' – but is not trying to dictate or take over his efforts. Because Matt is in control of this activity, he is very assertive towards other children who come and threaten to interfere with what he is doing. In an adult-initiated activity, the role of the adult is to fathom children's thinking and then support them to achieve their goals.

Ask yourself: *What does the child gain?*
See the end of the transcripts in Chapter 3 for ideas.

Transcript 6:3 'Frances and the well'
Three reception-age girls are playing in the outdoor sandpit. They are putting sand into a cement mixer. One of them, Frances, goes to find the teacher and brings her over. She gives her a bucket to hold. The teacher kneels down by the side of the sandpit and waits.

C: *(To the teacher)* What's that for? *(referring to the bucket)*

A: Frances asked me to hold it. I don't know what for.

C1: What's it for Frances?

C2: To make it a better well. To get it into the bucket. *(to the teacher)* The well's getting full.

A: Is it? And what's it full of?

C2: Water.

A: Full of water.

C2: It's *getting* full of water. And that's a sign to say, 'Only kids allowed', so that adults know.

A: OK. So adults aren't allowed to get water from the well?

C2: No... just children.

C1: And grown-ups!

C2: But the adults can get it for the children.

A: What about the adults getting drinks for themselves? What if they need a drink? What do they do?

C2: We'll have to build a bigger... umm... well. *(the girls continue filling the 'well' (the cement mixer) with sand)*

A: A bigger well for the adults?

C2: Yes.

A: So you've got to build two wells then.

C2: Yes... so that will take a big job! *(She fills a plastic container with sand to go and put it in the teacher's bucket. There follows activity while the girls are busy filling containers and the 'well'. Frances stands up.)* And then we'll put up another sign to say 'No kids allowed.'

A: Ahh, so there won't be any kids allowed in the adults' well?

C2: No *(she continues filling her container)*... But I'm just getting the sand... umm... for the adult well *(she puts the sand from her container into the bucket again)*.

A: It's getting heavier.

C2: Yes... but... no... but...

C1: Just pick it all out for the grown-ups.

C1: For... umm... the children.

A: Do you want to put that in there then? *(pointing to the 'well')*

C2: Just then it can... umm... go for the adults.

C1: We're making some cakes.

C2: No! They're the water for the well.

C1: You put it up here... to join.

C3: I've got some more here for the bucket.

A: You've got some more to go in here? It needs to go in the mixer... in the bucket?

C2: They're for all of the adults. That's for all of the adults *(continues filling)* and we're not allow... and we're not... and we're not... and we're not children we're adults.

A: Oh, we're adults now?

C2: We're pretending we're adults.

C1: We're all adults too.

A: OK.

C2: And no kids allowed for the adult well.

A: So this is the adult well I'm holding onto here?

C2: Yes. And you can be the children.

Analysis

There is quite a complex play theme here. Frances seems to be using the teacher as an audience to 'sound out' her thinking. The control of the play is (mainly) in Frances' hands. Right at the start, the teacher is unsure why she is holding the bucket and, even after quite a few questions seeking clarification, she remains unclear as to the purpose of the play (other than to 'fill the well'). It took until later in the day for Frances to explain that at Sunday school they had been asked to collect money for a well in an African village and that they had heard about the children having to walk miles to get water. The play in the sandpit is clearly Frances' attempt to make sense of this rather abstract scenario. Her friends are not as involved as she is. The other two girls are enjoying filling and emptying containers, but at one stage Frances' friend suggests that they are 'making cakes' as this, perhaps, makes more sense to her than the idea of a filling a well.

Because the girls control the play they speak much more than the practitioner. There is a great deal of complex thinking and reasoning, especially by Frances. The practitioner's questions try to clarify the purpose of the play, but do not really succeed because Frances is making things up as she goes along and the scenario becomes increasingly complex. In child-led play, the practitioner has to work hard to follow the threads of children's thinking when they themselves are not always clear about what they are trying to achieve.

Ask yourself: *What does the child gain?*

See the end of the transcripts in Chapter 3 for ideas.

Transcript 6:4 'Tanya's doughnut'

Grace, an NQT in her first term of teaching, has recently introduced play into her Year 1 classroom. Her initial training did not include how to support and develop play, and she is still learning about its potential. Tanya (C1) and four other girls have been making 'doughnuts' at the dough table. Sophie and Claire have taken their doughnuts to the teacher who has duly 'tasted' them and suggested they go into the oven. Tanya, a vulnerable, insecure child with poor language skills, has watched this interaction and, when the other girls leave, takes her own 'doughnut' to the teacher.

C1: This is yours *(handing teacher her doughnut)*.

A: Oh another one! You've made a much bigger one this time Tanya.

C1: Yes.

A: Is it the same? Is it a doughnut?

C1: Yes.

A: A bigger one?

C1: Yes.

A: What shape is this one?

C1: Uh... I don't know.

A: Don't know? Can you feel round the edge? *(running her finger around the edge of the 'doughnut')*

C1: No.

A: Are there any corners on it?

C1: *(Tanya runs her finger round the edge of the 'doughnut' and comes to a bit where there is an indentation.)* Yes.

A: Where are the corners? *(Tanya points to the indentation which creates two 'corners' in the edge of the doughnut.)* Yes – that's right. There is a corner there. Well done. *(The teacher then squashes the two 'corners' together so that the edge of the doughnut becomes continuous.)* What about if we put these two bits together... now are there any corners on it?

C1: Yes.

A: Where are the corners? *(Tanya runs her finger right round the circumference of the doughnut again.)* Or is it a line right around without any corners?

C1: Yes... yes.

A: So what shape is that?

C1: I don't know... like Molly what's her b...

A: *(Turning to the children on the dough table.)* Can anyone help Tanya to know what shape this is?

C2: It's a circle... a 2D one.

A: A circle, that's right. Can you say that word Tanya?

C2: A 2D one.

C1: Circle.

C2: A 2D one.

A: A circle, good girl. It's a 2D one.

C1: You've got your necklace on *(referring to the microphone round the teacher's neck).*

A: *(Now talking to C2)* What's a 3D circle?

C2: It's like a ball.

A: Like a ball. And what word... can you remember the word for that Molly? Beginning with 's'.

C2: I think I... *(Tanya turns to look at the camera)* I think I recognize that word cylinder.

A: Cylinder yes... I think that it looks to me like Mary-Anne and Miles are making cylinders *(Tanya turns to look at the camera again).*

Analysis

In this interaction, what starts as a child-led activity is hijacked by the teacher to make it adult-led. Tanya has gone to the teacher for reassurance and affirmation. She has seen the interaction with the first two girls and wants to have that same warm attentiveness from her teacher. Grace is less than confident that talking about doughnuts is acceptable for a Year 1 teacher, and so spots the possibility of giving Tanya a test on the names and properties of shapes. Tanya cannot answer the question about the shape of the doughnut and suddenly finds herself in a negative situation rather than a positive one. Not only does she not know the name of the shape that the teacher wants, but her doughnut – so lovingly offered – is not 'good enough' as a visual aid to demonstrate the properties of a circle and is tampered with by the teacher to support her teaching point. As Tanya increasingly fails to respond in the way that the teacher hopes, we find that Molly takes over answering the questions. Molly is an able child who knows not only about circles, but about 2D circles and cylinders (although not spheres). The interaction moves away from Tanya (who needs a skilled conversational partner to improve her language skills and communication, not just her emotional well-being), and the teacher talks increasingly to Molly, who is easier to talk to and knows the right answers. Tanya tries to get her teacher's attention back 'You've got your necklace on.', but this is ignored as the teacher is now back in her comfort zone of asking questions she herself knows the answers to. Tanya twice turns to the camera to see if anyone is paying attention to her. However, the teacher is now on track to achieve what she wants to achieve, rather than 'listening' to Tanya and responding to her needs.

Ask yourself: *What does the child gain?*
See the end of the transcripts in Chapter 3 for ideas.

Summary

Effective early years practitioners are very clear about the purposes of adult-led, adult-initiated and child-led learning. The young child benefits from all three experiences. They also benefit from practitioners who are sufficiently sensitive to adjust their role according to the learning taking place. When practitioners lead the learning they should not be frightened to steer the course of that learning, even if they take some detours while responding to children's thoughts and ideas. When children lead the learning, the role of the practitioner is to follow their lead – to respond to and support the child's thinking, and to be what the child needs them to be to achieve what the child wants to achieve. Sometimes that means that the best action a practitioner can take is to step back, to observe, and to remain silent in order for the child's thinking to develop. Sometimes it means becoming a co-player, a co-constructor of knowledge and understanding in the wonderful world of the young child's curiosity and imagination. Being clear about the different purposes of activities and experiences in a setting will help practitioners ensure that any interactions taking place will enhance, and not inter-fere with, children's learning. Effective practitioners are those who are light-footed enough to keep in step with the child and their learning needs. In the next chapter we consider how effective practitioners initiate and sustain interactions in a variety of contexts.

Self-reflection

1   Am I clear about the *purpose* of the different activities in our setting?

2   Do all those who monitor the quality of learning in our setting know about and understand the differences between adult-led and child-led learning?

3   Do I interact differently (and appropriately) with children when joining in their self-initiated activity as opposed to when I am leading the learning?

7

Sustaining effective interactions

A key role of the role of the early childhood educator is to sustain children's thinking and follow the momentum of their learning.

Introduction

The role of the practitioner in an effective interaction is to sustain a dialogue with the child rather than hold a monologue with themselves. Whether the practitioner initiates the conversation or seeks to sustain it, there should be an invisible thread running between the ideas, thoughts and feelings of the child and the responses of the adult. This thread lets the child know that they are being listened to and that their thinking is being valued. If the practitioner initiates a conversation at the wrong time, and about the wrong thing, it can break the threads to the child's thinking. If the practitioner responds to the conversational overture of the child, it can be equally challenging to sustain the flow of their thinking without taking it over. As we have seen in Chapter 6, it is necessary to be clear from the outset about whether the purpose of an activity or experience belongs to the practitioner or to the child. If it belongs to the practitioner, then there are legitimate reasons for steering and focusing a child's thinking on something specific that the practitioner deems valuable. However, when the activity or experience is child-led then the skilled practitioner aims to follow the flow of the child's thinking and to sustain the momentum of their learning. This chapter considers how effective practitioners initiate and sustain interactions that enhance children's learning.

Focus on babies and toddlers

Before babies develop language they develop an understanding of how language and communication works. For example, they engage in turn-taking behaviours that reflect the turn-taking of a conversation. Babies will suck vigorously at the breast or bottle when feeding, then pause, gazing at their carer, who talks to and maybe jiggles the baby in the pauses before the baby starts sucking again (Manning-Morton 1994). Colwyn Trevarthen (1974; 2011) calls such exchanges 'proto-conversations'. He describes babies as young as two months engaging in these 'conversations' and says they provide children with an understanding of the cultural vocabulary of communication.

Babies also develop an ability to follow the adult's attention. When environments and routines are predictable, babies show that they, in turn, can predict what the adult intends to do before they do it. For example, babies look towards the kettle as their bottle is being prepared. This ability means the practitioner can show the baby interesting things and also follow the baby's attention and talk about what they are looking at or pointing at.

As babies get slightly older – around 6–8 months – there is evidence that they are directly affected in their turn-taking by the emotional expressions of the person they are interacting with (Hobson 2002). For example, they smile less when that person is sad. So around this age, infants are perceiving and responding to the behaviour of other people in one-to-one interactions. They are developing what Hobson describes as 'increasingly rich and pleasurable forms of mutually sensitive interpersonal engagement' (p.42). It is around this age that babies become interested in play that has a pattern to it, such as 'peek-a-boo' and 'ring-a-roses'. Bruner (1983) suggests that these games provide a further framework for early turn-taking in communications between the infant and their caregiver. The games embody some important features of communication and in due course they provide a kind of scaffolding for the introduction of language itself as the infant is 'ready to take their role in the communicative dance of interpersonal exchange' (Hobson 2002: 58).

Initiating conversations

Adult-led learning

When a practitioner has planned for or seen the opportunity for learning, then they have a purpose in mind and the conversation they instigate is focused on that learning. If the activity or experience is pre-planned, then it seems to me that the introduction to that activity or experience needs to be quite direct.

For babies (one-to-one, not group):

'I can see you. I can see you in the mirror.'

'We're going down the road, past the shops, here's the post box.'

For 2- to 3-year-olds (one-to-one, not group):

'You're nearly there Jack. Shall I hold your hands this time to see if you can reach the top?'

'I'm going to dig this earth here and then we can plant the bulbs.'

For 4+:

'I thought it would be really helpful if we…'

'I watched you making your model yesterday and I thought you might want to know…'

'Today, I'm going to show you how…'

As we have seen in Chapter 6, it is all too easy to wrap up adult–led learning in such fancy ways (in order to make it more 'appealing') that we muddle children about what they are learning and why. The challenge for practitioners comes when, having initiated an interaction, the child's thinking goes off on another tangent altogether. There is no one way to manage this, but learning is often most effective when it has immediate relevance and meaning for the young child (Donaldson 1987; Nutbrown 2006; Athey 2007; Dowling 2013), and so following the threads of the child's thinking as they make unexpected connections is still appropriate. However, by following these threads it is important that the practitioner does not stray so far away from the purposes of the adult-led plan that its objectives are never met. This can result in the practitioner feeling pressured to interfere with child-led learning in order to 'cover' elements of the curriculum not successfully covered when they were planned (see Transcript 6:4). Often the child's tangential thinking can be acknowledged, responded to and then brought back to focus on the original purposes of the activity. Sometimes, however, their thinking – and the subsequent interaction – goes so far away from the practitioner's plan (and has such value in itself) that the practitioner needs to stay with the momentum of the child's learning and plan to return to her own objectives another day.

Child-led learning

When an activity or experience is child-led, the conversation springs from the child's thoughts, connections and feelings. The child may see something – e.g. an adult modelling a skill; may hear a story; may become fascinated by something, e.g. a caterpillar climbing a wall; may experience something, e.g. feelings of sadness because grandma is ill; and any of these can trigger thoughts and feelings that become very important to the child. The child initiates a conversation and the alert and responsive practitioner takes their turn to respond to and contribute to the child's opening comments or question.

Sometimes, however, the child's thoughts are internal and they do not need to talk at that moment. They are thinking something through, or just enjoying a feeling or sensation and living in the moment without need of conversation or commentary. At times like these, if the practitioner initiates a conversation, then the child's thinking is interrupted or distracted and this does not help the child's learning momentum. When children are engrossed in activity, or when they are deep in thought, then the best maxim is 'Don't speak until you are spoken to.' In this way, if the child chooses to say something, the practitioner knows that a conversation is welcomed. More than that, the child has given the practitioner the conversational opener. The practitioner is not guessing what the child is thinking about or what is fascinating the child, because what the child has said establishes this. All that remains is for the practitioner to respond to the child's contribution and to follow the child's train of thought and not take the child off on a tangent that suits the practitioner's purposes more than the child's.

> 66When a child is deep in thought, Don't Speak Until You're Spoken To.99

Whatever the context of a conversation, Pascal and Bertram (1997) describe the interaction between the practitioner and child as symbiotic, because not only does the adult's style of engagement directly affect the children's levels of involvement, but the children's involvement affects the adult's style of engagement. Malaguzzi (in Edwards et al. 1993: 79) says: 'Learning and teaching should not stand on opposite banks and just watch the river go by; instead, they should embark together on a journey down the water. Through an active, reciprocal exchange, teaching can strengthen learning how to learn.'

Sustaining interactions

In thinking about how to sustain an interaction, the participants in the Oxfordshire ACI Project found it helpful to reflect on the reciprocity of an effective exchange (see Chapter 10). Rather than just 'receiving' a child's comment or question, the practitioners became increasingly thoughtful about what they offered the child in return. While this depended very much on the child, the situation and the conversation taking place, there was evidence that, too often, practitioners ended an interaction when it could usefully have been continued. Practitioners found themselves saying 'Uh, huh', 'Lovely, 'Did you?' and, consequently, the interaction had nowhere to go. In the project DVD footage it was apparent that, in effective interactions, the practitioner offered something back to the child by way of a comment, an idea or piece of information which, if relevant to the conversation that the child was wanting to have, took the child's thinking further and enhanced their learning.

Babies   The baby grizzles because he is feeling hungry

      A: 'I can see you're miserable. Would you like some milk?'

      The baby kicks his legs excitedly

      A: 'You like that song don't you. It goes la-la la-la-la!'

2- to 3-year-olds   C: 'It won't go over the bump.'

      A: 'Sometimes if you make the car go faster it can get over bumps like that.'

      C: 'Shoes.'

      A: 'We need to put your shoes and coat on then we can go outside.'

4+   A: 'Will you tell me when it's time to go because I'd like to come for a ride.'

      C: 'Yeh.'

      C2:   'And a bit of oil.'

      A: 'Add a bit of oil, Daniel says. Don't forget the oil for your engine… to keep it working smoothly.'

C: 'Shall we mix water in the sand for the bricks?'

A: 'You could do. On the building site they mix sand with water in a big cement mixer to make the cement that helps the bricks stick together.'

In these examples, the practitioners return the child's thinking 'with interest':

- in emotional terms: *showing interest* in the child, their ideas and thoughts and feelings
- in dialogic terms: *adding interest* (adding something more) to what the child has offered.

The practitioner may offer the child:

- *vocabulary*: extending the child's single word contribution by offering a phrase or sentence in return
- *a question*: that clarifies what the child has said
- *a comment*: about a personal experience or a similar idea that the practitioner has had
- *some knowledge or information*: that the practitioner thinks might be helpful.

All of these strategies are those used by adults in natural, genuine conversations where both parties are concerned for the other and both see it is a responsibility to sustain the momentum of the dialogue. With young children, offering a conversational response 'with interest' is a far more effective strategy for sustaining interactions than constant questioning. It is as though the effective practitioner keeps opening up

children's thinking rather than closing it down; illuminating their ideas rather than simply interrogating them. As we shall see in Chapter 9, the use of too many questions (especially those to which the practitioner already knows the answer) often halts the flow of a child's thinking because questions are too frequently used to direct and to manipulate thinking and, all too often, put the practitioner in control of the interaction. Responding 'with interest', and offering a comment, statement or idea, encourages the child to think more deeply and allows them to maintain their own learning momentum.

Maintaining the learning momentum

Once a conversation has begun – whether initiated by the practitioner or the child – then there are several well-documented strategies for keeping the interaction flowing. During the Oxfordshire ACI Project, participants documented the following strategies most frequently as being effective in maintaining the child's learning momentum and keeping the 'threads' of a conversation between the adult and the child intact. Many were invaluable for offering the child a response 'with interest', thus sharing the exchange rather than dominating it. All of these strategies can be useful whether an interaction is adult-led or child-led, but some may be particularly suited to one context rather than another.

Commenting
Commenting is particularly valuable for practitioners working with children with little verbal language – very young children; those with English as an additional language; those with language delay (see Chapter 8). By commenting, words, grammar and figures of speech are reinforced and modelled by the practitioner. For example:

> 'My hands are getting colder in the water.'
> 'You're putting dolly to bed because she's tired.'
> 'The train is going through the tunnel. Is it coming out the other side yet?'

As with many strategies, 'commenting' can be overdone. When the practitioner speaks too much their words become like background music, and the child only notices when the sound is switched off. But used judiciously, commenting can enhance the crucial elements of speech, language and communication that we considered in Chapters 1 and 2.

Pondering
Pondering is an unthreatening way of posing a question. 'Pondering' suggests that the practitioner is interested in the question too, rather than she has the answer and is 'testing' the child. It also suggests that there will be a joint exploration or investigation, with practitioner and child co-constructing ideas and possibilities as their investigation proceeds. For example:

'I wonder if…?'

'I wonder why…?'

'I wonder whether…?'

> **"Planting an idea seems far more effective than demanding an answer."**

'I wonder' is a valuable question to use with young children as it opens up their thinking, rather than closing it down. 'I wonder' often plants an idea (rather than demanding an answer) to which the child can return when they make the relevant connections for themselves.

Imagining

Many young children have vivid imaginations, and it is vital that practitioners encourage their creative thinking in a whole range of contexts. Children need to be 'in someone else's shoes' (Duffy 2006) to imagine what it is like to be someone or do something outside their normal range of powers. Practitioners can help children to project into other people's lives, and to project into situations that they might never have experienced.

'What might it be like to…?'

'I can imagine…'

'Perhaps…'

'Let's pretend we…'

Being placed – or placing themselves – in an imaginary situation supports the development of children's creative thinking, which is so vital for developing their own ideas, using their imagination, and being original.

Connecting

It is crucial that practitioners help children make connections in their learning. Once the brain's neural connections are in place, the neurons are then able to communicate with one another and the brain can interpret the world in the light of experience. By reminding children of things that have happened, or that they have done in the past, we help them 'bring to mind' and exploit those aspects of their past experience that we know might be useful (Wood 1998: 97). It is much easier to remember something new if we can connect what is new to what is already known and understood. Jerome Bruner (1983: 183) once famously wrote that 'Learning is… figuring out how to use what you already know in order to go beyond what you currently think.'

'Do you remember how we planted the seeds under the soil? See… that's the top of the plant that is going to grow!'

'Do you remember when/how…?'

'It's just like when we/you…'

'If you can manage XX today, maybe you can try YY tomorrow.'

Thinking aloud

Sometimes asking children 'Why don't you try this…?' gets little response, whereas the more indirect 'I think I'll try this…' often leads to children following the practitioner's lead, thereby extending their repertoire of ideas. Young children respond to adults as role models (Rogoff 1990; Bandura 1977), and if a significant adult is seen trying or doing something then it often stimulates the child to copy. It also helps the child in their understanding of 'being a learner', that adults think things through and try things out as a result.

'I'm going to try…'

'I remember when I tried…'

'I did something like this before…'

Talking about feelings

It can be a great temptation, as caring adults, not to talk to children about their feelings. But research tells us that in order to manage feelings children have to confront them (Gerhardt 2010) and to be able to name them (Robinson 2014). Doing so, as situations arise naturally, is the best way to give children permission to express what they are feeling and that their feelings are OK.

'I think Sophie might be upset because she's missing her mummy too"

'I can see you're excited 'cos daddy's coming soon.'

'I think you're cross because you wanted that trike and Andrew got there first. Let's have a cuddle and then it will be your turn.'

Reflecting back to children

One way to show children that we have been listening to their thinking is to reflect back what they have said. Sometimes it is sufficient to repeat their own words. Sometimes they show us something through action and we give the action words. Sometimes we reflect back what the child has said and then embellish it.

'I was thinking what a good idea it was to make the witch into a good witch.'

'I think you've chosen the best bricks there because they've made the bridge far more secure.'

'I like your idea that the snail leaves a trail on the ground to move more easily. I think it also helps him to…'

Supporting the child to make choices and decisions

Often in our attempts to give children choice we make that choice too broad. Very young children may need their choices limited so that they become manageable. By supporting children's choices and decision making we help them increasingly to have control over their lives and its consequences.

'Would you like the red ones or the blue ones?'

'Do you think baby bear would rather have eaten his porridge or gone for that walk?'

'Would you like to use charcoal or chalk?'

As children get older their capacity for making choices increases, and so should the options offered by the practitioner.

Explaining/Informing

Sometimes children just need to be told something. Rather than be made to think about something or asked their opinion or told to go and fetch a book, they just need to be given an explanation or an answer. Practitioners can give reasons for why something has happened; they can explain outcomes; they can describe cause-and-effect relationships; they can justify actions and they can recognize problems and offer solutions.

'If you turn the saw like this you'll be able to cut right through.'

'The leaves have turned brown because they are dying and they'll fall off the trees so new leaves can grow.'

'Oh look. He forgot to tie his shoelaces and so he tripped over.'

'You have to wear your coat because it's cold outside.'

However, it is important that any such 'information' comes after the child has had the chance to show whether they already know this, or have had a go at something and want to be given the explanation.

Posing problems

Donaldson (1978) reminds us that young children tend to bring the concrete – what they know, understand and have experienced – to abstract situations and, therefore, sometimes 'reason' inaccurately because they bring this limited experience to bear. We can challenge children's thinking by posing problems which they can then solve in their own way and within their own capacities. These challenges need to be genuine, have meaning for the child, and be worth solving.

'Maybe there's a way of reaching the hook so Luke can fix it?'

'I wonder if there's a way to keep the grass dry in the den?'

'There must be a way to remember who's had a turn?'

Staying quiet

Finally, there are times to stay quiet. Times when children need to be given the opportunity to think rather than answer the practitioner's queries and questions. Time for the practitioner to stay attentive but not be intrusive. Time for the practitioner to watch and wait and wonder at what children are doing, thinking and learning.

All of these strategies can be used to offer children a response 'with interest'. All of them are valuable within a repertoire of strategies to maintain the learning momentum of an activity, experience or discussion. If the practitioner's comment or question, or the opportunity to make a connection arises from the contribution of the child, then the practitioner can be confident that they are supporting the child's thinking and not interrupting it. All of the strategies above, if used in the right way and at the right time, can enhance the child's understanding of the world around them.

Consolidating, extending and provoking thinking

As early childhood educators we know that **supporting** a child's learning is necessary, but not sufficient. It seems to me that there are three distinct ways in which practitioners enhance the learning of children; and all three have equal importance. The most effective practitioners help to **consolidate** children's learning, they **extend** children's learning and they **provoke** children's learning. Each has something unique to offer the child, and all three are necessary strategies in the dialogic armoury of the practitioner.

Consolidating children's learning

In an educational climate that has embraced the notion of 'next steps' with such alacrity, it is crucial to be reminded of the importance for young children of consolidation. For young children, the world is new and challenging and often bewildering. They need to revisit concepts, to practise skills, to learn fresh facts in a variety of situations and over long periods of time. That is why the concept of 'progress' is so challenging for early childhood educators. Sometimes a seed is sewn that takes root and flourishes many days, months, or even years later, rather than progress being apparent after one brief input. Progress in the early years goes in two directions. It *moves on* when the child is indeed ready for their 'next steps', but it also goes deeper as the child learns more, becomes more skilled, and makes more connections with something already familiar.

Piaget (1929) tells us that all new learning has to be assimilated into what is already known. Sometimes this is easily done. But sometimes children's existing knowledge needs to be shifted to make way for what they have just discovered. They have to rethink their view of the world and how they thought things were.

Transcript 7:1
Consolidating: Thinking and ideas
Nursery children in small group telling story of The Three Little Pigs

C (3:10): 'I know… I know… we could use the straw to make a nest.'
A: 'Yes, I see. If you use the straw to make a nest it'd be cosy and warm like our hamster in his cage.'

Transcript 7:2
Consolidating: Attitudes and dispositions
The teacher is helping a nursery boy (3:7) make his superhero cloak. He has done a lot himself, but is struggling to cut the final bit of material across the hem where it is thicker.

A: 'You did this much?' *(holding it up to show him)*
C: 'I'll try, I'll try… and do that bit like this. If you hold it like that I could cut it.'

A: 'How?'

C: 'I just go like.' *(and he 'air' cuts with his scissors)*

A: 'We've got to concentrate… watch your fingers.'

C: 'It's a bit stiff.'

A: 'Ohh… I don't believe it *(the scissors can't cut through).* We need to get to the end! Shall we try this way round.' *(The teacher turns the fabric onto its side.)*

C: 'Come on!'

A: 'You're nearly there. Open your scissors again.'

(The boy leaves, smiling broadly, to use his cape.)

C: *(Wearily)* 'You see what I could do some tomorrow? … Do some more of that tomorrow?'

A: 'Ahh… I don't know if your hand will be aching too much tomorrow… you've done so much cutting.'

C: 'Oooof. I think you need to…'

A: 'I think we're both exhausted.'

C: 'I'm exhausted because I did so much.'

A: 'I know. You've done most of it.' *(The teacher lays the fabric down on the carpet)*

C: *(Suddenly brightens)* 'Can I try and do it like that when it lies down?'

A: 'Yes, that might work.' *(She settles down leaning on her elbow to hold the fabric for him… he cuts through)*

       'Ooooo… that worked.' *(Claps her hands).* 'Brilliant. You did it! You've got your piece of fabric the right size.'

(The boy leaves, smiling broadly, to use his cape.)

Extending children's learning

However, if children only ever visit the familiar then they will not adequately extend their knowledge and understanding of the world and their skills and concepts will not develop as they should. Sometimes young children extend their own understanding by interacting with the environment and meeting challenges that have to be solved. Piaget (1929) believed that children's learning is at its optimum when their curiosity is *not fully* satisfied and that, therefore, the best learning experiences are those that keep children curious, make them wonder, and offer them real-life problems to solve, rather than just giving them information. Vygotsky (1978), on the other hand, while accepting Piaget's theory of the growth of concepts through experiences, believed that our understanding of the world was also drawn from the understanding of others, that 'The path from object to child and from child to object passes through another person.' (Vygotsky 1978: 30). Consequently, it is Vygotsky's work that has particularly influenced much recent thinking about the interactive nature of language, thought and understanding. Vygotsky argued that the role of the adult is to help the child accomplish things that they would otherwise not achieve alone. He claimed that without a natural ability to teach as well as to learn, human cultures would never have developed since they can only develop if the mature teach and the immature learn. One of the chief contributions Vygotsky made to educational thinking was his concept of the 'zone of proximal development', which is described (Wood 1998: 26) as 'the "gap" that exists for an individual (child or adult) between what he is able to do alone and what he can achieve with help from one more knowledgeable or skilled than himself'. Thus, Vygotsky saw a far more active and interventionist role for the practitioner than did Piaget for, as Vygotsky claims, 'learning awakens a variety of internal development processes that are able to operate only when the child is interacting with people in his environment' (1978: 90).

Sometimes practitioners in early years settings extend children's thinking by introducing them to something quite new: a new mobile; a new construction kit; a new mathematical concept such as halving or sharing; or a new idea about their feelings or relationships. Sometimes, practitioners extend children's thinking by taking something with which the child is already familiar and showing them, for example, how eggs in an incubator will hatch into chicks if they have the right conditions in which to thrive. Sometimes practitioners plan to extend children's learning (i.e. in an adult-led activity) and sometimes an opportunity presents itself in the middle of an activity or experience that the child has initiated. In both instances it is helpful to think: 'What else can I tell the child or show the child or say to the child that will add to their current understanding or extend their view of the world?'

Transcript 7:3

Extending: by adding information

A group of children are playing in the outside house. Will is making food for the baby the teacher is holding for him. Will asks the teacher to taste the food.

     A: Is it OK for the baby to have some too? Is it safe for the baby?
C (4:10): Yeh it's safe... I'll get a spoon.
     A: Cos if you have big bits in food babies can choke on them, can't they?

(The boy 'feeds the baby' which is still on the teacher's lap, taking great care to scoop up little bits at a time.)

Transcript 7:4

Extending: by talking about your own experiences

A reception teacher is talking to a girl about the bus she is making from junk modelling materials.

C (5:1): One, two, three, four (wheels) and a wheel on top!
     A: What's the wheel on top for?
     C: A spare one.
     A: In case they have an accident... or in case the tyre pops?
     C: In case the tyre pops.
     A: My car's got a spare tyre... and it's inside my boot, not on the top.

Provoking children's learning

Finally, effective practitioners use interactions to **provoke thinking**. The notion of 'provocation' has become embedded in the practice of early childhood educators as a consequence of the influence of the Reggio Emilia approach to early learning (see, for example, Katz 1993). While sparking children's interests and inspiring them to pose questions and discover solutions is a fundamental tenet of British nursery education, the use of the word 'provocation' to describe the process originated in the preschools in Northern Italy, where 'provocations' are seen to arise from children's questions; from an event; from a story; from a question posed by an adult; from the environment; from an object, or from a problem to be solved. The fundamental premise is that the world around the child offers many learning opportunities that sometimes need a trigger (or provocation) to capture their interest and engage their thinking.

I am using the word 'provocation' in a different way here. I believe the notion of provocation takes children's thinking beyond being 'extended'. To extend thinking suggests that the educator builds on and enhances what is already known. It suggests something quite sequential and logical about the next steps of understanding or learning a skill. The word provocation seems to me to have an element of surprise. It is as though thinking has been 'caught out' – as though we have met something unexpected that does not necessarily fit with our current understanding of the world. Piaget has explained how, when humans learn something new, they assimilate it into what is already known. Sometimes it is easy and the pieces of information – the new and the old – fit together logically and easily. Sometimes however, the new challenges the old. What we thought we understood is knocked off balance by what we now know. Piaget refers to this as cognitive conflict (Piaget 1985). The child enters a state of disequilibrium, Wood explains, as new understandings are 'brought into question by the reality of events' (1998: 56) and the child struggles to accommodate this new, unexpected reality until he finds a mental solution that restores his equilibrium. As Wood explains, 'some accommodations require dramatic changes in the structure of the child's understanding of the world' (1998: 54), though the very struggle eventually makes the learning and understanding all the more robust.

To provoke young children's thinking is to offer them something unexpected and outside their cognitive 'box', something that challenges them to rethink their existing view of the world and with which they have to grapple to come to a satisfactory mental solution. Claxton (1997) argues that the process of coming to know develops from uncertainty. This causes children to be cognitively turned upside down so that they have to work harder to think of what to do or what to say. When a practitioner provokes children's thinking, the child is met with a situation that surprises and, to begin with, baffles them. In order to make sense of the situation they have to think creatively so that the situation is resolved.

> **"Sometimes a child needs to be temporarily baffled to provoke higher-order thinking."**

Practitioners can provoke children's thinking either in a planned situation (an adult-led context) or spontaneously. But it is important that the practitioner knows the child sufficiently well to ensure they are not overly confused or upset by the provocation. Some children are simply too unsure of themselves or of their relationship with the practitioner to have their cognitive world turned upside down. Equally, no child (and no adult) likes to be constantly provoked. There is nothing more aggravating or unsettling than everything you say being turned on its head so you feel unsure of everything or unwilling to say anything for fear you will get a provoking response.

These three kinds of interactions – consolidating, extending and provoking – just as with the three learning contexts for children in Chapter 6, need to be sensitively balanced. For the majority of the day, children need to feel secure: 'I recognize this'; 'I understand/can do this'; 'I'm really good at this – watch' for some of the day (as long as it is at an appropriate moment for the child) it is good to be extended: 'I didn't know that'; 'How do I...?'; 'What will happen if I...?' Finally, it is good to be a little provoked: 'Oh... what do I do now?'; 'I thought you were going to say...'; 'Oh no, my idea won't work!' Having watched countless practitioners work in countless settings, I see children taken to a completely different level of thinking by sensitive and judicious provocation, so that their ideas are really sharpened and they become truly creative in their search for solutions.

Transcript 7:5

Provoking: posing an unexpected problem

A large group of nursery children are involved in 'cat play'. They have told the teacher that she is the 'cat mum'. A child comes up to the teachers and says:

C (3:4): Mummy, mummy I've hurt my paw.

The teacher takes a wooden block from her pocket to phone the vet.

A: Hello, mummy here. One of the cats has hurt her paw. Can we have an appointment? *(Then she looks worried and says:)* Oh really... Oh... Oh... Oh... OK... well I'll ring tomorrow then. *(Turning to the girl)* Do you know what the vet said? The vet is ill. So they can't see any animals.

The girls look confused for a moment, then one of them says: 'I'm a vet, I know what to do.' – and the play continues.

Transcript 7:6

Provoking: saying something unexpected (deliberately using humour)

A student teacher is reading a group of nursery children 'The Very Hungry Caterpillar' (Carle 1969). The children know the story well and are calling out bits of the text they know and can anticipate. The student turns to the page where the caterpillar builds a cocoon around himself, and she 'reads'...

A: 'Then he nibbled a hole in the cocoon, pushed his way out and... he was a beautiful... elephant.'

The children are stunned into silence for a minute and then roar with laughter and get busy telling her why she is wrong and why it is a butterfly and couldn't possibly be an elephant!

> **Analysing your own practice: Consolidating, extending and provoking learning**
>
> • The practitioner is clear about the difference between consolidating, extending, and provoking learning.
> • The practitioner is not only concerned with 'next steps'; progress in the early years goes 'deeper' as well as 'further'.
> • (Where appropriate) the practitioner responds 'with interest' to what the child has said.

Body language

The transcripts above show how effective practitioners consolidate, extend and provoke children's thinking. But success in supporting children's thinking and learning does not end there. There are two further factors that impact on the effectiveness of an interaction between a practitioner and a child. The first is **body language** and the second is **tone of voice**.

Research has demonstrated that body language has the greatest percentage of impact when it comes to communicating messages to another person. The research of Albert Mehrabian, undertaken in 1971, is often quoted to demonstrate this. Mehrabian's research claimed:

• Words (the literal meaning) account for 7 per cent of the overall message.
• Tone of voice accounts for 38 per cent of the overall message.
• Body language accounts for 55 per cent of the overall message.

However, it is important to note that Mehrabian himself later wrote that the 7 per cent figure can be misleading as it could imply that the words we say are of relatively little importance. His original research was concerned with feelings and attitudes, and he later wrote that 'Unless a communicator is talking about their feelings or attitudes, these equations are not applicable.'

The fact remains that the messages we give through our bodies are powerful and can contradict the words that we say. Young children are very astute. They know that if a practitioner says 'How lovely' as they walk by, that their interest is only slight. In order to give children a secure feeling of our interest in them, practitioners must stop, listen and respond. Stopping means getting down to the child's own level so the child believes the practitioner has 'all the time in the world'. Listening means being quiet so the child can say what they have to say, without the practitioner guessing or assuming and trying to hurry the child along. Responding means keeping the child's thinking or learning momentum buoyant by reacting and responding 'with interest' to what the child has said to show they have listened and understood and are engaged.

Body language is clearly very hard to exemplify in writing, but the Oxfordshire practitioners attempted to summarize what they saw on their DVD material in written form to try and express what effective practitioners *do* to sustain a conversation, as well as what they actually *say*.

Analysing your own practice: Body language

- The practitioner displays warm attentiveness.
- The practitioner's eyes are alert and show interest; they are focused on the child.
- The practitioner's body is relaxed, but leaning towards the child.
- The practitioner does not break away from an interaction to take notes or make assessments (see Chapter 5: the practitioner should do this once the interaction is over).

Tone of voice

The other feature of non-verbal communication, which it is hard to describe in words, is tone of voice. The Oxfordshire Project participants noted that when an interaction was considered effective, the practitioner spoke to the child in ways that demonstrated their warm attentiveness – but the tone of voice was neither patronising nor condescending. One participant said that the effective practitioners used a tone of voice that they would use with an adult friend, a tone of voice that they did not keep just for interacting with young children. The only exception to this, of course, is 'motherese', where the parent or practitioner engages the baby by deliberately talking in a higher pitched voice in shorter and simpler sentences, often repeating the same thing over and over again (see Chapter 2). Interestingly, tests show that babies choose to listen to mothers talking to infants over mothers talking to adults (Gopnik et al. 1999: 129). Their preferences have nothing to do with the actual words mothers use, but they seem to choose it because it is a sort of 'comfort language'. However, those practitioners working with slightly older children the Oxfordshire project team identified as being the most tuned in to their children, and most effective in their interactions, used a tone of voice described as 'genuine', 'respectful', and 'normal'.

Analysing your own practice: Tone of voice

- The practitioner's voice is not patronising.
- The practitioner's voice is natural.
- The practitioner's verbal response is genuine.
- The practitioner's tone of voice is respectful.

Transcript: sustaining effective interactions

Transcript 7:7 'Terri and girls in the gazebo'

Two 3-year-old girls are in the gazebo in their nursery garden with their teacher. One of the girls is writing a sign that says 'Don't', and the teacher is sitting next to her. The girl is cross that some boys trampled on the newly planted bulbs the day before, and wants to tell them not to do it again. The conversation has turned to the snails that they saw in the garden.

C1: *(Is rubbing some paper over the teacher's forehead.)* Do you like snails, Terri?

A: Well... I do like snails actually. I know a lot of people don't like them going on their...

C: There's slime on your forehead!

A: Well there would be... if there was a snail on me. They need slime don't they, to move along.

C2: Why do they need slime?

A: Hmm?

C2: What does slime do?

A: Why do they need slime? Because their bodies are very soft and delicate *(both girls are listening intently)*. They haven't got any bones to protect them, so they produce the slime so that when they're going along *(she demonstrates on the table)*, perhaps over bumpy ground or sharp stones, their skin is protected

C2: By the slime?

A: Yes. It stops them being hurt. We've got our skin to protect us and we've got our bones.

C: But we've got two layers of skin.

A: Have we?

C: Yes... like koalas.

A: I didn't know that koalas had two layers of skin.

C: And we've... 'cos they're animals.

A: Mmm… we are, we are.

C: Do you need a plaster or a haircut? Do you madam?

A: Madam… I do actually need a plaster. Look, or something, I've got a lump on that finger. What do you think you could do about that?

C: That means you might have to go to the fifteenth floor of the hospital, emergency part, erm… emergency part, and the, and the hospital will chop your finger open. But don't worry… remember what you did with a little boy one day? You took him to the hospital to get his finger sewed on *(the teacher realizes what she is talking about, and nods slowly)*

A: I did tell you about that didn't I? That really happened. A little boy did get the top of his finger chopped off.

C: I think it was…

A: It was the daddy of the little boy. It was Charlie's daddy.

C2: Well do you know what – look, you don't actually have two layers of skin because look… blood! *(she holds up her wrist which has a scratch)*

A: It's actually not coming out though. I think that that's the second layer of skin *(pointing)* that Evie is talking about.

Analysis

This transcript shows how attentive practitioners have to be to the twists and turns of children's thinking and conversation. From snails to koalas to manicures to fingers being chopped off, this teacher moves effortlessly to follow the girls' thinking and to make appropriate responses. Some of the teacher's answers are complex. But she knows the girls well and can see they are listening. There is a significant difference between the explanation in this transcript and the one about batteries in Transcript (5:2). In this instance, the girls have asked for an explanation, and therefore have a vested interest in the teacher's answer. They also show their understanding by asking a follow-up question of their own 'By the slime?'. In Transcript 5:2, on the other hand, the boy wants to play, but instead gets an explanation he didn't ask for and isn't interested in. The interaction with these two girls is sustained because of the close, warm relationship the practitioner has (the close body contact is evidence of that in that she doesn't flinch or move away, for example, when the first child wipes paper over her 'slimy' forehead). She tunes in to each change of theme; the problems she sets are genuine ('I've got a lump on that finger… What do you think you could do about that?). Her tone of voice is respectful and she treats the girls as conversational equals.

Ask yourself: *What does the child/children gain?*
See the end of the transcripts in Chapter 3 for ideas.

Summary

Sustaining interactions with young children is challenging and complex. It requires practitioners to be alert at all times to the signals and messages being sent by children and being thoughtful and intelligent about how best to respond. Through their responses, effective practitioners consolidate, extend and provoke children's thinking, and they need to know their children well, and have observed them with care in order to pick the right strategy at the right time. As this chapter has shown, there are many different ways in which interactions can be initiated and sustained. But the overarching message is clear:

- Say only what is necessary.
- Mean what you say.
- Don't speak if it will interfere with learning.

In the next chapter we consider children who do not want to talk to us, and see what strategies seem to work to encourage the reluctant talker.

Self-reflection

1   Do I dominate interactions, rather than sustain them?

2   Do I consolidate, extend and sometimes provoke children's learning at appropriate times?

3   Does my body language and tone of voice encourage children to talk to me?

8

Interacting with children who might not want to interact

There are children who do not want to interact with us... and (regrettably) some children with whom we do not want to interact

Introduction

When we think about young children, we usually think of them brimming over with things to say and chattering happily to communicate their thoughts and feelings. Yet, in our early years settings, there are children who, for a variety of reasons, find communication far more difficult; children who cannot or will not use their voices to tell us how they feel or what they think. When the Oxfordshire project team were analysing their DVD footage it became apparent that the same children often appeared in shot, interacting readily with different practitioners on a range of issues. These were children who clearly enjoyed the company of adults and enjoyed interacting with them; children who were used to sharing their thoughts with an appreciative audience and who felt that they had something worthwhile to say. These children were usually those who had homes where talk was valued and where the children were valued *as* talkers. The DVD footage shows not only that these children talk more readily to practitioners, but that practitioners talk more readily to them. It is clearly easier to interact with the children who are easiest to interact with – not only because it means that conversations flow more readily, but also because these more talkative children make practitioners feel as though they are effective as communicators. Once the project team noticed how easy it is to be drawn to the children who like to talk, they made a special effort to identify those children in their settings who were reluctant talkers and to research what needed to be done to improve the quality of their interactions with them. This chapter focuses on more reluctant talkers and the strategies attempted to encourage them to communicate.

> ❝It is easiest for practitioners to interact with those children who are easiest to interact with.❞

Focus on babies and toddlers

We have seen in previous chapters that young children are driven to form close attachments to their primary caregivers as a biological necessity (Bowlby 1969). The baby has a fundamental need to feel safe and secure, and 'attachment' refers to the relationship that is forged between baby and caregiver, according to the comfort that the caregiver brings when the baby is at his most distressed. By about seven months, babies will usually show secure attachment behaviour by being very wary of strangers and clinging on to their main caregiver at all costs. Bowlby believed that the main ingredient for developing secure attachments is parenting characterized by warmth, sensitivity, responsiveness and dependability (Underdown 2007). Where interactions are not warm, responsive or consistent then babies will act out their distress. This acting out may be aggressive, with hyperactivity or challenging or attention-seeking behaviour. Or it may be passive, with the infant appearing self-reliant and resistant to comfort from adults, or happy to accept help from *any* adult rather than one main caregiver (O'Connor 2013).

The baby who does not react to and interact with their main caregiver has already learned that, for some reason, this adult is not to be relied upon to offer the comfort the baby seeks. Yet feeling connected to someone else is fundamental to our emotional health (O'Connor 2014). The child who does not have consistent positive feedback from the person they most depend on will come to believe that they do not 'matter enough' to anyone, and will live with what O'Connor refers to as 'intolerable' stress and anxiety.

The child who has been neglected or who has had multiple disruptions to their attachments will be most in need of sensitive interactions from knowledgeable practitioners. This is often challenging because even these very youngest children may already be displaying behaviours that make them harder to respond to in positive ways. If a young child has been let down by their primary caregiver it can be harder for them to accept love and care from anyone else, for fear of being let down still further. It is easy to assume that the child who has insecure attachments must be looking to find someone to latch onto emotionally. However, young children with insecure attachments often reject what it is they most want. They turn away from close care and attention for reasons of self-preservation – steeling themselves to be rejected before it actually happens. Babies and toddlers with insecure attachments are most in need of sympathetic and therapeutic practitioners who can begin to build the positive neural connections that come from repeated patterns of positive nurturing.

Reluctant talkers

Most children talk quite naturally, and cannot wait to use their more sophisticated communicative powers. However, there are some children for whom interaction and communication are, or become, increasingly difficult. They lack the confidence or the will to enter into the vibrant exchange of news, ideas, thoughts and feelings that their peers seem to relish.

Children who are quiet or shy

Young children who are just starting in an early years setting are often quiet, even when they are reported to be chatty and communicative at home. It may simply be that the child needs time to grow in confidence in a new place, surrounded by new people. Some children lack experience in talking to unfamiliar adults and children, and will need sensitive help to join in a group activity or to participate in an interaction where they have to compete for adult attention. Initially, these children may respond most positively to being with one attentive adult they know best – probably their Key Person (see Elfer et al. 2012). They may be keen to join in with group activities, but should not be put 'on the spot' by being asked to go first. Shy children may be more concerned than other children about how practitioners will react to them; particularly whether the practitioner will approve or disapprove of what they are doing or saying. It is important that practitioners neither attempt to coerce quiet children to join in, or make too much fuss if they do. Quiet children often lack confidence. The effective practitioner will give them time to observe others in action before expecting them to participate. As with all reluctant talkers, the key is not to pressurize. The shy child needs to be reassured that their early years setting is a safe place in which to talk, when they are ready.

Johnson and Jones (2012) remind us that many reluctant talkers are highly aware of possible negative reactions to what they might say or do. Sometimes this is because they lack confidence or have low self-esteem and expect that nothing they do will be right. However, sometimes it is because they are perfectionists and believe that whatever they do *has* to be right or people will think negatively about them. Either way, this can lead to children feeling very anxious about making mistakes and, say Johnson and Jones, 'a negative reaction from an adult or another child, no matter how small, can confirm that they were right in feeling this' (2012: 9). When we talk to each other, what we say is rarely perfect; there are bound to be mispronunciations, or times when what we say does not make sense to the listener. Alexander (2008) suggests that this is the very power of talk over the written word, that it is 'transitory', we offer half-baked ideas, off-the-cuff thoughts, can change our minds as soon as we have spoken, rephrase or reframe an idea as soon as it leaves our mouths. It is the very ephemeral nature of talk that makes it an ideal companion to thinking. Whereas the written word is recorded forever in its current form, talk can respond rapidly and flexibly to whatever thoughts and feelings we currently have. Whereas confident talkers do not worry if they make mistakes when talking to other people, the quiet or shy child is often overanxious that what they say will somehow be 'wrong', and so they need time and sensitive support from practitioners to become more confident and to join in conversations and interactions without negative repercussions.

> **"It is the very ephemeral nature of talk that makes it an ideal companion to thinking"**

There is no doubt that fear of saying the wrong thing will usually end up in silence. While a shy or quiet child is building up their confidence it can be more effective to encourage them to join in with others in less direct ways. The Communication Trust's 'Hello' campaign' (www.thecommunicationtrust.org.uk/hello), launched in 2010 to increase understanding of how important it is for children and young people to develop good communication skills, suggested that shy and quiet children can gain greater confidence by:

- activities that are playful and encourage smiles and laughter
- joining in songs and rhymes
- manipulating a puppet or soft toy (it is easier to whisper to Bear than to answer yourself)
- pretending to be someone else (who has more confidence and *can* speak when spoken to).

This campaign advocated the rights of children to remain silent and participate in an interaction by listening and doing something instead of speaking. At the start of building a relationship with the child the practitioner can put words to the child's actions and to the facial expressions that are used. Often a nod or shake of the head by the practitioner can signal that they have understood what the child is attempting to convey, and the child will gain confidence through their meanings being shared and understood. If early interactions can

> **"The key with reluctant talkers is not to pressurize them to speak."**

proceed in this non-verbal way, then children inhibited by their speech are saved from painful silences and requests to repeat themselves. The quietness of young children is often a temporary response to uncertainty. These sensitive non-verbal interactions will usually lead to increasingly verbal exchanges with attentive practitioners, and also with other children. If those responding are patient and do not expect or demand a verbal contribution from the child, then most shy and quiet children will eventually emerge as confident talkers and willing communicators.

Children with speech and language difficulties

Some children who are reluctant talkers are made insecure by having a developmental delay in their speech and language. Having a language delay means that these children take longer to understand and use words and sentences than other children. They do go through the normal stages of language development expected of all children, but they do so later than most. Children who have language delay find it difficult to listen to people talking, especially in large groups. Their vocabulary is often limited, making it difficult to describe things, explain their ideas and answer questions. Generally, children with language delay sound like children who are much younger. They make errors in the articulation of sounds in words and in the construction of phrases. Their sentence structures are often very simple, containing maybe only a few words, and they make quite truncated statements – e.g. 'Me play here.' They usually use the simple present tense to express themselves and their speech has an absence of complexity. They often echo or repeat what other children have said because they are using the other person as a model and to give them confidence.

There is a wide variation in how fast different children develop speech and language. Many who cause their parents concern catch up quickly once they attend an early years setting where there is plenty to talk about, practitioners who make time to interact, and children with well-developed language skills to play and talk with. However, language delay can be caused by difficulties with a child's hearing, and it is essential that everyone is aware if children are hearing well or not. Other children may have specific language difficulties and will then need the specialist support of a speech therapist or other professional.

Children with selective mutism

Selective mutism is a complex childhood anxiety disorder characterized by children's inability to speak and communicate effectively in select social settings, such as a nursery or school. These children *are* able to speak and communicate in settings where they are comfortable, secure, and relaxed, such as the home. Most children with selective mutism are diagnosed between 3 and 8 years of age, but it is frequently not until they enter nursery or school that their condition becomes more obvious. Children with selective mutism have an actual fear of speaking and of social interactions where there is an expectation to speak and communicate. This anxiety is so strong that children often describe experiencing an actual physical blockage in their throats, which is caused by muscular tension. It is when children are expected to speak, to interact, to respond 'on demand' rather than when they choose, and when they are expected to talk very publicly, that they become overwhelmed by their anxieties.

Not all children with selective mutism manifest their anxieties in the same way. Some may be completely mute and unable to speak or communicate to anyone in a social setting; others may be able to speak to a select few, or perhaps whisper. Some children may stand motionless with fear as they are confronted with specific social settings. Less severely affected children may look relaxed and carefree, and are able to socialize with one or a few children, but are unable to speak and communicate effectively to their practitioners or in front of most of their peer group.

> **"All expectations for verbalisation should be removed as this will lower anxiety and place the selective mute in control of when and whether they chose to interact."**

Children with selective mutism need specialist support to help them overcome their anxieties and to learn to manage effectively in social situations. The main goals of any treatment will be to lower anxiety, and increase self-esteem, social confidence and communication. Practitioners in early years settings need to ensure that these are their goals also. Specialists advise that emphasis should never be on getting the child with selective mutism to talk. All expectations for verbalisation should be removed as this will lower anxiety and place the child in control of when and whether they chose to interact. Many of the strategies for supporting children with non-verbal communication (below) will apply to those with selective mutism.

NHS UK (www.nhs.uk) recommends that, most of all, those working with young children need to reduce their levels of anxiety by creating a positive environment for the child. This means:

- not letting the child know you are anxious
- reassuring them that they will be able to speak when they are ready

- concentrating on having fun
- praising all efforts the child makes to join in and interact with others (such as passing and taking toys, nodding, pointing)
- showing no surprise when the child speaks, but responding warmly as you would to any other child.

Children with autism

Autism Spectrum Disorder (ASD) is a condition that affects social interaction, communication, interests and behaviour. It includes Asperger Syndrome. ASD can cause a wide range of symptoms which are often grouped into two main categories:

- *Problems with social interaction and communication* – including problems understanding and being aware of other people's emotions and feelings; it can also include delayed language development and an inability to start conversations or take part in them properly.
- *Restricted and repetitive patterns of thought, interests and physical behaviours* – including making repetitive physical movements, such as hand tapping or twisting, and becoming upset if set routines are disrupted: (http://www.nhs.uk/conditions/autistic-spectrum-disorder/pages/introduction.aspx).

Children with ASD are often affected by other mental health conditions such as Attention Deficit Hyperactivity Disorder (ADHD), anxiety or depression, and about half of those with ASD also have varying levels of learning difficulties. Autism features can often be recognized in children before the age of 2 or 3 years. However, for many, the signs will only become more noticeable as they get older.

For children with Autism Spectrum Disorder, communication development happens differently and more slowly than for typical children. Many children with autism may not even understand *why* they should communicate with other people, let alone how to do so effectively. They develop anxiety about talking to other people, and often develop strategies for avoiding the feelings of discomfort that they experience when in a group or when addressed face-to-face. Because of the sensory challenges associated with the disorder, children with ASD might seem more interested in environmental sounds, like the whirring of a fan or a vacuum, than in the sound of people talking. They may seem distracted or even seem not to hear what people say.

Typically-developing children learn a great deal about language, communication and interaction through imitation. As we saw in Chapter 2, observations of mothers and their newborns reveal both baby and mother imitating each other's sounds, gestures and facial expressions. Children with ASD do not naturally imitate in the same way as other children. They either do not imitate at all or, when using language, they imitate in whole sentences (called echoes) without always understanding the meaning of the things they are saying. Among children who do not use echoes, first words are often delayed and are sometimes unusual (like numbers or letters of the alphabet). Children with high-functioning autism or Asperger Syndrome may have an extensive vocabulary and use long sentences, but when it comes to social communication, much more is required than the ability to use words. Body language, facial expressions, eye gaze, tone of voice – all these non-verbal clues often tell us more about what people think and feel than the words they use (see Chapter 7). To be successful communicators, children need to know how to interpret and respond to non-verbal cues and how to use these cues themselves. Researchers have concluded that the lack of natural capacity to imitate has an effect on other areas of the development of a child with ASD, such as language outcomes, play skills and, most significantly, joint attention (Ingersoll 2008; 2012).

Learning to imitate actions with toys and objects is the first step in learning to imitate people, because object imitation is easier for children with autism than other forms of imitation, such as imitating gestures, facial expression, or sounds (Ingersoll 2008). However, it is not only interactions with adults that have to be supported and modelled. All children learn a great deal from interacting with their peers (Reszka et al. 2012). Weitzman and Greenberg (2002: 185) suggest that 'Through peer interaction, children develop the ability to see things from another person's point of view. They learn to make compromises, to resolve conflicts, and to share, collaborate, and cooperate with others. They also learn how to negotiate and assert themselves… in order to become well-adjusted human beings, children need to interact with other children.' Children with autism, however, are less likely to initiate social exchanges or respond to others' initiations. For this reason, their ability to acquire the skills above is jeopardized, and they may 'be at an increased risk of social isolation and rejection by their peers' (Reszka et al. 2012: 40).

Reszka and colleagues looked for associations between the children's social behaviours and the contextual features of the classroom and found that the children with ASD engaged more frequently with peers:

- *In the 'Book area' and while engaged in book-related activities*–books may offer a concrete means for initiating and sustaining social interaction (such as showing pictures or talking about the book topic).
- *In the 'Food/Snack area'– this* is in contrast to typically-developing children, who tend to engage less with peers during meals. Meal times are socially structured, and children sit in close proximity to their peers. These features may facilitate peer interaction among children with autism.
- *During large motor activities (e.g. swinging, riding bikes, pushing and pulling wagons, etc)*– as large motor activities are often a preferred activity for children with autism, this may have contributed to the increase in social interaction.
- *In small groups with one or two peers, or in large groups (three or more peers) when an adult was present*–the finding that the children with autism interacted in large groups when an adult was present is contrary to findings from other studies in which children with autism and other disabilities interacted more in small group settings.
- *During child-initiated activities*–the authors recommend that 'allowing children to choose their activities and providing opportunities for self-direction may be especially important in promoting the development of independence for children with disabilities and social interaction among children with disabilities and their peers' (Reszka et al. 2012: 53).

Children with English as an Additional Language (Eal)

It has been estimated that around two-thirds of the world's population speak at least two languages, and there are many who speak more than two (Baker 1996). When children arrive in our settings already competent in a language other than English this should be cause for celebration. Research is suggesting that bilingualism has many benefits, for example:

- Bilingual children are better able to focus their attention on relevant information and ignore distractions (DCSF 2008b; Poulin-Dubois et al. 2011).
- Bilingual learners have been shown to be better at planning and solving complex problems than monolinguals (Marcos 1998; Paradis et al. 2011).
- The effects of aging on the brain may be diminished among bilingual adults (DCSF 2008).

What is important for early years practitioners to remember is the difference between being able to communicate, and being able to communicate in English. Most bilingual and multilingual children arrive in our settings already able to communicate effectively. It is English they have to learn, not communication.

Like all other children, those with English as an additional language are actively seeking to make sense of their environment and, slowly but surely, this will involve using the language. However, it can take two years to achieve conversational fluency (DfES 2007), and so practitioners need to understand the role they play in

> **"It is English that EAL children need to learn, not communication."**

supporting children's moves towards confidence and competence in their new language. Often, young children learning a new language will go through what is known as a 'silent period' when they are not yet confident to speak (Lowry 2011). But, as with the language development of babies, there is a time lag between a child understanding the meaning of a word or phrase and using it. Children learn language by hearing it and then by wanting to use it to communicate. Carroll and O'Connor (2009) remind us that we do not stop talking to a baby just because they cannot talk back. Even when they are silent, children with EAL are still hearing and receiving English, and working out important aspects of their new language, such as where one word ends and where another begins. It is vital that during this time EAL children are surrounded by the words, phrases and structures of their new language in order to be ready to imitate and vocalise, when they feel ready to do so. If they receive the right kind of support, children often emerge from this stage as chatty individuals who then learn their new language by talking a lot, in order to repeat and rehearse what they have heard. The advice, says Tassoni (2013), is never to push a child to speak until they do so freely.

Children usually learn their first language in the home. Surrounded by talkers they hear language being used for real purposes, in meaningful contexts, and are encouraged to join in and experiment with sounds and words. Exactly the same experiences are needed for learning a second language. To access the curriculum, *second language learners need* (adapted from Carroll and O'Connor 2009):

- A relaxed, unpressurized, welcoming environment indoors and out that feels safe. The outdoors in particular (especially Forest School) provides the freedom many children need in order to take risks with language.
- Routines that quickly provide them with emotional security and predictable language – for example 'going home time'.
- Visual clues that enhance their understanding of the language being used – 'It's snack time now' – with a picture to represent what the words mean.
- Time to just 'stand and stare' to take things in slowly and make sense of them.
- Lots of opportunities (when they are ready) to engage physically and mentally in self-initiated play activities that provide cognitive challenge at the right developmental level, which is likely to be richer than their level of English.
- Lots of opportunities to engage in free-flow play alongside their peers, from whom they will hear and learn language, and with whom they may be most confident to try our their first words.

Practitioners need to ensure that they offer second language learners:

- Warm attentiveness – someone who is close by and who is clearly interested in what they are doing.

- Responses to their non-verbal actions and gestures, helping them feel accepted and understood.
- Sensitive, enthusiastic and encouraging feedback when they try to make themselves understood.
- Opportunities to feel included and part of the group without feeling pressure to join in or contribute (never deny a child involvement in an interaction because you think he or she doesn't understand).
- Time to process what has been said to them and to think through what they want to say.
- Mime, action and gesture – as tools for *all* children – so as to facilitate collaboration between themselves and the EAL child, and between children.
- The use of simple and repetitive language that models fundamental vocabulary.
- Opportunities to share simple books, especially baby books with repetitive vocabulary and clear images.
- Use of props for books and rhymes.
- The opportunity to share their focus of interest with adults and other children in collaborative ways that don't rely on shared language.

English language learners especially benefit from wait time (see Chapter 9), requiring more time to process the language than they are often given. Effective practitioners acknowledge the hard work involved in operating in an unfamiliar language (Carroll and O'Connor 2009). So, as well as offering differentiated support that suits the individual language and communication needs of the EAL child, and giving the child all the time he needs to comprehend a question or comment and formulate a response, practitioners need to offer the child plenty of opportunities to rest and relax their brains at different points in the day so they are ready for the next burst of intense concentration that communicating in an unfamiliar language requires.

Sensitive practitioners also recognize children's right to use their first language with peers and adults, particularly when it scaffolds their thinking, and to hear key words from their home language – particularly phrases that soothe or keep their families in mind, such as 'Mummy's coming soon'; or survival language, like 'toilet?' or 'hungry?'

Carroll and O'Connor (2009) suggest that practitioners have a responsibility to build up their own knowledge of new and unfamiliar languages.

Practitioners need to:

- Make sure they know the correct pronunciation of children's names (and those of their parents). It can make the world of difference for a child's sense of identity and self-esteem.
- Provide bilingual support wherever possible and encourage bilingual practitioners to share their expertise: maybe by challenging monolingual staff to learn a new phrase or song every week and supporting them to practise and get the pronunciation right.

Most of all, effective practitioners acknowledge that the ability of EAL children in using English is not representative of the levels of their cognitive, emotional or social development. Interactions with young EAL children should, above all, be relevant and meaningful to their stage of development and draw on what is interesting and absorbing them at the time.

Signing as a form of communication

An increasing number of settings are introducing signing as a way of supporting all children to communicate in ways that do not require verbal interaction. Signing can be valuable for children who are reluctant to talk for the range of reasons explored above. It is also valuable in settings where any child is deaf or hard of hearing.

For children without, or with limited, verbal language, signing is a fast and effective way of communicating with others. Signing makes use of standard hand movements and gestures, enabling children to make themselves understood as well as helping them understand what is being said to them. When children have speech and/ or language problems, signing can help to make their messages clear. Signing can be used alongside or instead of speech. For children with delayed speech development, signing can:

- provide a way to communicate while their speech develops
- reduce frustration and behaviour difficulties

- help them understand the meaning of words
- help them develop more complex thinking skills.

There are different signing systems in use in the UK, but the most common are British Sign Language and Makaton. British Sign Language (BSL) was recognized by the British government as a language in its own right in March 2003, and is the first or preferred language of much of the deaf community within the UK. The language makes use of space and involves movement of the hands, body, face and head. It is a visual-gestural language with its own grammar and principles which are completely different from the grammatical structure of English. BSL has regional variations too. Someone using BSL in Scotland, for example, may use different gestures than someone in Somerset.

If a child comes into an early years setting using BSL, then their family will be using this communicative tool in the home and practitioners will be able to draw on their expertise and also attend one of many courses across the UK that teach the language. For further information and a list of possible courses for practitioners, see http://www.british-sign.co.uk/.

Makaton is a language programme using signs and symbols to help a wider range of people communicate than BSL. It was designed to support adults and children with learning difficulties to communicate, but is now increasingly used more widely for children who are learning to speak. Makaton uses signs (gestures), symbols (pictures) and speech to aid communication. Signs are used, with speech, in spoken word order, which helps provide extra clues about what someone is saying. The signs can be used to help people who have no speech, or whose speech is unclear. The symbols can help people who have limited speech and those who cannot, or prefer not to, sign. The signs and symbols can be used either as a main method of communication or as a way to support verbal communication and the development of early language. With Makaton, children and adults can communicate straight away using these signs and symbols. Many people then drop the signs or symbols naturally at their own pace, as their speech develops.

Analysing your own practice

These are the features of effective practice that the Oxfordshire practitioners identified in analysing their interactions with those who are reluctant to interact:

Features of interactions where reluctant talkers are encouraged to speak

- Children are not pressurized to speak until they are ready.
- Children are included in conver`sations that have meaning for them (although not forced to contribute).
- Children's play, activity and interests are noticed and commented on.
- Any attempt by the child to speak is listened to and waited for patiently.

- Any words offered by the child are passed back, maybe with the addition of more words to enrich the child's language – e.g. 'Mum go shop'; 'Yes – mum's gone to the shops for some bread.'
- The child isn't cross-examined or put on the spot to answer or speak.

Features of interactions where reluctant talkers are discouraged from speaking

- Children are forced to speak.
- Children are placed in social situations where they have a 'turn' to speak, whether they want to or not.
- Practitioners become impatient if the child does not reply, as though they are being disobedient.
- Other children make fun of the child who does not choose to or cannot speak.
- Children's home languages are not encouraged in the setting.

Transcripts: children who do not want to talk

Transcript 8:1 'Helen and Nadeem's picture'

Nadeem is in Year 1. English is his second language and he is new to the school. The teacher knows not to pressurize him to talk and sits alongside him, drawing, to see if that encourages conversation. In the end however, the desire to 'fill the silence' over-whelms her and this does not encourage Nadeem to communicate.

The teacher sits on the same table and takes a piece of paper. She doesn't say anything. Nadeem stops drawing and looks at her somewhat suspiciously. The teacher doesn't look up, but keeps drawing. After another 40 seconds Nadeem again looks at the teacher uncertainly. She doesn't look at him. He looks at her picture and then turns back to his own. After 55 seconds Nadeem looks at the teacher again. This time she looks up and smiles at him. She leans towards his picture but then doesn't say anything.

At 1 minute 13 seconds the teacher again leans over to Nadeem's picture and says:

A: That's lovely

Another child comes up to show the teacher something she has done. She nods and smiles at this child, but doesn't say anything. She goes back to drawing. Nadeem looks up at her to check what she is doing. At 1 minute 58 seconds she says:

A: Nadeem, you're very good at drawing aren't you? What are you drawing there (although it is clearly a house).
C: A house.

A: A house? It's lovely *(Nadeem goes back to his drawing)* I'm going to try and draw a house. Can I try as well?

C: Yes *(he doesn't look at her).*

A: Is it anybody's house or is it your house?

C: My house.

A: Your house.

They draw for another 15 seconds in silence and then the teacher looks over again at what Nadeem is doing. This time she doesn't say anything, then goes back to her drawing. After another 1 minute 9 seconds the wind from the open door blows her picture onto the floor. She gets up to retrieve it.

A: Oh my picture fell on the floor Nadeem *(he smiles shyly).* What do you think? *(he looks at her uncertainly).* What do you think? *(he doesn't answer).* Any good? Or is yours better? *(he looks down at his own but doesn't answer).* Not sure?

At 4 minutes 41 seconds Nadeem looks up at her again and then quickly looks down. At 5 minutes 10 seconds the teacher says:

A: Do you know, I really like drawing Nadeem *(Nadeem doesn't look up).*

At 5 minutes 26 seconds Nadeem looks up and the teacher looks across at his picture once more:

A: Is that your house as well?

C: That's a big house.

A: It's much bigger than that one isn't it? *(pointing)*

C: I can make a really bigger house.

A: Can you?

C: Yes.

A: Are you going to do it on there? *(pointing) (he doesn't answer).* Are you going to make a *really* big house? *(he doesn't answer).* Do you want... are you going to do it on here or on another piece of paper? *(he doesn't answer but goes back to his picture).* Or are you going to finish this one off? *(he doesn't answer).*

Analysis

Here we have a teacher and a child, but neither are relaxed. The teacher has understood that Nadeem shouldn't be forced to speak to her, but has failed to grasp that she needs to talk to him. It would have helped if she had told him why she sat down with him and what she was going to do, which would have made him less suspicious. She should have commented on her drawing – and his – rather than asking him questions to which she already knew the answer (and he knew she knew, which made the situation even more confusing for him). Because the questions were pointless, the answers were monosyllabic, so Nadeem wasn't practising or extending his vocabulary. When Nadeem did open up a little (about the second house) the teacher didn't sustain the interaction by offering some personal comment or informative statement, but closed the interaction down with a 'Can you?'. In the end, because she was getting so little in return, the teacher found herself asking an endless series of questions, none of which received a reply. Nadeem was left feeling uncomfortable and was unlikely to look forward to another interaction of the same ilk with his teacher. Children who are reluctant to talk need meaningful reasons for doing so. This interaction left both adult and child keen for it to end.

Ask yourself: *What does the child gain?*
See the end of the transcripts in Chapter 3 for ideas.

Transcript 8:2 'Kate and Louise's bus'
Louise is a reception class child who does not choose to talk at carpet times or in any formal learning situation in front of other children. Her teacher sees her making a model on her own and kneels alongside the craft table to see if a conversation flows more easily there.

C: I'm making a bus for the food

A: A *box* for food or a *bus* for food?

C: A bus for food... and these are the wheels... one, two, three, four... and a wheel on top.

A: What's the wheel on top for?

C: A spare one.

A: In case they have an accident.... or in case the tyre pops?

C: In case the tyre pops.

A: My car's got a spare tyre... and it's inside my boot, not on the top.

C: My dad's car hasn't...

A: Your dad's car hasn't got a spare tyre?

A: No... I've got two dads. I've got a stepdad called Frank who like picks me up. And I have another dad who lives at my nanny Debbie's... that's his mum's.

A: That's his mum's, yes.

C: Yeh, that's my nanny.

A: That's right. That's what happens in lots of families. *(Louise works on in silence for a while.)* So my mum's mummy is *my* grandma. I don't call her nanny, I call her grandma.

C: Well that one is my nanny.

A: Yes I don't call her nanny, I call her grandma.

C: She's got a dog that's called Spot *(she stops her model and looks at the teacher).* But it's died and he had a sore belly so its, so it's died now *(she goes back to the model)* like my nanny died and my mummy's mum.

A: Your mummy's mum died too? That happens sometimes when you get poorly or when you get old. My grandma's got a dog and her dog's called Charlie.

C: My, my nanny's dog is called, called Spot. Now she's staying at my Auntie Kate's house.

A: Nanny stays at Auntie Kate's house?

C: No, she lives at the same house. She, she works at Sainsbury's, and I some-times go there for shopping.

A: Yeh, I sometimes go to Sainsbury's for shopping. I sometimes go to Tesco's for shopping. I don't really like going shopping.

Analysis

This conversation about Louise's nanny and the complex personal arrangements within her family life continued for several more minutes, getting more and more detailed. Louise was more willing to interact with the teacher because she had her undivided attention (rather than vying for attention on the carpet with others), and because she was doing something with her hands (a very imaginative 'bus' using a whole range of skills in its construction) which gave her confidence as she spoke. The teacher's body language (getting down to the child's level) and her conversational style (attentive but not intrusive) led Louise to feel more relaxed and willing to interact.

The teacher's use of genuine questions to clarify her understanding of what Louise was saying ('A box for food or a bus for food?') and then offering personal information ('My car's got a spare tyre…') kept the conversation flowing, rather than Louie feeling overwhelmed by an interrogation about the model (e.g. 'How many wheels does the bus have?'; 'What are you going to use to make the tyres?'; 'Where is the bus going?' – and so on). If Louise continues to have relaxed extended conversations of this nature in a one-to-one situation she may in time be less reluctant to respond to the teacher in a larger group situation.

Ask yourself: *What does the child gain?*
See the end of the transcripts in Chapter 3 for ideas.

Summary

There are a number of different reasons why children may be reluctant to interact. We have seen that this may be because they are shy, because they are anxious, or because they simply have not yet learned the language. What is clear is that we cannot ignore these children because they are difficult to talk to or because we achieve more satisfactory interactions talking to talkative children. All practitioners need to identify those children who do not choose to interact and find strategies that will support them to communicate more readily. The message from the experts who specialize in supporting the communication of reluctant talkers is very consistent: do not pressurize a reluctant talker to talk. Pressure will only make a child more reluctant and hold back their development. Reluctant talkers need to be bathed in a warm bath of language, included in contexts where talk has value and purpose and to experience an emotional environment where they are given the security to speak – when they are ready. In the next chapter we see how questioning young children can often inhibit rather than encourage interactions, and that some questions, for young children, simply get in the way of learning.

Self-reflection

1 Have I identified the children in my setting who are reluctant to talk?

2 Do I understand why they might be reluctant?

3 Do I have the expertise to support them, or do I know who to turn to for help?

9
Questions that work and questions that don't

Questions often interrupt the flow of children's thinking and interfere with their learning

Introduction

In this country there is a long tradition of educators asking questions of children. Indeed, the role of questioning is as old as the first accounts we have of the teaching process (Harrop and Swinson 2003). It is clear that questioning is an important skill that we use throughout life to find out more and to understand better. But the question posed by this chapter is why, when questioning is associated with problem-solving (de Bono 1992), with the creative thinking process (Beetlestone 1998), and with the construction of children's own understanding of the world (Isaacs 1930; Tizard and Hughes 1984), are most of the questions posed in our nurseries and classrooms asked by the practitioner rather than the child? Why, when in the early years we espouse child-initiated learning and independent enquiry, do practitioners use questioning strategies that frequently take control of learning away from the child and place it back into the hands of the adult? In this chapter we consider questions that work with young children and questions that don't, and the strategies that practitioners can use as alternatives to questioning.

Focus on babies and toddlers

During our analysis of the impact of questioning on young children's learning it was assumed by the Oxfordshire ACI Project participants that they would ask more questions of children as they grew older. It was assumed there would be a steady increase in the number of questions asked from very few in the baby-rooms (where children would be unable to answer), peaking in Year 2 classrooms where teachers would be driving through an external agenda. This was not the case. In their study, the Oxford-shire practitioners found the highest number of questions being asked in the baby-rooms, with Key Stage 1 classrooms coming a close second. Practitioners in baby and toddler rooms asked a myriad of questions such as:

'Shall we go and have some sleep now?'

'Do you want your nappy changed?'

'Are you missing your mummy?'

Now clearly the practitioners did not expect the babies to answer, and would have been shocked if they did, so it was interesting to discuss why questions were such a prevalent form of communication with such young children. Those who worked in the baby-rooms said, on reflection, that they posed questions because they were attempting to interpret the child's sounds, gestures or cries. The questions recorded in the baby-room showed practitioners trying to tune in to the baby's efforts to com-municate and guessing, as best they could, what the baby was trying to tell them. As we saw in Chapter 3, this became so much easier when the practitioner knew the baby well and was able to make a more informed assumption about what their differ-ent cries might be trying to convey.

Questions in the baby-room serve as an internal dialogue for practitioners. Because they do not expect the baby to answer, practitioners use questioning to interrogate their own thinking and to ask the baby questions that they are really asking them-selves. 'What does this baby need?'; 'Am I right that his nappy needs changing?'; 'Is she grizzly today because a tooth is coming through?' Coupled with the use of 'moth-erese' (see Chapter 2), questioning lets the baby know that they are the focus of attention and that this is an adult trying to tune in to their needs. Asking a baby ques-tions also offers opportunities for early turn-taking. When the attentive practitioner asks a question, they watch or listen for the baby's 'reply', searching for a smile, or gurgle, a movement of the legs or head that signifies that the baby is 'answering', thus giving the practitioner the opportunity to take another conversational turn. The asking and answering of questions in the baby-room involves both practitioner and infant in a proto-conversation where turn-taking plays a vital role.

Why do we ask questions?

Much seems to depend on who is doing the questioning. Tizard and Hughes (1984) suggest that asking questions is a child's way of making sense of the world. Children ask many questions, often internally, and their questioning is dependent on curios-ity, an attitude which Johnson suggests is 'essential to learning' (2007: 81). However, educators often have a different purpose. Their questioning is often used to check up on what children already know and can recall, rather than leading them to what they might come to know.

> **❝**Questioning is often used to check up on what children already know, rather than leading to what they might come to know.**❞**

In real life, we ask questions when we are perplexed. We ask questions when we do not understand something or when we want to understand it in more depth. Yet practitioners repeatedly ask questions to which they already know the answers. They ask questions to confirm a hypothesis they already hold (this child knows/does not know this). They ask questions sometimes to reassure themselves that they have done a good job. In doing so, practitioners often undermine the creative, investigative intent of the child and curb the child's curiosity in order to satisfy their own objectives.

Who asks the questions?

Jim Dillon believes that in educational contexts, 'Normal practice is to induce in the young answers given by others to questions put by others.' (1990: 7), and that: 'Typically the teacher is found to speak more than any other person and more than all others combined.' (1981a: 51). It seems irrefutable that in nurseries and classrooms in this country, the person asking most of the questions is the practitioner. Given that learning often springs from curiosity and that curiosity stimulates questioning, why isn't the quality of teaching in our nurseries and classrooms judged on the questions children's raise, rather than the questions adults pose?

The work of Harrop and Swinson (2003) reveals that the imbalance between the number of questions asked by children and the number of questions asked by practitioners has a long history. Some 100 years or more ago, Stevens (1912) investigated the number of questions asked by teachers and found high school teachers in the USA were asking about 400 questions per day. He found virtually no questions asked by children, directly, were concerned with learning. Later, Floyd (cited by Gall 1970) found an average of 348 questions a day from primary-grade teachers. Brown and Edmondson (1984) noted a number of similar studies and concluded that, on average, teachers ask around 100 questions an hour. More recently the work of Galton et al. (1999) gives an estimate of some 16 per cent of classroom time being devoted to teachers asking questions. This is in stark contrast to conversations in the home. The research of Tizard and Hughes (1984) and Wells (1983), comparing conversations in the home and at school, revealed that teachers asked a far larger proportion of questions than did mothers. In the home, mothers tended to *respond* to the questions of the child far more than to initiate questions of their own.

> **❝**Why isn't the quality of teaching in our nurseries and classrooms judged by the questions children raise, rather than the questions adults pose?**❞**

The data from the Oxfordshire ACI Project, analysed some 100 years after Stevens' research at the beginning of the last century, shows that things have not changed significantly. Of the questions recorded in a five-minute sample taken from each participant setting, practitioners asked 94 per cent of the questions posed, and children only 6 per cent; and of the questions children asked, only 2.3 per cent were to do with learning.

Why is it then, that practitioners feel the need to ask so many questions? Why are they seemingly more interested in questions of their own, rather than questions posed by the child? My observation is that far from redressing the balance between questions raised by the adult and the child, the current use of questioning as part of the educator's repertoire has become relentless. Observing in baby-rooms though to Year 2 classes, it seems that practitioners feel obliged to fill any available silence with questions; to interrupt a child's investigation with questions; to pepper any supposed interaction with questions. Yet these observations also reveal how often these questions used, I am sure, by the practitioner with the intent of enhancing or extending learning more often do the opposite. Data from the Oxfordshire ACI Project show that, frequently, questions:

- *dismiss* children's thinking
- *sidetrack* children's thinking
- *muddle* children's thinking
- *interrupt* children's thinking.

Transcript 9:1 Dismissing children's thinking
Circle time in the nursery with three-year-olds. Children have to say how they are feeling and place their name card in the appropriate container.

>   A: How are you feeling today Saeed? Where are you going to put your name today? In the happy tray or the sad tray?
> C (3:4):   Sad.
>   A: Are you? Are you sure? You are smiling today. You are smiling and look so happy! Why are you going to put your card in the sad tray today?

Saeed takes his card from the 'sad' tray and puts it in the 'happy tray'.

Transcript 9:2 Sidetracking children's thinking
A group of nursery aged girls are filling buckets with water from the outside tap and pouring them into a large sandpit. Fiona has been watching the water disappear.

> C (4:9):   It's gone, it's gone!
>   A: Yes, the sand has absorbed all the water. Look it's wetter now.
>   C: Tell the police an', an' put the thief in prison!
>   A: Look now. All the water has been absorbed! Isn't that amazing?

Transcript 9:3 Muddling children's thinking
Whole-class reception 'plenary' session. Teacher holds up a rectangle.

>   A: What is this?
> C (5:1): A square.
>   A: It's not *quite* a square, is it Daisy?
>   *(Waits, but no answer)*

A: What's the square got?
(No answer)
A: What makes the square special?
(No answer)
A: What *hasn't* the square got?
(No answer)
A: Goodness, I thought you understood this.

Transcript 9:4 Interrupting children's thinking
Not long after 9/11, three nursery age boys are building towers from lego and then smashing them down to the ground, only to build the towers up again. The teacher kneels down alongside them.

A: Wow – they're big towers!
C (3:8): They're big towers and the aeroplane's gonna crash them and... and...
A: Whose tower is the tallest do you think?

Different types of questions

It is important to acknowledge that there are different kinds of questions and that different questions are suited to different purposes. One of the most widely disseminated myths about questioning is that 'open' questions' are good questions, while 'closed' questions are bad questions. Johnson (2007: 88), for example, states that 'effective teacher questions are those that are open-ended', and there are many other examples of blanket statements about the efficacy of 'open-ended' questions. In this next section, I want to challenge this simplistic proposition. Different questions have different purposes and practitioners need to be sensitive about using the right question at the right time.

Open questions and closed questions

The most common distinction between questions that practitioners pose is between 'open' questions and 'closed questions'. Different researchers use slightly different definitions to describe the difference between these two types of question, but the most commonly accepted distinction between them is as follows:

Closed questions have only one answer (the answer is often short, and often 'Yes' or 'No').

Examples: *'Do you think this will go faster now?'*

             'Was the owl frightened in the dark?'

Open questions have different possible answers (none of which is necessarily the 'right' one).

Examples: *'What might happen if we lift this up higher?'*

             'I wonder where bubbles go when they pop?'

The Oxfordshire Project data reveals that early years practitioners can ask an open-ended question when what they really want is a closed answer. In other words, although the practitioner already has an answer in their head that they want or expect, they then pose their initial question in a way which suggests that the answer is not known, or has many possibilities. Children are then confused and potentially disheartened when they are told their answer is wrong (see, for example, Transcript 6:1).

Higher-order and lower-order questions

The simplistic assumption that 'open' questions are good and 'closed' questions are bad may arise from the belief that open questions demand higher-order thinking while closed question are seen as requiring only lower-order thinking. The term 'higher-order thinking' means that the child is required to do more cognitive processing than simply recalling facts or knowledge (lower-order thinking). This kind of thinking is seen as more valuable and educationally significant for children because it affords them the opportunity to apply what they know and to analyse and evaluate what they are thinking in different situations. In higher-order thinking, children are required to think something through, to reason, to make some mental decisions, to use their imagination or to hypothesize.

A summative definition of these two types of questions might be as follows:

Higher-order questions: those that require the manipulation of information and reflection. For example:

> *'I wonder what love looks like?'*
> *'What makes you happy/sad?'*

Lower-order questions: those that require the recall of information. For example:

> *'Would you like porridge or Cheerios?'*
> *'What does the hairy hat-man say?'*

In understanding the gradation between lower and higher forms of thinking, people frequently draw on the work of Benjamin Bloom (see Bloom et al. 1956) whose goal in developing his taxonomy (or hierarchy) of questions was to encourage educators to focus on the following domains (1) cognitive (knowing/head), (2) affective (feeling/heart), (3) psychomotor (doing/hands). His belief was that in order to achieve higher-order thinking, the learner needed to have attained prerequisite knowledge and skills at lower levels (Dalton and Smith 1986; Orlich et al. 2004).

In their analysis of the Oxfordshire data, project participants recorded three other kinds of questions asked frequently by early years practitioners:

- 'known' questions
- pointless questions
- managerial questions.

Known questions

'Known' questions are described by Durant (2013) as those questions practitioners ask, but to which they already know the answer. While higher-order thinking may challenge children to think beyond the facts and knowledge they have to apply their thinking more creatively and critically, there are inevitably times when practitioners need to know what children know, or what they have remembered. As we saw in Chapter 6, one purpose of adult-led learning is to clarify what children already know in order to plan what they need to know next, and one straightforward way of doing this is to ask them a question. This kind of question is almost certainly a 'known' question in that the practitioner already knows the answer, but wants to be sure that the child does also. The important point about these kind of questions (as with most closed questions) is that they should only take up a small part of the questioning repertoire of the practitioner. Regrettably, as we shall see below, this appears not to be the case.

Practitioners need to be sensitive to the fact that, for young children, asking a question to which the answer is 'known' and (frequently) obvious can be very bemusing. I am always reminded of Sonnyboy in Jacqui Cousin's book, *Listening to Four Year Olds,* who scathingly responds to his teacher's meaningless questions with a question of his own: 'Why do you keep asking the kids questions when you knows all the answers? Like... like... what colour is it then? You can see for yourself it's red... so why do you keep asking them?' (Cousins 1999: 30). It is only when children arrive in an educational setting (rather than the home) that they are asked questions of this kind. It must be somewhat bewildering to find that adults are so unsure of things they need to ask questions that are so obvious and, often, so banal.

Pointless questions

A number of questions were recorded in the Oxfordshire data that were somewhat pointless. Pointless because, had the practitioner really tuned in to what the child was thinking and doing, the answer was apparent in the actions of the child.

> *Examples:*   'What are you going to do with your lid?' (when the child was already putting it on the tube).
>
> 'Is the dragon going to hurt the princess?' (when the small world dragon is already sweeping the princess into the air and away).

It is at moments like this that young children will give you a look. A look that says, 'Why are you asking me that?'; 'What has that got to do with anything?' These kind of pointless questions seem to come about for two main reasons. Firstly, because practitioners have not tuned in to the child and their thinking sufficiently well to deduce what the child is investigating or exploring or playing, without asking a question that interrupts them. Secondly, because practitioners are afraid of silence. There seems to be something in the psyche of early years practitioners (as well as teachers of older children) that compels them to fill moments of silence and to fill them, usually, with a question. As we shall see later in this chapter, sometimes silence is golden, and to ask a question merely to make ourselves feel as though we are doing our job is to create an ethos where questions appear to children to be relentless and interfering.

Managerial questions

As the project children got older, more of the practitioner questions were concerned with management. They were posed to keep control, to organize, and to ensure the smooth running of the nursery or classroom:

> *Examples:*   'Would you like to come and sit on the carpet now?'
>
> 'Would you please put your books in your trays ready for literacy?

Sometimes these questions are intended to bring about a change in behaviour e.g. *'Do you think that's a kind thing to do to William, Ben?'* Sometimes it is in order to keep control of a discussion. Dillon (1981a) suggests that most questioning involving a practitioner and group of children offers a picture of 'one in control of the discourse of many'. In other words, questioning can steer a conversation; it can alter the course of a conversation; it can halt or introduce new topics and ideas to a conversation; and it keeps the adult firmly in control.

Using questioning as control

Practitioners have quite unique control over the talk that takes place in their setting. In any nursery or classroom, particularly when a group of children are together, it is the practitioner who decides who can speak; the topic of conversation; for how long any child may speak; when to begin a conversation, and when to bring it to an end. Tizard and Hughes (1984: 279), in their research into conversation in the home and at school, concluded that 'the didactic, teacher-directed mode of interaction characteristic of later schooling was already established in the nursery. This no doubt reflects the underlying power relationship between teacher and child. The children seem to learn very quickly that their role is to answer not ask questions.' Wood et al. (1980: 77) suggest that children's learning interests are often inadvertently undermined by 'the power structure of adult-child conversations'. Wood and his colleagues drew on transcripts of talk between practitioners and children to highlight these structural inequalities. While making full concession for the higher levels of sophistication in the adult's conversational repertoire, they found that 40 per cent of the total of all 'moves' made by the adult when interacting with children were composed of questions classified as 'controlling' moves. In the same analysis, the researchers found that children's questions totalled only 7 per cent of their 'moves'. Wood and his colleagues found that the adults' tendency to 'ignore children, talk over them and generally dominate proceedings', was the single most striking feature of their recordings (p.65). They went on to conclude that the adult's tendency to overuse 'controlling' moves, such as questions, and their preoccupation with managing conversations, had definite consequences for the way children responded or participated in classroom talk. For example, those practitioners found to use a high level of controlling moves were often approached by children with managerial intentions. Those who raised more open-ended questions, which stimulated children's curiosity, were more likely to be met with further questions from the children.

Dillon suggests that when questioning is used as control in this way, that 'a question-answer relationship fosters dependency, passivity and reactivity' (1981a: 53). It is questioning as control that very often draws on closed questioning techniques to keep the power in the hands of the practitioner but, subsequently, leaves children's contributions mired in a swamp of lower-order thinking.

> **Am I asking this question for myself or for the child?**

Children's answers

> **'Questions are only as good as the answers they get.' (Brown and Edmondson 1984)**

Not all questions demand to be answered. We have seen that some questions are *rhetorical*. Especially with young babies, the questions posed are those asked by the practitioner as they try and interpret the baby's signals and cues, rather than to actually elicit information. Some questions are *hypothetical*: they pose possibilities or plant an idea that can be thought about, dwelt on, and returned to in the child's own good time. Such questions do not demand an answer on the spot and they do not put the child under pressure for a response. In his book, *Hare Brain, Tortoise Mind* (1997), Claxton suggests that the quality of thinking and ideas is enhanced when children are given time to respond more slowly, to come to conclusions over time, and to test out ideas at their own pace.

Children's attempts to answer questions

Research has shown how hard children try to make sense of a practitioner's questions, even when those questions have been deliberately constructed to be nonsense. In some intriguing and illuminating research in the 1980s, Donaldson et al. asked young children a series of questions to which there are no answers, such as: 'Is milk bigger than water?'; 'Is red heavier than yellow?'; 'One day there were two flies crawling up a wall. Which fly got to the top first?' The researchers found that the children were ingenious at trying to make sense of a question and, invariably, supplying an answer. However nonsensical (to the child) the question might be, the child seems to believe it is their job to try to make sense of what the adult is saying (see Transcript 5:2).

Listening to children's answers

Considering how many questions educators ask, one would think that they would be very practiced at listening to answers. But research has shown that the hardest thing for someone asking a question to do is to listen to the answer they receive. It seems to be particularly difficult for educators, who all too often ask a question with the answer they want to hear already firmly in their mind. This closes them to the range of possible answers they might hear, or stops them from receiving an unexpected answer with interest, rather than annoyance.

So, it is extremely difficult to listen to an answer when you are waiting for the 'right' answer. It is also difficult to listen when you are too busy thinking about the next question. When practitioners are more interested in the questions they ask than the answers children give, then the space between asking one question and the next is taken up by formulating a question, rather than listening to an answer (see Transcript 9:1).

'Wait time'
It would significantly help practitioners to listen to children if they learned to wait longer between asking a question and expecting an answer. Back in 1974, Rowe reviewed numerous studies which demonstrated that the wait time in classrooms between the answer given by a child and the next question posed by the teacher was less than one second. Rowe (1974), and others in the field, recommended a 'wait time' of between three and five seconds; yet, some ten years later, Swift and Gooding (1983) claimed that it had proved to take arduous training for teachers to increase their pausing or 'wait time' even to two seconds.

Further research (Rowe 1986) has demonstrated that increasing the time between asking a question and expecting an answer to between three and five seconds brings about the following benefits:

- an increase in the number of correct answers
- an increase in the length of responses

- an increase in the incidence of speculative responses
- an increase in responses from pupils of lower ability
- an increase in the frequency of pupils' own questions
- more interaction between pupils
- a decrease in 'No' answers and 'I don't know' responses.

It appears that there are two important 'wait times'. Firstly, after the practitioner poses a question, and secondly, after the child gives their response – to see if there is more to come. The problem seems to be that, too often, practitioners ask questions which do not demand answers that take time to formulate. We saw earlier in this chapter that the questions most frequently asked in educational contexts are those that do not take too much thinking time because they are concerned with recall and knowledge: 'What is this called?'; 'What happens when...?' So one reason why practitioners do not habitually wait long enough for answers is that they are not asking enough questions that demand higher-order thinking.

Another reason why practitioners do not wait long enough for answers is because questions are too often asked of large groups of young children, and waiting for the answer often leads to a loss of engagement and subsequent control of the group whose interest is not maintained. Practitioners press on from one question to the next as a control mechanism, rather than displaying a genuine interest in the answers that are forthcoming.

Questions that work and questions that don't

Questions that work

Having analysed the different questions asked in the Oxfordshire Project, there seemed to be three types of questions that worked well if practitioners were trying to sustain interactions with children and to extend or provoke their thinking.

1   **Showing interest/Clarifying** (following up something that has already been said):
    e.g. *'So it sounds as though you live in the roof?'*
    'Did Matilda go to the party too then?'
2   **Pondering** (encouraging creative thinking):
    e.g. *'I wonder where bubbles go when they pop?'*
    'I wonder if bear felt better when the light came on?'
3   **Posing possibilities** (planting an idea):
    e.g. *'Maybe you need to find something for Johnny to stand on?'*
    'Do you think another block might help keep it steady?'

All of these questions are genuine and meaningful. The practitioner wants to know the answer and does not know it already (although they might be able to have a jolly good guess). The questions are intended to open up possibilities, rather than close thinking down to one desirable answer.

The Oxfordshire DVD material suggests that merely 'asking an open-ended' question is not the solution to an effective interaction. We can see that some of the questions above are 'closed' but, used for the right purpose and at the right moment, can be effective in sustaining a conversation. The right question at the right time depends on the purpose of the question, whether or not it demands an immediate answer, and whether that answer is already in the practitioner's head.

Questions that don't work

The Oxfordshire DVD material also shows the result of questions being asked in the wrong way at the wrong time: a closed question being asked when the practitioner wants an open answer or vice versa; a question that interrogates children's thinking, rather than illuminating it. When questions put children on the spot, or make them fearful that they do not know the right answer, then they employ a range of avoidance strategies. The data has many examples of children shrugging – 'I don't know'/'I don't care'; ignoring – 'Question… I didn't hear any question'; walking away – 'Please get off my back'; as well as trying to answer – 'I don't understand, but this is the best I can manage'.

The data also shows that most questions that are asked remain concerned with what children *know*, rather than what children *think*. Finding out what children know makes practitioners feel pleased that their teaching has been effective and that they can move on to the next steps of learning. Finding out what children think demands practitioners who are open to answers, who wait for answers, who are fascinated by answers, and who are responsive to answers. Creative and critical thinkers are those who can work things out for themselves, who find solutions to problems, who use their initiative and who contribute ideas, all of which are skills that flourish where learning is enriched, rather than simply checked. It is imperative that, in early years classrooms, practitioners ask more questions to find out what children think, rather than merely what children know.

> "Too many questions are concerned with what children know, rather than what children think."

Our data suggests that practitioners should ask fewer questions, and that those that *are* asked are chosen carefully for their intended purpose. However, if practitioners are to ask fewer questions then what strategies have been found to be more effective in sustaining children's thinking?

Alternatives to questioning

Making statements

Offering alternatives to questioning is not new. Dillon (1990: 177) advocates the greater use of what he terms 'declarative statements', responses to which he claims 'promise to be longer and more complex than answers to questions'. The data from the Oxfordshire ACI Project found the use of statements by practitioners, rather than questions, led to a number of positive outcomes:

- Children did not look anxious, as though they were expected to answer there and then.
- Children did not stop what they were doing to answer, but carried on their activity while thinking.

- Children's responses were often unexpected, the statement having triggered some connected, but not necessarily predicted, thinking.
- Often, children came back with a statement of their own.

These findings confirmed those of research projects aimed at enhancing children's expressive language (e.g. Wood et al. 1982; Wood and Wood 1984) where children were found to respond to statements with greater length and quality than to questions. Hubbell's (1977) review of various studies of children at home, in clinic, and in school revealed that questions and commands are 'inhibiting stimuli', rather than facilitative, with nursery-age children responding to questions with 'a smaller vocabulary and little discussion' (Hubbell 1977: 219). In another study of preschool children age 3 – 4 years, paired in conversational sessions with a teacher, the children responded to statements with greater length and initiative than to questions, whether open or closed (Wood and Wood 1983). Boggs (1972) sociolinguistic research with 6- and 7-year-old children, found that by making statements and comments rather than asking questions, the children's responses were nearly three times longer than to questions. In addition, when the researcher changed to statements and comments, the children responded by asking more questions when not being questioned themselves.

"When we change from questions to statements, children talk to us for longer and ask more questions themselves."

Figure 9.1 shows the range of statements practitioners can make to effectively contribute to an interaction:

For most of the Oxfordshire practitioners, making statements instead of asking questions took a considerable amount of 'retraining'. It seemed to be habitual to ask questions at every opportunity and to see this as the primary way to extend children's thinking. Yet the more skilled the project participants became in making statements rather than posing questions, in adding something 'with interest' to what the child had said (see Chapter 7) rather than interrogating it, then the richer their interactions became and the longer and more intricate became the children's contributions.

Commenting
A: Hmm, I think that's a bigger brick this time.
A: That grey paint has made the stormy sky look so realistic.

Layering/Embellishing
C: My mum's gone to the market.
A: Yes, there's a market in town on Wednesdays.

Offering an alternative view of the world
C: My mum says the best babies are breast-fed.
A: Sometimes there are good reasons why mums feed their babies with milk from a bottle. My babies were bottle-fed because...

Talking about the future
C: My baby's asleep.
A: When your baby wakes up she won't be tired any more, will she?

Planting an idea
A: I really like the giraffe on your T-shirt.
Ch: Maybe you can buy one too?
A: Do you know, I don't have any clothes with animals on. Perhaps they make those just for children.

Adding something personal
C: My cat got sick and he's gone away to be better.
A: My cat went to the vet with his bad leg. It made me feel so sad.

Giving information
C: What does that say? (on the bottom of her T-shirt)
A: That says 'copyright'. Copyright means no one else can make a T-shirt that looks just like that because that would be copying – and that's not allowed.

Addressing misconceptions
C: That can't be someone's house, it's too high.
A: Actually, some people live in flats and apartments and they are often taller than houses because lots of people live in the same building.

Figure 9.1 Making statements instead of asking questions

Fillers and Phatics

A further contribution, alternative to questioning, is the use of fillers and phatics. These are the sounds and single words that simply show you are listening to the speaker. So contributions such as 'Mmm, 'Really', 'uh-huh…', which are frequently accompanied by positive body language such as nodding the head, often elicit a further contribution from the child; whereas asking a question often brings the interaction to a close once that question has been answered.

In studies of both deaf and hearing children – Wood et al. (1982) and Wood and Wood (1983) – reported that the use of phatics by teachers enhanced the length and initiative of children's responses more than questions, whether open or closed. Wood and Wood (1984: 45–6) noted that 'fewer questions and more phatics were met by children giving more spontaneous contributions, elaborated answers, and asking questions themselves'. Following a question, however, children often stop commenting themselves because they think the practitioner has gone into interrogative mode and they then simply wait for the next question to come along. Dillon suggests that one of the big problems with questioning is that it can lead the child to be 'silently cooperative as a pupil' (1990: 46), and simply wait for the next question to be asked.

Silence

Research into the asking of questions and alternatives to questioning in a variety of contexts – classrooms, criminal courts, therapy sessions – reveals that, against all expectations, people respond positively to silence. They respond to silence with both further thought and more complex thought. Yet silence is incredibly hard to achieve, especially in a busy nursery or classroom where practitioners feel they are being judged if they do not constantly intervene in children's activity and thought processes. It can be difficult to think something through when distracted by someone else speaking – and yet how often are children asked a question only for the practitioner to fill their thinking time with further elaboration or, worse still, another question.

Equally important as silence is the 'second silence', when the speaker is stuck or still thinking. It is crucial at this juncture, Dillon says, to allow the silence to continue and not to 'help them out'. The sustained expression of thought is marked by hesitations, false starts, and pauses in speech. And 'It is at these precise points', suggests Dillon (1990: 201), 'that practitioners habitually enter in to ask a question… Were the practitioner to maintain silent at this juncture, he would probably hear not only further talk but richer talk.' Indeed, claim Matarazzo et al. (1968: 375 – 6), the frequency of response 'increases systematically with the length of interviewer silence'.

Analysing your own practice

These are the features of effective practice that the Oxfordshire practitioners identified in relation to 'Questions that work and questions that don't':

Features of interactions where questions work

- The right question is asked for the right learning moment.
- Questions are asked because the adult is interested and wants to know more.
- Questions are asked to which the adult doesn't know the answer (other than when 'checking' knowledge and understanding in an adult-led context).
- Questions require children to think, rather than merely to know.
- Questions lead to further activity, enquiry or thinking (but not necessarily right at that moment).
- Questions are followed by long pauses to give the child time to think and respond.
- More questions are asked by the child than the adult.

Features of interactions where questions don't work

- The adult asks a question but doesn't wait for the answer (walking past).
- The adult asks a question but doesn't give time for an answer (immediately asking another question).
- The adult asks a question and then ignores the answer (it wasn't 'right'; it wasn't 'worth' acknowledging).
- The adult asks a question and then demands an answer (interrogation).
- The adult asks a question and then answers it themselves.
- The adult asks a question that is unnecessary (and interrupts learning).
- The adult asks a question when what the child wants is an answer.
- The adult asks too many questions.

Transcripts: questions that work and questions that don't

Transcript 9:5 'Simon and Saeed's model'
Saeed (3:9) (C1) and his friend Faisal (C2) are constructing a castle from Lego pieces. This is familiar play to them (they have been friends since starting nursery) and play to which they return repeatedly. They do not speak much because they know what they are doing and work together quietly but with purpose. After they have been playing for about 20 minutes, the teacher comes up to them:

A: What are you doing boys?
C1: Making a castle
A: Is it a special castle?
No answer
A: Who have you made the castle for? I expect it's for a dragon or a princess? Is it?

The boys look at her but do not answer

A: I can see a prince coming along to rescue a princess from your castle. Is it finished yet? Shall I get you some people from the small world box? A prince and princess? Would you like that?

The boys do not respond

C2: Come on Saeed, let's go out.

Analysis

The boys are engaged in purposeful play. Play with which they are confident and familiar. They do not actually need adult intervention because they are achieving their own goals for their own purposes very successfully. The teacher does not stop and watch and listen before intervening. She presumes that the focus of the boys' attention is on creating a 'story' around their castle. In fact they were simply 'building'. They were enjoying the familiar routine of constructing what was quite a complex model and were also enjoying each other's company. They had previously been engaged in a rather boisterous, whole-group session of 'Letters and Sounds', and seemed to have returned to their castle for some quiet downtime. By speaking without tuning in to the boys' play, the teacher interfered with both the mood of the play and its purpose. Because the teacher believed that asking questions would somehow enhance the learning she actually interfered with it. Firstly, she distracted the boys from their play by asking 'What are you doing?', when some quiet observation would have answered that question. Then she persisted with a line of questioning that was attempting to manipulate the boys towards the purpose she had already assumed to be *their* purpose. She was not sufficiently sensitive to pick up that the boys were not responding with enthusiasm for or interest in the exchange, and that she had, in fact, stopped the play and taken its momentum away. She is uncomfortable with the boys' lack of engagement with her and so fills the silences with further questions. Rather than continue to be interrogated in this way, the boys chose to leave.

Ask yourself: *What does the child gain?*

See the end of the transcripts in Chapter 3 for ideas.

Transcript 9:6 'Kristen and the buried treasure'

The teacher in this Year 1 class has put some hidden 'treasure' in a builder's tray filled with pink sand. The children have been told to find the treasure and put it into their own individual bowls. Alongside the 'treasure' there are plastic pincers, intended to develop the children's fine motor skills (the objective of the activity).

C: I got lots of treasure.

A: You've got loads? What do you think they all are? *(the question is not answered)*

C2: I've got even loads.

A: You've got even more? How do you know you've got even more Joe?

C: Umm... 'cos I found some... and I'm very good at finding things.

A: You were very good at finding it. What do you think you'll be able to do to...?

C2: I'm thinking there must be... oo... oo.

A: Oo.

C: Yeh.

A: Have you used... *(picking up a pair of pincers)*. What do you think these are for?

C: Umm... umm... I think...

A: What do they help people do?

C3: *(The two girls have been continuing to 'find treasure' very excitedly)* Are we going to find any more, Tanya? *(They look in each other's bowls)*

C1: Yeh – there's lots in there.

C2: Put them in there... an' hiding them in there... an' then...

A: Mmm.

C1: *(Showing her bowl to the teacher)* I got... I got lots of treasure.

A: Right. What do you think those things... what are all these things Tanya?

C1: It's all... it's a lot of treasure.

C2: I can't find...

A: It's a lot.

C2: I can't find some.

A: I think you might have found them all. But I wondered what they did? Why are they in there, do you think?

C2: I think Lois got all of them.

C1: No. I haven't. There's lots more.

C2: I think there's one more now.

A: What do you think Mrs Rogers put them in there for? Why do you think she put them in there? *(the two girls stop and look at her, unsure)*. What does it help you to do?

C3: Umm... pick them up?

A: 'Cos you pick them up *(Joe pours all his 'treasure' into Lois's bowl)*. Oh that's kind of you Joe. Are you sharing with Lois? *(he doesn't answer)*. Who do you think has got the most now Joe?

C2: Umm... her *(pointing at Lois. He stands up and leaves)*.

Analysis

The children were given something quite enjoyable but straightforward to do (finding the treasure). The teacher's constant questioning interfered with this activity and the children were not interested in the direction she wanted to take their learning. Rather than building on their enthusiasm and their comments – 'I got lots of treasure' – the teacher repeatedly returned to her objectives which were concerned with the development of fine motor skills: 'Why are they (the pincers) there?'; 'What are they for?' Both questions seemed irrelevant to the children who only answered a question once with any thought ('What does it help you to do?' – 'Umm... pick them up?'). The teacher was busy thinking of the next questions to ask and failed to hear the children's answers, or tune in to their lack of engagement. In this activity, the children had to spend more time tuning in to the teacher's questions than she spent tuning in to theirs.

Ask yourself: *What does the child gain?*

See the end of the transcripts in Chapter 3 for ideas.

Summary

It seems that the use of statements rather than questions often sustains an interaction between practitioners and children. Whereas questions often put children's thinking (and them) 'on the spot', making a statement, planting an idea, offering an alternative idea, seem to enrich children's thought processes and encourage them to speak – and think – more, and in more complex ways. The use of statements contributes helpfully to the strategy of responding to the child 'with interest', sustaining the turn-taking of an effective interaction, while a question (and its answer) so often brings an interaction to an end. The secret to asking questions that have purpose and value is to ask *yourself* this question first: 'Am I asking a question that's useful for me or for the child?'

Self-reflection

1 Do I only ask questions to which I know the answer?

2 Do my questions encourage children to think, or do they only check on what children know?

3 Do I ask questions to steer learning in the direction I want it to go?

4 Do I interrupt children's learning with too many questions?

10

The attributes of effective practitioners

'Not words, but virtues are her main qualifications.' (Montessori 1967)

Introduction

In this final chapter we consider the attributes displayed by those practitioners who consistently interact effectively. In the analysis of the Oxfordshire ACI Project material, certain practitioner attributes revealed themselves repeatedly as the DVD footage was viewed and then discussed – attributes that seemed to lead most readily to a mutual learning encounter between the practitioner and the child.

Not surprisingly, the most effective practitioners were those who were fascinated by young children – what they said, what they were thinking, what they were trying to do. Those practitioners who were less engaged simply did not take the time it takes to tune in to the children's thinking and respond to their ideas. These were practitioners who, for one reason or another, felt pressurized to follow their own agenda, rather than become attuned to the agenda of the child. The age of the children involved in the interactions made little difference. There were simply some practitioners who were more concerned with making their own contributions to an interaction, rather than responding to the contributions of the child. This chapter examines why some practitioners are consistently effective when interacting with young children and, in the process, demonstrates why teaching in the early years is such a special – and specialist – occupation.

Focus on babies and toddlers

When the Oxfordshire ACI project began, it was assumed that the attributes of effective practitioners would vary according to the age group the practitioners were working with. The project team's assumption was that the attributes necessary when working with babies and toddlers, for example, would differ from those needed to work with children higher up the school system. In the end, following many months' analysis and discussion, it was found that there was no difference between the attributes of effective practitioners, whatever the age of the children they worked with. As has already been explained in this book, any difference between how practitioners interact effectively was to do with the purpose of an interaction – whether it was meeting the purposes of the practitioner (adult-led) or the purposes of the child (child-led) – and nothing to do with the age of the children involved. Practitioners who interact effectively with young children are practitioners who display very similar characteristics.

The attributes of effectiveness

At the beginning of the Oxfordshire Project, I undertook a literature review to identify what others believed to be the attributes of effective early years educators. Drawing on a wealth of material, certain attributes appeared repeatedly in the literature and were used as yardsticks in the project analysis. By the end of the project, some four years after we began, the same attributes remained strong indicators of the likelihood of a practitioner engaging in effective interactions. Whatever the age of the children involved, there were seven attributes which manifested themselves in the way practitioners engage effectively with young children's thinking:

1 Being attentive.
2 Being sensitive.
3 Being responsive.
4 Being respectful.
5 Being genuine.
6 Being a good role model.
7 Being at ease in the company of children.

Being attentive

In her MA dissertation, Sue Vermes (2008) used the phrase 'warm attentiveness' to describe the way the expert practitioner, the subject of her study, communicated her interest in and respect for the child in her company, and that child's conversation. This phrase, better than any other, seems to summarize the manner in which all of the most effective practitioners in the Oxfordshire study interacted with their children. The disposition to be 'warm' is critical in all relationships with young children who thrive on the care, empathy and sensitivity of the practitioners who work with and play alongside them. Children sense whether adults truly care about them and enjoy being with them, and this creates the foundation for successful relationships leading, in turn, to both practitioners and children being sufficiently relaxed for an interaction to flow (see Chapter 3).

The word 'attentiveness' suggests a practitioner who is alert to and interested in what is going on, but not necessarily intervening. It confirms the importance of practitioners who wait, watch and wonder (see Chapter 6) before deciding when or whether to interact. It reminds practitioners that to engage with children does not necessarily mean speaking to them. Positive body language, a smile, a nod or a filler (see Chapter 9) when the child looks towards the practitioner, can sometimes do more to keep the child's learning momentum going than a verbal contribution. This does not mean, of course, that the practitioner cannot speak! What it does establish, is that 'being attentive' is the first step. Being attentive leads to observation and active listening, both (as we saw in Chapter 5) necessary stages before making a decision about when and whether to interact. Sometimes silence is golden. The practitioner who waits, watches and wonders is more likely to say the right thing at the right time and to interact rather than interfere.

In adult-child interactions, *being attentive* shows itself in the following ways:

- practitioners genuinely care about and are interested in children
- practitioners exude warmth when they interact with all children (and not just those who are easy to talk to)
- practitioners are alert to every conversation that comes along
- practitioners show attentiveness in their body language and in the sensitivity of their interactions.

Being sensitive

In his work on a process-oriented approach to learning and teaching, Laevers (1994) highlights the importance of the way in which adults interact with children. He believes that these interactions are key to the achievement of well-being and involvement. One of the dimensions he highlights in his 'Adult Style Observation Schedule' (ASOS) is sensitivity, which he sees as being responsive to the emotional needs of the child. He suggests that practitioners have to be sensitive to the child's:

- *need for respect*: giving the child a feeling of being valued and equally important in an interaction
- *need for attention*: listening to the child, acknowledging their need for focused time and attention
- *need for security:* recognizing and responding to the child's insecurities and uncertainties
- *need for affection:* responding to the child with warmth and genuine interest
- *need for affirmation*: being positive about a child's achievements and efforts and empowering the child with a sense of agency

- *need for clarity*: ensuring the child knows what is expected and is not having to tune in to the adult's agenda
- *need for understanding*: ensuring the child is known well and responding to their different and highly individual needs.

Practitioners who are sensitive are alert to the differences in their children's needs day by day. They tune in very quickly to changes in mood and signals that suggest that a child may have more need of them today than other days. Sensitive practitioners sense changes in behaviour and reactions and make themselves available to give the child emotional support if and when it is needed. They are empathetic to the child whose behaviour may be upsetting them as well as others. Effective practitioners are also sensitive to the child's learning needs–that today this child needs one-to-one attention, whereas yesterday they managed their learning independently. They are sensitive to the child's agenda, whatever that might be.

In adult-child interactions, *being sensitive* shows itself in the following ways:

- practitioners tune in to the child swiftly at the start of each day
- practitioners are attentive to the child's agenda and to their needs
- practitioners understand that the child's interests need to be addressed before any adult agenda is introduced
- practitioners respect the child, their feelings, their conversation and their thinking.

Being responsive

Dillon (1990) explains how it is all too easy to listen to what a child says and not respond, or to respond in a superficial way. If the practitioner's mind is full of the many things that have to be done in the day, then responses can be curt – 'Uh huh'; 'How lovely' – without the practitioner truly engaging with the child at all. These responses are different from the phatics and fillers described in Chapter 9. The practitioner uses phatics and fillers to sustain the child's learning momentum, while in the example above, the practitioner is showing that the child does not have their full attention, the response is not inviting an exchange and the interaction is not sustained. Being responsive means that the practitioner must want the interaction to take place, must consider it sufficiently important to stop, get down and listen to what the child is trying to say, must put their own agenda temporarily on hold as they engage with the child and theirs. Being responsive rests on what Margaret Donaldson (1978) describes as the practitioner's ability and willingness to 'de-centre' – in other words, the practitioner's willingness to see the child as more central to the learning experience than the practitioner themselves.

The quality of responsiveness lies in the skill of the practitioner to respond to the child in different ways. Firstly, as we have seen, the response must be sensitive to the individual child and their particular needs. But the response must also be appropriate to the situation. Sometimes, and in different situations, the practitioner is asked to respond by: giving an answer; making connections; commenting; asking a question; addressing misconceptions; clarifying; provoking; modelling; offering an alternative viewpoint; elaborating or embellishing. Rose and Rogers (2012) suggest the term 'the plural practitioner' to describe these many and varied roles undertaken when working with young children. The effective practitioner moves from one role to another with ease, nimble on their feet and alert to what is required to sustain and extend their interactions.

In adult-child interactions, *being responsive* shows itself in the following ways:

- Practitioners are interested in the child and what they might have to say.
- Practitioners stop, get down, and listen to the conversational openers that come their way.
- Practitioners show through their warm attentiveness that they are giving the child time and attention.
- Practitioners chose the most effective response to keep the momentum of an interaction going.

Being respectful

Young children will always be more likely to engage with practitioners who treat them with respect. Being respectful means taking children's ideas and opinions seriously.

It means asking what they think and then responding to their answers with interest, reacting to and acting on those answers if appropriate. Over the past decade there has been considerable research into listening to the voices of children, brought about by the perceived failure of authorities to listen to what children – particularly those in crisis – are saying, and acting upon it. These concerns about the unheard voices of children brought about the *Every Child Matters* agenda (DfES 2004), focusing on five outcomes identified by children and young people themselves to make their voices heard:

1 Being healthy.
2 Staying safe.
3 Enjoying and achieving.
4 Making a positive contribution.
5 Achieving economic well-being.

The fact that these outcomes are now enshrined in law (The Children Act 2004) means that all those working with young children need to heed the call that 'The child's voice should be heard and account taken of their wishes and feelings.'

Being respectful means recognizing that the child is an individual in their own right, with their own feelings, beliefs, attitudes, concerns and interests. When practitioners respect children then they work harder to tune in to all of these individual characteristics. The young child has their own embryonic view of the world, how it works and their own place within it, and the respectful adult is intrigued by this child's-eye view and does their best to tune in to it and respond accordingly. Being respectful means not only listening to the child's ideas and point of view, but acting upon them if necessary, sometimes amending the practitioners' agenda completely in order to respond to the agenda of the child.

In adult-child interactions, *being respectful* shows itself in the following ways:

- Practitioners offer the child plenty of opportunities to put across their own ideas, to form their own opinions, and to express their feelings.
- Practitioners listen attentively to what the child has to say and respect their contribution.
- Practitioners respond to the child with due concern and interest.
- Practitioners act upon what the child has said, if appropriate.

Being genuine

The need for practitioners to be genuine in their interactions is emphasized in the work of Carl Rogers (1902–87), the American psychologist who was leading among the founders of the humanistic approach (or client-centred approach) to psychology. Rogers (1951) claimed that students learn more and behave better when they receive high levels of understanding, caring and genuineness, than when they are given low levels of them. He suggested that being genuine meant that the practitioner is not presenting a façade. And he claimed that patients or clients saw through any false attempts to extract information and responded most readily and openly to practitioners who seemed genuinely interested in them than those whose persona was more aloof and where the practitioner was almost 'playing a part'.

In educational contexts, messages about genuineness are often manifest in both body language and tone of voice. A practitioner may say something positive or encouraging, but if their body language is 'distracted' then the child gets the feeling that the response is not genuine. Likewise, the practitioner may use a tone of voice that is rather too gushing and unnatural, and the child again senses that they are being treated in a way that is somewhat patronizing. There is a difference here, of course, when practitioners are working with babies. As we have seen in Chapter 2, the sing-song, high-pitched tone of voice, and exaggerated facial expressions of 'motherese' are universally used by adults to capture infants' attention and help them to keep focused on interacting. But when children sense that a practitioner's response is not genuine then they come to believe that any contribution on their part is some sort of game, rather than a genuine dialogue. They come to believe that they are taking part in an interaction which is being manipulated by the practitioner and, therefore, that they are expected perhaps to respond in the way the practitioners expects, rather than in the way they might choose.

In adult-child interactions, *being genuine* shows itself in the following ways:

- Practitioners are genuinely interested in young children, what they have to say, and what they are thinking.
- Practitioners respond to the child with body language and a tone of voice that demonstrates that genuine interest.
- Practitioners comment on and embellish what the child has said 'with interest'; they do not interrogate it.
- Practitioners maintain interactions that serve the learning purposes of the child.

Being a positive role model

Early childhood educators are acutely aware that they act as role models for young children. Many practitioners will have stories of children who come to nursery wearing earrings just like their Key Person's; or teachers will hear their own instructions and tone of voice mimicked in the role-play area; or parents will say (sometimes in exasperation) that everything at home is ruled by what the practitioner says should or should not happen: 'Miss Smith says that we must roll up our sleeves before we wash our hands.' Bandura (1977) suggests that social learning begins with imitative learning which is subsequently internalized. The child's construction of the world and how it works is founded upon the behaviour of other people who are considered significant, and which the child then internalizes. Lois Malaguzzi (1993) says, 'We must know that children... do not acquire the art of becoming friends or teachers of one another by finding models in heaven or in manuals; rather, children extract and interpret models from adults, when the adults know how to work, discuss, think, research and live together.'

Early childhood educators model:

- *Language*: by using, commenting on and extending children's vocabulary.
- *Behaviour*: by acting in ways that children should emulate e.g. listening; taking turns; being respectful; being fair.
- *Thinking*: by making explicit the process of thinking – 'I really need to think about this more'; 'If I think for a while I might remember how to do this' – and so on.
- *Learning*: by making explicit the ways in which learners go about making sense of the world – e.g. by writing lists to aid memory; changing one's mind and improving an idea; going to look for a book to check information – and so on.

In adult-child interactions, *being a good role model* shows itself in the following ways:

- Practitioners are sensitive to the impact of their own actions on the actions of the child.
- Practitioners use language carefully and consciously to enhance the child's vocabulary and their use of language to communicate.
- Practitioners are aware of their own behaviour and behave in ways that they would be happy for a child to emulate.
- Practitioners make explicit the process of thinking and learning so children understand these are lifelong skills.

Being at ease in the company of children

One would think this hardly needs saying, but there is no doubt that effective early years educators and those who engage in the most effective interactions are those who take a pleasurable interest in the child and in their conversation. Such practitioners will always put the interaction with the child before any other more trivial task they had planned to do. They will always stop, get down, and listen to the child's conversational opener, however insignificant it may appear to be. They will show respect for and interest in the child, their family, their news, their fascinations, their concerns. This interest will manifest itself, not in a smile and a nod and a 'Uh-huh', but through a genuine question to clarify what the child has said – comments to show they have been listening, or a personal anecdote to embellish what the child has said and to 'add interest' to the interaction.

Such warm attentiveness comes from enjoying and being relaxed in the company of young children (Chapter 3). This serves as a reminder that not all people – not all practitioners – are cut out to work with young children. To enjoy the company and conversation of young children, a practitioner has to enjoy unpredictability; they must relish spontaneity; they must be flexible; they must be quick at thinking on their feet; they must love the outdoors and prefer dialogue to monologue. They must understand that interactions with young children will give them the evidence of learning, development and progress that they need, far over and above anything that tick-sheets and record books will reveal. In short, effective practitioners must like young children. Being at ease in the company of a young child means that both practitioner, and child, will be relaxed. This, as we have seen, is an indicator of interactions that flow effortlessly, and an indicator of a practitioner who is more concerned with revelling in the learning journey of the child than stressing about arriving at some destination.

In adult-child interactions, *being at ease* in the company of young children shows itself in the following ways:

- Practitioners find young children and their spontaneous, idiosyncratic thinking fascinating.
- Practitioners are happy to go with the flow of young children's thinking and (if appropriate) to abandon (even if only temporarily) what is planned.
- Practitioners are relaxed, so children are at ease in their company.
- Practitioners appreciate the journey of learning and are not constantly trying to arrive at a destination.

The importance of reciprocity

While these are the attributes that seem to be common among practitioners who achieve the most effective sustained interactions with children, it is important not to stop at this stage of the analysis. To put the spotlight only on the practitioner is to see only half of the story. Much of the literature about adult-child interactions is informed by Vygotsky's (1978) sociocultural theory that 'human learning presupposes a specific social nature and a process by which children grow into the intellectual life of those around them' (p.88). An effective interaction takes two, and it is the response of the child to the practitioner as much as the practitioner to the child that leads to an interaction of value and purpose. The practitioner and the child share experiences and knowledge of the other and, says Wells (2009), attempt to understand the meaning intended by the other and to express their own meanings in ways 'which will be understood against the background of shared information'. Wells refers to this meaning-making as reciprocity, a term also used by Claxton (2002) as one of his 'Four Rs of Learning Power'. For Claxton, reciprocity signifies being 'ready, willing and able to... learn with others' (2002: 17), demonstrated by an ability to get inside the minds of the other person. As Boyd and Markarian (2011: 517) have argued, 'it is the perceived function of the talk in a situated, social context, not its decontextualized form, that determines its effectiveness'.

The notion of reciprocity suggests an equal contribution from both parties or, at least, a contribution that leaves both parties feeling involved in and satisfied by the exchange. As we have already seen in Chapter 9, the problem in many school classrooms in particular is that talk is what Cazden (2001) describes as 'asymmetrical'. She suggests that in a typical classroom the most significant asymmetry lies in the control of the right to speak. While teachers have the right to speak at any time and to any person – to fill the silence; to interrupt any other speaker; to speak across one child to another; to speak at any volume or using any tone of voice – the child does not have the same rights. Indeed, in most classrooms children would be chastised for any attempt to behave in such ways. So, it can be seen that reciprocity lies heavily in the hands of the practitioner and their willingness to engage in interactions that have meaning, purpose and relevance for the child as well as for themselves.

There have been different ways of illustrating the reciprocity between adult and child which may be helpful in recognizing the efficacy of an interaction. The first is the notion of a **dance**. Colwyn Trevarthen (1974), in his ground-breaking work on the interactions between mothers and their newborn infants, describes the rhythm and sequence of action and response being like a dance, as one leads and the other follows in imitating sounds and gestures. In discussing this analogy, the Oxfordshire practitioners decided the relevance for early childhood educators was that it does not matter who leads the 'dance' – in other words, who initiates the interaction – as long as the other person follows doing the same dance. The person instigating the 'dance' may chose a tango but, however good the dancers are, the 'dance' will not be effective if the other person is trying to waltz. For the conversational dance to be effective, both adult and child must engage in joint attention and a shared experience.

A second analogy is that of a **see-saw** (or scales), used by The Hanen Centre (see Weitzman and Greenberg 2002), a Canadian charitable organization providing parents, carers, early childhood educators and speech-language pathologists with training and materials to help young children develop children's language, social and literacy skills. The Hanen materials describe ways to help children learn the rules of conversation, including turn taking. They encourage practitioners to 'treat any reaction such as a wriggle, a smile, a kick, a burp, a sound or a stare as if the child has taken his turn'. The purpose of illustrating this point using a see-saw or scales is that, for an interaction to be effective, both participants need to have similar input. The see-saw does not work as a piece of play equipment unless it goes up and down in equal measure. If one partner is too heavy (i.e. they talk too much) then the other participant does not have the opportunity to join in or contribute to the interaction and is left stranded in mid-air and frustrated. An effective interaction means that both adult and child take their turn in a flow of ideas and feelings where the threads of thinking are sufficiently balanced.

The third analogy draws on a game of **ball**. Lois Malaguzzi (1992) suggests that an interaction mirrors a game of ball between at least two players. He says, 'The ball is passed always along. At times the children throw it, at times we do.' In a similar way to Trevarthen, Malaguzzi believes that either the adult or the child can start the conversational ball game but, in both cases, must pass the ball in such a way that the other person wants to keep the game going. As the more experienced 'player' the adult has the greater responsibility to pass the conversational ball in such a way that the child is both able to and motivated to receive it, and pass it back. What the Oxfordshire practitioners noticed was how often children passed them a conversational ball which they then put down in favour of a new 'ball' (conversation) of their own. The skill of effective practitioners is in keeping the ball game going, using the same ball.

Interaction as 'improvisation'

While finding all of these analogies interesting, the Oxfordshire practitioners found none of them quite adequate. We would like to suggest that only the notion of 'interaction as improvisation' comes close to capturing the intricacies of an effective learning encounter between an early years educator and a child. Whether viewed within a musical context, in dance, drama or in art, 'improvisation' (involving at least two people) comes closest to explaining the transformative nature of an effective interaction when a practitioner's contribution enhances the learning of a child and, frequently, vice versa. Like improvisation, an effective interaction has the power to change relationships as well as knowledge and understanding. Like improvisation, effective interactions are complex — both activities requiring the utmost concentration and demanding the complete involvement of both parties. There is no right or wrong way to contribute to an improvisation or an interaction, but all contributions need to connect with the other person and need to be responded to sensitively and appropriately in order to sustain the quality of what is created. In an interaction, just as in improvisation, the more experienced partner needs to pay particular attention to the contribution of the other in order to link what is said, or played, to the less experienced contribution. Like improvisation, an effective interaction shows both spontaneity and freedom. There is a fluidity

about improvisation that replicates the flow of a natural and genuine conversation between the practitioner and child. According to the mood of those involved, what is initiated, and what response it brings, will differ from day to day, moment to moment. There are no preconceived notes or steps, and yet many of the improvised paths are familiar, drawing on past experiences in creating something new and relevant to the moment. Like effective interactions, improvisation often begins with a simple motif, a basic exchange that then becomes enhanced and embellished the longer the encounter lasts, in accordance with the skill and commitment of those involved. The nature of improvisation with somebody else is quite different from improvisation by one person alone. Both parties learn from it and through it, and the contribution of both is vital to the success of both the process and the outcomes. Just like shared play differs from individual play there are far more possibilities, more options, a greater interplay of ideas and more diverse outcomes when the improvisation, or interaction, involves two.

Interacting not interfering

This book has examined the ways in which effective practitioners interact with children to support and extend their thinking, their learning and their development. It has drawn on the detailed, painstaking analysis of practice undertaken over four years by a group of Oxfordshire practitioners committed to improving their own practice for the benefit of the children they work with. Much of the analysis came from repeated viewing of many hours of DVD footage and the refining and synthesizing of the data that took place as result. The findings from the project are multilayered. Many features overlap and, inevitably, key messages from the project permeate different chapters in this book. However, in discussing and refining the data, we sometimes found it helpful to capture our thinking in more manageable ways, through diagrams and prompts. So, to conclude this book I would like to share some of these with you as a way of summarizing the findings of the Oxfordshire Adult-Child Interaction Research Project, as well as summarizing the key messages of this book.

Firstly, we agreed that the **aim** of the project was:

'To improve the quality of adult-child interactions.'

We decided that the **purpose** of any interaction was:

'To consolidate, extend or provoke children's learning and development.'

We arrived at a **key question** to ask about any interaction in order to analyse its effectiveness:

'Did the child gain something positive from this interaction that they might not otherwise have had?'

We agreed that '**something positive**' was not necessarily cognitive, but that it could be:

Cognitive: 'That cardboard gets soggy and falls apart when it gets into water.'
Social: 'If I hold this still then Ricky can send the car faster down the ramp.'
Emotional: 'Jenny says my gran will come for me when she's back from shopping.'
Dispositional: 'If I stick at something I can usually do it in the end.'
Metacognitive: 'I need to change my plan 'cos my idea isn't working.'

Note: *this is phrasing children's thinking in adult language.*

We believe that a **key strategy** for sustaining an interaction is to respond to the child 'with interest':

- *Being interested in* what the child says, feels and thinks.
- *Adding to* what the child says, feels and thinks with a comment, clarifying question, or statement that sustains the interaction further.

Analysing your own practice

As an outcome of the Oxfordshire ACI project, the participants identified key features to look for when analysing the quality of an interaction. There were concerns over this kind of analysis because it could make what is a highly complex and sophisticated activity (an interaction with a child) appear too straightforward. However, after much discussion it was decided that if practitioners were to analyse their own practice – or indeed to analyse the practice of others – then there had to be some attempt to capture the features of effective practice that might be observed when an interaction was taking place. Each chapter in this book has a section on 'Analysing My Own Practice' which is specific to the particular subject matter of that chapter. Here, we present two sets of prompts that attempt to sum up all that has been learned through our project, and which has been useful for individual practitioners, as a basis for whole-staff discussions and as a monitoring tool for those senior leaders and managers looking for evidence of effective early years practice. Figure 10.1 summarizes 'What to look for' in evaluating the quality of adult-led learning, and Figure 10.2 summarizes 'What to look for' in child-led learning.

Adult-Led Interactions

The Child:

'The child gains something positive from the practitioner that s/he might not otherwise have had.'

- is left with something positive from the adult s/he didn't have before: social; emotional; cognitive; dispositional; metacognitive
- remains engaged and focused on the adult
- appears to find the interaction relevant and meaningful
- is demonstrating own ideas and raising own questions
- has plenty of opportunities to contribute
- looks relaxed and comfortable
- is confident of/in the adult's attention/help
- has the time s/he needs to respond.

The Practitioner:

'The adult <u>focuses</u> on the child's thinking.'

- shows a desire to get to know the child better (cognitively)
- pauses long enough to tune in to the child's thinking during the activity
- gives the child the time necessary to respond to questions and challenges
- is attentive, both physically and mentally
- contributions are affirming and constructive
- contributions are genuine and natural, while keeping the child's thinking focused
- tone of voice is respectful
- uses a range of strategies that are fit for purpose and relevant to the child's needs
- is respectful of and responsive to the child's ideas and opinions
- does not break away from an interaction to take notes
- offers a positive interactional role model – listening; responding with interest; building on ideas
- manages interruptions sensitively without losing the flow of the conversation
- takes a pleasurable interest in the child's thinking and ideas
- is sensitive to the child's level of interest and involvement.

Figure 10.1 Effective adult-led interactions: What to look for

Child-Led Interactions

The Child:

'The child gains something positive from the adult that s/he might not otherwise have had.'

- is left with something positive from the adult s/he didn't have before: social; emotional; cognitive; dispositional; metacognitive
- remains engaged and focused on the adult
- appears to find the interaction relevant and meaningful
- is demonstrating own ideas and raising own questions
- has plenty of opportunities to contribute
- looks relaxed and comfortable
- is confident of /in the adult's attention/help
- has the time s/he needs to respond
- is confident to instigate/initiate an interaction
- leads the interaction for as long as s/he wants.

The Practitioner:

'The adult <u>follows</u> the child's thinking and intentions'

- shows a desire to get to know the child better
- watches and waits long enough to tune in to the child's thinking
- gives the child the time necessary to respond
- is attentive, both physically and mentally, but not intrusive
- contributions are affirming and constructive
- contributions are genuine and natural
- body language is attentive and tone of voice is respectful
- uses a range of strategies that suit the conversational purpose and the child's needs
- is respectful of and responsive to the child's ideas and opinions
- does not tell the child what to think
- does not break away from an interaction to take notes
- offers a positive conversational role-model – listening; responding with interest; building on ideas
- manages interruptions sensitively, without losing the flow of the conversation
- takes a pleasurable interest in the child's company and conversation
- is sensitive to the child's level of interest and involvement.

Figure 10.2 Effective child-led interactions: What to look for

Transcripts: the attributes of effective practitioners

Transcript 10:1 'Heather and Izzy at the craft table'

It is the start of the morning session in a state nursery school. Two three-year-old girls have gone to the craft table and the teacher joins them there.

A: Sorry, Eva, I didn't hear what you said when I asked why you were late.

C: *(Putting glue on a tissue box)* Well I didn't dress so quick.

A: You didn't dress quickly. Did you get dressed by yourself though? *(Eva nods)* That's the most important thing really, isn't it?

C2: *(Cutting masking tape for a card)* 'Cos, 'cos I wasn't late this morning.

A: You weren't late. Did you come here for breakfast Izzy?

C2: Yes.

A: I thought I saw you. And Tina? *(her sister)*

C2: Yes.

A: This morning. Just after I had my breakfast I came here and I saw you eating yours.

C2: Yes, that was Tina. But who did you see with Tina?

A: *(Teacher 'thinks' for a moment)* Hmm... Miss Andrews.

C2: Miss Andrews.

A: And you.

C2: And Simon.

A: *(Teacher 'thinks' again)* Umm... yes... Simon *was* here, you're right, because as I came in the door I saw Simon's mummy and Simon's sister going in to their car.

C2: And... and... do you know what I saw?

A: What did you see?

C2: I saw Simon's sister, she was holding a bag with Mickey Mouse on it.

A: Ahh, perhaps she was taking that to her own nursery or daycare. 'Cos I think Simon's mummy goes off to work, doesn't she?

C2: Or, or, or, or...

A: Or to do some jobs.

C2: Or, or stay at home.

A: Or stay at home if she's got things to do at home. Or have a rest! *(They grin at each other)*

C1: You know who else is going to come to my party?

C2: Me!

A: Izzy.

C1: And Freda.

A: Where is Freda today?

C2: She, she, she's on holiday.

A: Oh, she's on holiday. That's right... her mummy did tell me, but I forgot. *(Look-ing at Izzy)* You're good at remembering things aren't you?

C2: Uncle Geoffrey... Uncle Geoffrey... he bought this *(her T-shirt)*, he bought this from, er, the Lake District. The Lake District.

A: Ahh... there's a lot of sheep in the Lake District. That might be why you've got lots of sheep on your T-shirt. It's like a souvenir of the place that he went to, to help him remember – and help you remember. Can I see the writing... *(reads)* 'Do you think he's seen us?' *(Izzy looks down)*

C2:   What does that say? *(pointing to the small writing underneath)*

A: Oh, underneath that says 'Copyright'... ooh, I've just got to read around your tummy.

C1:   Megan, Megan...

A: *(Turning to C1)* Yes, just a moment, we're just reading this writing... *(she reads)* 'Copyright... Rannerdale Ltd. That means that nobody else can make a T-shirt just like that one, because that would be copying... and that's not allowed.'

Analysis

This transcript has many examples of the characteristics of effective interactions outlined in previous chapters. In particular, this teacher is skilled at responding to children 'with interest', enriching the child's contribution by helping her make connections in her current knowledge and understanding, and by adding something more to her existing knowledge and understanding.

When Eva says she was late, the teacher turns it into a positive point: 'Did you get dressed by yourself though?' *(Eva nods)*. 'That's the most important thing really, isn't it?' **Affirming a positive disposition/celebrating independence**

Izzy says she wasn't late. The teacher doesn't just say 'Well done you', but adds a further question: 'Did you come here for breakfast Izzy?' **Asking a question to sustain the interaction.**

The teacher then adds something personal: 'Just after I had my breakfast I came here and I saw you eating yours.' **Saying something personal to make the exchange mutual**

Izzy shows *her* engagement in the interaction by passing the conversational ball back to her teacher: 'But who did you see with Tina?'

On a number of occasions the teacher draws attention to metacognitive thinking. She models 'thinking': 'Hmm...' (pausing to 'think')... Miss Andrews. Then later: 'Umm... yes... Simon was here, you're right.' **Modelling thinking**

The teacher reinforces Izzy's positive view of herself: 'Umm... yes... Simon *was* here, you're right, because as I came in the door I saw Simon's mummy and Simon's sister going in to their car.' Then later: 'Oh, she's on holiday. That's right... her mummy did tell me, but I forgot. *(looking at Izzy)* You're good at remembering things, aren't you?" **Affirming a positive dispositions/contributing to child's self-esteem**

When Izzy says, 'I saw Simon's sister, she was holding a bag with Mickey Mouse on it.' The teacher doesn't say 'How lovely', and leave it there. She says, 'Ahh, perhaps she was taking that to her own nursery or daycare. 'Cos I think Simon's mummy goes off to work, doesn't she?' **Enhancing knowledge and making connections**

The teacher and Izzy enjoy the humour of passing ideas:

A: 'Cos I think Simon's mummy goes off to work, doesn't she?

C2:   Or, or, or, or...

A: Or to do some jobs.

C2:   Or, or stay at home.

A: Or stay at home if she's got things to do at home. Or have a rest! *(they grin at each other)* **Enhancing their positive relationship**

When Izzy shows the T-shirt her Uncle Geoffrey has bought in the Lake District, the teacher doesn't just say 'How nice of him' (or similar). Instead she makes connections in Izzy's understanding of the world and gives her new information.

A: 'Ahh... there's a lot of sheep in the Lake District. That might be why you've got lots of sheep on your T-shirt. It's like a souvenir of the place that he went to, to help him remember – and help you remember.' **Enhancing knowledge and making connections beyond the 'here' and 'now'**

The teacher deals with the interruption from Eva by acknowledging her, 'Yes, just a moment, we're just reading this writing...' – but without interrupting the flow of her interaction with Izzy at that point: 'Copyright... Rannerdale Ltd.' That means...'

Izzy again shows her engagement with the interaction by asking what the small writing on her T-shirt says and the teacher is able to add more new information: 'Copyright... Rannerdale Ltd. That means that nobody else can make a T-shirt just like that one, because that would be copying... and that's not allowed.' **Enhancing knowledge by giving new information**

The teacher in this transcript takes many opportunities to consolidate and extend the children's knowledge and understanding, yet is always following their thinking and the direction they want the interaction to take.

Summary

Interactions with young children offer both the practitioner and the child untold riches in terms of learning and development. For the practitioner, a child's communicative contributions offer an insight into what is interesting the child, where his understandings and misunderstandings might be, and what he wants to discover about the world. For the child, a sensitive and responsive practitioner offers opportunities to build relationships, to learn more language, to rehearse the skills of communication, and to enrich thinking.

Throughout this book we have seen that the quality of interactions between practitioners and children is dependent on the responsiveness of the practitioner to the thinking of the child. The level of a child's engagement with a practitioner depends on whether the practitioner is sufficiently fascinated by the child to help consolidate or extend their thinking; whether the practitioner is sufficiently attentive so that the child is encouraged to maintain their learning momentum; and whether the practitioner is sufficiently skilled to say just the right thing at the right time for the child to want to pass back the conversational ball.

Interacting with a young child is challenging but endlessly rewarding. Practitioners share the emerging thinking and understanding of each unique learner in their care as they engage with and make sense of the world in which they are growing up. The more attentive and sensitive practitioners are in their relationships with children, the more likely it is that they will interact effectively rather than interfere with children's learning. In order to be effective, what children need most is a practitioner's time and attention. Nothing should matter more to any practitioner than to make time for interacting with their children.

Self-reflection

1   Am I sensitive, responsive, respectful, and a good conversational role model?

2   Am I at ease in the company of young children? Do I find them fascinating?

3   Do I prioritize 'warm attentiveness' over and above all other aspects of my practice?

Appendix
The Oxfordshire Adult–Child Interaction Project 2010–14

Scope and methodology

The Oxfordshire Adult-Child Interaction Project[*] involved 18 early years practitioners (14 at any one time) working with children from six months to six years, one of whom was male (working in a baby room). The practitioners were recommended to the project either by their headteacher/manager or by a member of the local authority advisory team. The criterion for inclusion in the project was a willingness to be open and reflective about practice and a willingness to deconstruct elements of current practice in order to bring about change.

Each project practitioner was paired with a 'buddy' so that there were two practitioners working with each designated age group of children. These ages were 6 months to 1 year; 1–2 years; 2–3 years; 3–4 years; 4–5 years; 5–6 years; 6–7 years. By pairing in this way, discussions were age- and stage-specific, as well as cutting across ages when the project team were together, to encompass the whole of the Early Years Foundation Stage in England (0–5 years) and Key Stage 1 (5–7 years). These discussions took place at twice-termly project meetings (approximately every 10 weeks).

The provocation for discussions was digital video footage, gathered from all project participants once every term (three times per project year) for two years, with more limited and focused recordings taken in Years 3 and 4. By its conclusion, the project had gathered 120 pieces of footage of between 20–45 minutes duration according to the circumstances and the age of the children. Each session of filming was followed by post-observation analysis between the practitioner and the project coordinator who had been responsible for the filming.

The project followed a cycle of action research, where practitioners identified aspects of their practice that they wanted to develop, took action to do so, and then reflected on the impact their action had made. This cycle of self-reflective enquiry was stimulated by the analysis, at individual and group level, of the DVD footage. Alongside the filming and subsequent analysis, practitioners considered various existing theories that might illuminate, explain or justify the project's emerging findings. Finally, from

---

[*]*'Interacting or Interfering? The Oxfordshire Adult-Child Interaction Project'*

the commencement of the project, each practitioner kept a research log describing, from their own perspective, the development of their thinking and practice and what had impacted upon these.

Each stage of the project was cumulative. Discussion was informed by scrutiny of the DVD footage, which in turn was challenged by theory and by further analysis of transcripts. Several important themes emerged over the lifetime of the project that have, ultimately, formed the basis of the chapters in this book. These themes appeared over and over again during discussions and observation of the DVD footage, and helped refine and define the thinking of the group as a whole. As the post-observation analysis became more perceptive over time, the project participants increasingly highlighted where observations of their own practice coincided with the themes and issues emerging from the group as a whole.

Throughout the project, the role of the coordinator was participative. The role involved leading discussions and summarizing thinking. It also initially involved reading around and suggesting complementary theories. However – over time – the project participants found and recommended reading to each other. The coordinator participated in the 120 post-observation analysis sessions, keeping a record of what was notable according to the practitioner involved, and of themes and ideas that appeared to be common across a number of practitioners.

Throughout the lifetime of the project, the research was governed by a steering group. The group had representatives from the neighbourhood university (specializing in early years education) and from the local authority. We were also fortunate to have three expert practitioners, one representing those working with children Birth–3, another whose expertise was chiefly with children 3–7 years, and finally a representative from the project participant team. The role of the steering group was to maintain the focus of the project, to challenge emerging models and theories, and to keep an overview of finances and dissemination.

Ethical considerations

The project had a number of ethical issues to address. The first being the relationship between the project participants and the coordinator. In all but two cases the coordinator was known previously to the project participants in a role that included monitoring and evaluation. It was critical to establish a more collaborative relationship where both parties jointly constructed and scrutinized theories and where neither was seen as expert or to be in judgement over the other. This was mainly achieved by establishing early on that the coordinator would not make any evaluative comments during the post-observation analysis. The evaluation was entirely in the hands of the practitioners, including when to pause the footage and when to comment. The role of the coordinator was to keep notes about the issues raised by the individual practitioners and to maintain a record of issues that were emerging between all the practitioners.

The next issue concerned the filming of young children. Prior to the commencement of filming, permission was sought from all parents of children within the setting. Parents received not only a letter asking for their permission, but also a detailed explanation of the purposes and proposed outcomes of the project and the use to which the video footage would be put. This permission was sought every term as new children were taken into the project settings. When the coordinator was filming, the practitioners alerted her to those very few children for whom permission had not been granted although, being very young children, it was difficult at times to keep those children away from the camera and, as a result, some footage could not be used.

The final consideration concerned the use of the DVD footage for purposes outside of the project. At the commencement of the project each participant practitioner signed a project 'commitment' which was countersigned by the manager or headteacher of the practitioner's setting. This included an agreement that the outcomes of the project – transcripts, DVD footage and logs – could be shared with other practitioners, outside of the project, for staff development purposes.

Conclusions

The iterative process of this project clearly shows the impact of various elements of the action research process on each other. Nevertheless, while theory and reflection impact upon practice, the research evidence still confirms that changing educators' beliefs – or at least what they say they believe – is easier than changing practice itself. However, the project also shows that change is most likely when practitioners are confronted by their own practice in post-observation analysis, and when what they say is challenged by what they are seen to do on the screen.

For those working with early years practitioners in professional development programmes, the use of DVD footage would potentially appear to be highly influential, even when the footage is of other practitioners and not themselves. Evaluative feedback from training and conferences where this project's material has been used always contains comments about the usefulness of seeing other practitioners at work. Whenever the project material is shown to others I thank (in their absence) the project participants who were willing to have their work filmed and scrutinized in this way. Without them, the project would not have borne such rich fruit.

References

Ainsworth, M.D.S., Blehar, M.C., Waters, E. and Wall, S. (1978) *Patterns of Attachment.* Hillsdale, NJ: Erlbaum.

Alexander, R. (2008) *Towards Dialogic Teaching: Rethinking Classroom Talk*, 4th edn. York: Dialogos.

Andrews, M.A.W. (2013) Ask the brains, *Front Psychology*, 4: 578. Published online 30 Aug 2013. doi: 10.3389/fpsyg.2013.00578

Athey, C. (2007) *Extending Thought in Young Children*, 2nd edn. London: Paul Chapman Publishing.

Baker, C. (1996) Perceptions of language, *European Journal of Cultural Studies*, 7(1): 45–50.

Balint, M. (1992) *The Basic Fault: Therapeutic Aspects of Regression.* London: Routledge.

Bandura, A. (1977) *Social Learning Theory.* London: Prentice-Hall International.

Basic Skills Agency (2002) *Summary Report into Young Children's Skills on Entry to Education.* London: Basic Skills Agency.

Beetlestone, F. (1998) *Creative Children, Imaginative Teaching.* Buckingham: Open University Press.

Behne, T., Carpenter, M. and Tomasello, M. (2005) One-year-olds comprehend the communicative intentions behind gestures in a hiding game, *Developmental Science*, 8(6): 492–9.

Benenson, J.F. and Dweck, C.S. (1986) The development of trait explanations and self-evaluations in the academic and social domains, *Child Development*, 57: 1179–87.

Bernstein, B. (1971) *Class Codes and Control Vol. 1: Theoretical Studies Towards a Sociology of Language.* London: Routledge.

Bernstein, B. (1973) *Class Codes and Control Vol. 2: Applied Studies Towards a Sociology of Language.* London: Routledge.

Bernstein, B. (1977) *Class Codes and Control Vol. 3: Towards a Theory of Educational Transmissions.* London: Routledge and Kegan Paul.

Bion, W. (1962) *Learning from Experience.* London: Heinemann.

Bishop, J. (2001) Creating places for living and learning, in L. Abbott and C. Nutbrown (eds) *Experiencing Reggio Emilia: Implications for Pre-school Provision.* Buckingham: Open University Press.

Blanden, J. (2006) *Bucking the Trend – What Enables those who are Disadvantaged in Childhood to Succeed later in Life?* London: Department for Work and Pensions.

Blasi, A., Mecure, E., Lloyd-Fox, S. et al. (2011) Early specialization for voice and emotion processing in the infant brain, *Current Biology*, 21(14): 1220–4.

Bloom, B.S., Engelhart, M.D., Furst, E.J. et al. (1956) *Taxonomy of Educational Objectives: The Classification of Educational Goals.* New York: David McKay Company.

Boggs, S. T. (1972) The meaning of questions and narratives to Hawaiian children, in C. Cazden, V. John and D. Hymes (eds) *Functions of Language in the Classroom.* New York: Teachers College.

Bowlby, J. (1969) *Attachment and Loss Vol. 1: Attachment.* New York: Basic Books and Hogarth Press.

Bowlby, J. (1988) *A Secure Base: Clinical Applications of Attachment Theory.* London: Routledge.

Boyd, M.P. and Markarian, W.C. (2011) Dialogic teaching: talk in service of dialogic stance, *Language and Education,* 25(6): 515–34.

Bredekamp S. (ed.) (1987) *Developmentally Appropriate Practice in Early Childhood Programs Serving Children from Birth through Age 8.* Washington, DC: NAEYC.

Bronfenbrenner, U. (1979) *The Ecology of Human Development.* Cambridge, MA: Harvard University Press.

Brooker, L. (2002) Starting School: *Young Children Learning Cultures.* Buckingham: Open University Press.

Brown, G.A. and Edmondson, R. (1984) Asking questions, in E.C Wragg (ed.) *Classroom Teaching Skills.* London: Routledge.

Bruner, J. (1966) *Towards a Theory of Instruction.* London: Harvard University Press.

Bruner, J. (1980) *Under Five in Britain.* London: Grant McIntyre.

Bruner, J.S. (1983) *Child's Talk.* Oxford: Oxford University Press.

Cairns, K. (2002) *Attachment, Trauma and Resilience: Therapeutic Caring for Children.* London: BAAF.

Carle, E. (1969) *The Very Hungry Caterpillar.* London: Penguin Books.

Carroll, T. and O'Connor, A. (2009) All about … bilingualism, *Nursery World,* 7 May 2009: 17–22.

Cazden, C. (2001) *Classroom Discourse: The Language of Teaching and Learning.* Portsmouth, NH: Heinemann.

Chapman, R.S. (2000) Children's language learning: an interactionist perspective, *Journal of Child Psychology and Psychiatry and Allied Disciplines,* 41(1): 33–54.

Chilvers, D. (2006) *Young Children Talking: The Art of Conversation and Why Children need to Chatter.* London: Early Education.

Claxton, G. (1997) *Hare Brain, Tortoise Mind.* London: Fourth Estate.

Claxton, G. (2002) *Building Learning Power.* Bristol: TLO Ltd.

Clegg, J., Hoiis, C. and Rutter, M. (1999) Life sentence, *Royal Society of Speech and Language Therapists Bulletin,* 571: 16–18.

Coster, F.W., Goorhuis-Brouwer, S.M., Nakken, H. et al. (1999) Specific language impairments and behavioural problems, *Folia Phoniatricia et Logopaedica,* 51(3): 99–107.

Cousins, J. (1999) *Listening to Four Year Olds.* London: The National Early Years Network.

Cross, T.G. (1977) Mothers' speech adjustments: the contribution of selected child listener variables, in C.E. Snow and C.A. Ferguson (eds) *Talking to Children: Language Input and Acquisition.* Cambridge: Cambridge University Press.

Csikszentmihalyi, M. (1990) *Flow: The Psychology of Optimal Experience.* New York: Harper Row.

Cunningham, J. (2004) Children's humor, in J. Cunningham and W. G. Scarlett. *Children's Play.* Thousand Oaks, CA: Sage Publications.

Dalton, J. and Smith, D. (1986) *Extending Children's Special Abilities: Strategies for Primary Classrooms.* Melbourne: Curriculum Branch, Schools Division.

De Bono, E. (1992) *Serious Creativity.* London: HarperCollins.

De Hann, M., Johnson, M.H., Maurer, D. et al. (2001) Recognition of individual faces and average face prototype by 1 and 3 month old infants, *Cognitive Development,* 16: 1–20.

Department for Children, Schools and Families (2008) *Every Child a Talker: Guidance for Early Language Lead Practitioners.* London: DCSF. Available at http://webarchive.

nationalarchives.gov.uk/20130401151715/https:/www.education.gov.uk/publications/
eOrderingDownload/DCSF-00854-2008.pdf.

Department for Children, Schools and Families (2009) *Learning, Playing and Interacting.*
Nottingham: DCSF.

Department for Education (2012a) *Developing a Communication Supporting Classrooms
Observation Tool.* London: BCRP.

Department for Education (2012b) *Revised Statutory Framework for the Early Years Foundation Stage.* London: DfE.

Department for Education and Skills (2002a) *Study of Pedagogical Effectiveness in Early
Learning (SPEEL).* London: DfES.

Department for Education and Skills (2002b) *Researching Effective Pedagogy in the Early
Years.* Research Brief No. 356, June 2002. London: DfES. Available at http://www.dfes.
gov.uk/research/.

Department for Education and Skills (2004) *Every Child Matters: Change for Children.*
London: DfES.

Department for Education and Skills (2007) *Practice Guidance for the Early Years Foundation Stage.* London: DfES.

Department for Education and Skills (2008) *Statutory Framework for the Early Years
Foundation Stage.* London: DfES.

Dillon, J.T. (1981) To question or not to question during discussion: questioning and discussion, *Journal of Teacher Education,* 32(5): 51–5.

Dillon, J.T. (1990) *The Practice of Questioning.* London: Routledge.

Dockrell, J., Lindsay, G., Mackie, C. and Connolly, V. (2007) Constraints in the production
of written text in children with specific language impairments, *Exceptional Children,*
73: 147–64.

Dockrell, J., Sylva, K., Huxford, L. et al. (2008) *I CAN Early Talk programme: An evaluation
of two local authorities.* London: I Can.

Donaldson, M. (1978) *Children's Minds.* London: Fontana.

Donaldson, M., Grieve, R. and Pratt, C. (1983) *Early Childhood Development and Education.* Oxford: Blackwell.

Dowling, M. (2010) *Young Children's Personal, Social and Emotional Development,* 3rd
edn. London: Sage.

Dowling, M. (2013) *Young Children's Thinking.* London: Sage.

Dubiel, J. (2014) *Effective Assessment in the Early Years Foundation Stage.* London: Sage.

Dudek, M. (1996) *Kindergarten Architecture.* London: Chapman and Hall.

Duffy, B. (2006) *Supporting Creativity and Imagination in the Early Years.* Maidenhead:
Open University Press.

Durant, R. (2013) The key to good questioning: ask fewer, better questions, *Optimus Education,* London: Optimus Education. Available at http://www.optimus-education.com/
print/key-good-questioning-ask-fewer-questions.

Dweck, C.S. (1976) Children's interpretation of evaluative feedback: the effect of social cues
on learned helplessness, *Merrill-Palmer Quarterly,* 22(2): 105–9.

Dweck, C.S. (2012) *Self-theories: Their Role in Motivation, Personality, and Development.*
Hove, East Sussex: Psychology Press.

Edwards, C., Gandini, L. and Forman, G. (eds) (1993) *The Hundred Languages of Children: The Reggio Emilia Approach – Advanced Reflections.* London: Ablex Publishing
Corporation.

Elfer, P., Goldschmied, E. and Selleck, D. (2012) *Key Persons in the Early Years: Building
Relationships for Quality Provision in Early Years Settings and Primary Schools,*
2nd edn. London: Routledge.

Emde, R.N. (1989) The infant's relationship experience: developmental and affective aspects, in A.J. Sameroff and R.N. Emde (eds) *Relationship Disturbances in Early Childhood*. New York: Basic Books.

Feinstein, L. and Duckworth, K. (2006) *Development in the Early Years: Its Importance for School Performance and Adult Outcomes*. Wider Benefits of Learning Research Report No. 20. London: Institute of Education.

Fisher, J. (2002) *The Foundations of Learning*. Buckingham: Open University Press.

Fisher, J. (2013) *Starting from the Child*, 4th edn. Maidenhead: Open University Press.

Flavell, J. (1976) Metacognitive aspects of problem-solving, in L. Resnick (ed.) *The Nature of Intelligence*. Hillsdale, NJ: Lawrence Erlbaum Associates.

Flewitt, R. (2005) Is every child's voice heard? Researching the different ways 3-year-old children communicate and make meaning at home and in a pre-school playgroup, *Early Years*, 25(3): 207–22.

Froebel, F. (1908) *The Education of Man*. New York: Appleton and Co.

Gable, S. (2010) *Communicating Effectively with Children*. Columbia: University of Missouri.

Gall, M. (1970). The use of questions in teaching, *Review of Educational Research, 40:* 707–21.

Galton, M., Hargreaves, L., Comber, C. et al. (1999) *Inside the Primary Classroom 20 Years On*. London: Routledge.

Gerhardt, S. (2004) *Why Love Matters: How Love Shapes a Baby's Brain*. Hove, East Sussex: Brunner-Routledge.

Gerhardt, S. (2010) *The Selfish Society: How we all Forgot to Love One Another and Made Money Instead*. London: Simon and Schuster.

Goddard Blythe, S. (2005) *The Well Balanced Child*. Stroud: Hawthorn Press.

Goldschmied, E. and Jackson, S. (1994) *People Under Three: Young Children in Day Care*. London: Routledge.

Goleman, D. (1995) *Emotional Intelligence*. New York: Bantam Books.

Goouch, K. and Powell, S. (2013) Orchestrating professional development for baby room practitioners: raising the stakes in new dialogic encounters, *Journal of Early Childhood Research*, 11(1): 78–92.

Gopnik, A., Meltzoff, A. and Kuhl, P. (1999) *How Babies Think*. London: Weidenfeld and Nicolson.

Harrop, A. and Swinson, J. (2003) Teachers' questions in the infant, junior and secondary school, *Educational Studies*, (29)1: 49–57.

Hart, B. and Risley, T. (2002) *Meaningful Differences in the Everyday Experiences of Young American Children*. London: Paul H. Brookes.

Hart, K.I., Fujiki, M., Brinton, B. et al. (2004) The relationships between social behaviour and severity of language impairment, *Journal of Speech, Language and Hearing Research*, 47(3): 647.

Hastings, N. and Schwieso, J. (1995) Task and tables: the effects of seating arrangements on task engagement in primary schools, *Educational Research*, 37(3): 279–91.

Hedges, H. (2012). Vygotsky's phases of everyday concept development and the notion of children's 'working theories', *Learning, Culture and Social Interaction*, 1(2): 143–52.

Heschong, L., Wright, R.L., Okura, S. et al. (2002) Daylighting impacts on human performance in school, *Journal of Illuminating Engineering Society*, 31: 101–14.

Heyman, G.D., Dweck, C.S. and Cain, K.M. (1992) Young children's vulnerability to self-blame and helplessness: relationship to beliefs about goodness, *Child Development*, 63: 401–15.

Hobson, P. (2002) *The Cradle of Thought: Exploring the Origins of Thinking*. London: Pan Books.

House, R. (ed.) (2011) *Too Much, Too Soon? Early Learning and the Erosion of Childhood.* Stroud: Hawthorn Press.

Hubbell, R.D. (1977) On facilitating spontaneous talking in young children, *Journal of Speech and Hearing Disorders,* 42: 216–31.

Hughes, J.L. (1923) *Froebel's Educational Laws for all Teachers.* London: D. Appleton & Co.

Ingersoll, B. (2008) The social role of imitation in autism: implications for the treatment of imitation deficits, *Infants & Young Children,* 21(2): 107–19.

Ingersoll, B. (2012) Brief Report: Effect of a Focused Imitation Intervention on Social Functioning in Children with Autism, *Journal of Autism and Developmental Disorders,* 42: 1768–73.

Isaacs, N. (1930) Children's 'why' questions, in S. Isaacs, *Intellectual Growth in Young Children.* London: Routledge and Kegan Paul.

Isaacs, S. (1929) *The Nursery Years.* London: Routledge.

Jarman, E. (2009) *Communication Friendly Spaces in Children's Centres.* London: A&C Black.

Johnson, J. (2007) Questioning, in J. Johnson, J. Halocha and M. Chater, *Developing Teaching Skills in the Primary School.* Maidenhead: Open University Press.

Johnson, M. and Jones, M. (2012) *Supporting Quiet Children.* Birmingham: Lawrence Educational.

Karmiloff-Smith, A. (1995) The extraordinary journey from foetus through infancy, *Journal of Child Psychology and Psychiatry,* 36: 1293–315.

Karmiloff-Smith, A. (2010) Face to face, *Nursery World,* 15 July 2010.

Karmiloff-Smith, A. (2012) 'TV is bad for children' – less emotion, more science please!, in P. Adey and J. Dillon (eds) *Bad Education: Debunking Myths in Education.* Maidenhead: Open University Press.

Katz, L. (1993) What can we learn from Reggio Emilia?, in C. Edwards, L. Gandini and G. Forman (eds) *The Hundred Languages of Children: The Reggio Emilia Approach to Early Childhood Education.* Norwood, NJ: Ablex Publishing Corporation.

Kaye, K. (1982) *The Mental and Social Life of Babies.* Chicago: The University of Chicago Press.

Knez, I. (1995) Effects of indoor lighting on mood and cognition, *Journal of Environmental Psychology,* 15: 39–51.

Kogan, N. and Carter, A.S. (1996) Mother–infant re-engagement following the still-face: the role of maternal emotional availability in infant affect regulation, *Infant Behaviour and Development,* 19: 359–70.

Kutner, L. (2013) *Humor as a key to child development, Psychology Central website.* Available at http://psychcentral.com/lib/humor-as-a-key-to-child-development/ [Accessed 27 May 2015].

Laevers, F. (1994) *The Leuven Involvement Scale for Young Children.* Experiential Education Series No 1. Leuven: Centre for Experiential Education.

Laevers, F. (ed.) (2005) *Well-being and Involvement in Care Settings: A Process-oriented Self-evaluation Instrument.* Leuven: Kind & Gezin and Research Centre for Experiential Education.

Lancaster, Y.P. and Kirby, P. (2010) *Listening to Children,* 2nd edn. Maidenhead: Open University Press.

Lee, W. (2008) *Speech, Language and Communication Needs and Primary Aged Children.* I CAN talk series, issue 6. London: I CAN.

Lee, W. (2010) *Skills for Work, Skills for Life.* London: I CAN.

Lees, J. and Unwin, S. (1997) *Children with Language Disorders.* London: Whurr Publications.

Locke, A., Ginsborg, J. and Peers, I. (2002) Development and disadvantage: implications for early years, *International Journal of Language and Communication Disorders*, 37(1): 3–15.

Lowry, L. (2011) Bilingualism in Young Children: Separating Fact from Fiction. Available at http://www.hanen.org/Helpful-Info/Articles/Bilingualism-in-Young-Children–Separating-Fact-fr.aspx [Accessed August 2015].

Malaguzzi, L. (1992) *A Message from Malaguzzi* [video transcript]. Reggio Emilia, Italy: Reggio Children.

Malaguzzi, L. (trans. L. Gandini) (1993) For an education based on relationships, *Young Children*, 49(1): 3.

Malaguzzi, L. (1997) Shoe and meter, in Reggio Children (ed.) *Shoe and Meter*. Reggio Emilia, Italy: Reggio Children.

Manning-Morton, J. (1994) Communicating, *Nursery World*, Part 8; Birth to Three: Your guide to developing quality provision.

Manning-Morton, J. and Thorp, M. (2001) *Key Times: A Framework for Developing High Quality Provision for Children under Three Years*. London: Camden EYDCP/University of North London.

Marcos, K.M. (1998) Second language learning: everyone can benefit, *The ERIC Review*, 6(1): 2–5.

Matarazzo, J., Wiens, A., Matarazzo, R. et al. (1968) Speech and silence behaviour in clinical psychotherapy and its laboratory correlates, in J. Shlien (ed.) *Research in Psychotherapy Vol. 3*. Washington, DC: American Psychological Association.

McCabe, P.C. (2005) Social and behavioural correlates of pre-schoolers with specific language impairment, *Psychology in Schools*, 42(4): 373–87.

McColl, S.L. and Veitch, J.A. (2001) Full spectrum fluorescent lighting: a review of its effects on physiology and health, *Psychological Medicine*, 21: 949–64.

McGurk, H., Caplan, M., Hennessey, E. et al. (1993) Controversy, theory and social context in contemporary day care research, *Journal of Child Psychology and Psychiatry*, 34(1): 3–23.

Meadows, S. (1993) *The Child as Thinker: The Development and Acquisition of Cognition in Childhood*. London: Routledge.

Mercer, N. and Hodgkinson, S. (eds) (2008) *Exploring Talk in School*. London: Sage.

Mercer, N. and Littleton, K. (2007) *Dialogue and the Development of Children's Thinking: A Sociocultural Approach*. Abingdon: Routledge.

Montessori, M. (1967) *The Discovery of the Child*. New York: Ballantine Books.

Morrell, J. and Murray, L. (2003) Parenting and the development of conduct disorder and hyperactive symptoms in childhood: a prospective longitudinal study from 2 months to 8 years, *Journal of Child Psychological Psychiatry*, 44: 489–508.

Moses, L.J., Baldwin, D.A., Rosicky, J.G. and Tidball, G. (2001) Evidence for referential understanding in the emotions domain at twelve and eighteen months, *Child Development*, 72(3): 718–35.

Mott, M.S., Robinson, D.H., Walden, A. et al. (2012) Illuminating the effects of dynamic lighting on student learning, *Sage Online Publications*. doi: 10.1177/2158244012445585. Available at http://sgo.sagepub.com/content/2/2/2158244012445585.

Moylett, H. and Stewart, N. (2012) *Understanding the Revised Early Years Foundation Stage*. London: Early Education.

Murray, L. (2014) *The Psychology of Babies: How Relationships Support Development from Birth to Two*. London: Constable and Robinson.

Murray, L. and Trevarthen, C. (1985) Emotional regulation of interactions between two-month-olds and their mothers, in T.M. Field and N.A. Fox (eds) *Social Perception in Infants*. Norwood, NJ: Ablex.

Nakamura, J. and Csikszentmihalyi, M. (2002) The concept of flow, in C.R. Snyder and S.J. Lopez (eds) *Handbook of Positive Psychology*. Oxford: Oxford University Press.

National Assessment Agency (2007) *Additional Guidance on Completing Foundation Stage Profile Assessments*. London: NAA.

Nutbrown, C. (2006) *Threads of Thinking*, 3rd edn. London: Sage.

O'Connor, A. (2008) Reference points, *Nursery World*, 2 October 2008.

O'Connor, A. (2013) *Understanding Transitions in the Early Years*. London: Routledge.

O'Connor, A. (2014) *Health and Wellbeing*. London: Practical Pre-School Books.

Office for Standards in Education (2011) *The Impact of the Early Years Foundation Stage*. Manchester: Ofsted. Available at http://dera.ioe.ac.uk/2155/1/The%20impact%20of%20 the%20Early%20Years%20Foundation%20Stage%20(09FEB11).pdf.

Orlich, D., Harder, R., Callahan, R. et al. (2004) *Teaching Strategies: A Guide to Effective Instruction*, 7th edn. Boston, MA: Houghton Mifflin.

Oxfordshire County Council (2006) *Are You Listening to Me? Oxfordshire Babies Speak Up for Themselves*. Oxfordshire: OCC Publications.

Paradis, J., Genesee, F. and Crago, M. (2011) *Dual Language Development and Disorders: A handbook on Bilingualism and Second Language Learning*. Baltimore, MD: Paul H. Brookes Publishing.

Pascal, C. and Bertram, T. (1997) A conceptual framework for evaluating effectiveness in early childhood settings, in M.K. Lohmander (ed.) *Researching Early Childhood, vol. 3: Settings in Interaction*. Gothenburg: Göteborg University, Early Childhood Research and Development Centre.

Phillips, A., Wellman, H. and Spelke, E. (2002) Infants' ability to connect gaze and emotional expression to intentional action, *Cognition*, 85(1): 53–78.

Piaget, J. (1929) *The Child's Conception of the World*. London: Routledge and Kegan Paul.

Piaget, J. (1985) *The Equilibration of Cognitive Structures: The Central Problem of Intellectual Development*. Chicago: University of Chicago Press.

Poulin-Dubois, D., Blaye, A., Coutya, J. et al. (2011) The effects of bilingualism on toddlers' executive functioning, *Journal of Experimental Child Psychology*, 108(3): 567–79.

Recchia, S.L. (1997) Social communication and response to ambiguous stimuli in toddlers with visual impairments, *Journal of Applied Developmental Psychology*, 18: 297–316.

Reggio Children (2001) *Making Learning Visible*. Reggio Emilia, Italy: Reggio Children and Project Zero.

Reszka, S.S., Odom, S.L. and Hume, K.A. (2012) Ecological features of preschools and the social engagement of children with autism, *Journal of Early Intervention*, 34(1): 40–56.

Roberts, R. (2002) *Self-esteem and Successful Early Learning*, 2nd edn. London: Hodder & Stoughton.

Robinson, M. (2003) *From Birth to One*. Buckingham: Open University Press.

Robinson, M. (2008) *Child Development from Birth to Eight*. Maidenhead: Open University Press.

Robinson, M. (2009) *The Wonder Year: First Year Development and Shaping the Brain*. Newcastle-upon-Tyne: Siren Films.

Robinson, M. (2014) *The Feeling Child*. Abingdon: Routledge.

Rogers, C. (1951) *Client-centered therapy: Its Current Practice, Implications and Theory*. London: Constable.

Rogoff, B. (1990) *Apprenticeship in Thinking*. Oxford: Oxford University Press.

Rogoff, B. (2003) *The Cultural Nature of Human Development*. Oxford: Oxford University Press.

Rojas, N.L. and Chan, E. (2005) Old and new controversies in the alternative treatment of attention-deficit hyperactivity disorder, *Mental Retardation and Developmental Disabilities Research Reviews*, 11(2): 116–30.

Rojas-Drummond, S., Torreblanca, O., Pedraza, H. et al. (2013) Dialogic scaffolding: enhancing learning and understanding in collaborative contexts, *Learning, Culture and Social Interaction*, 2(1): 11–21.

Rose, J. (2006) *Independent Review of the Teaching of Reading*. London: DfES.

Rose, J. and Rogers, S. (2012) *The Role of the Adult in Early Years Settings*. Maidenhead: Open University Press.

Roskos, K. and Neuman, S.B. (2002) Environment and its influences for early literacy teaching and learning, in S.B. Neuman and D.K. Dickinson (eds) *Handbook of Early Literacy Research*. New York: The Guildford Press.

Rowe, M. (1974) Wait time and rewards as instructional variables, *Journal of Research in Science Teaching*, 11: 81–94.

Rowe, M. (1986) Wait time: slowing down may be a way of speeding up!, *Journal of Teacher Education*, 37: 43.

Rowe, M. (2012) A longitudinal investigation of the role of quantity and quality of child-directed speech in vocabulary development, *Child Development*, 88(5): 1762–74.

Schofield, G. and Beck, M. (2006) *Attachment Handbook for Foster Care and Adoption*. London: BAAF.

Schweinhart, L.J., Barnes, H. and Weikhart, D.P. (1993) *Significant Benefits: The High/Scope Perry Preschool Study Through Age 27*. Ypsilanti, MI: High/Scope Press.

Selleck, D. (2006) Key persons in the Early Years Foundation Stage, *Early Education*, 50: 11–13.

Senju, A. and Csibra, G. (2008) Gaze following in human infants depends on communicative signals, *Current Biology*, 18: 668–71.

Siraj, I., Kingston, D. and Melhuish, E. (2015) *Assessing Quality on Early Childhood Education and Care: Sustained Shared Thinking and Emotional Well-being (SSTEW) Scale for 2–5 year-olds Provision*. London: IOE Press/Trentham Books.

Siraj-Blatchford, I., Sylva, K., Muttock, S. et al. (2002) *Researching Effective Pedagogy in the Early Years*. London: DfES.

Smith, P.K., Cowie, H. and Blades, M. (2010) *Understanding Children's Development*, 4th edn. Oxford: Blackwell.

Snowling, M. and Stackhouse, J. (eds) (2006) *Dyslexia, Speech and Language: A Practitioner's Handbook*. Dyslexia Series. Chichester: Whurr.

Sommerville, J. and Woodward, A. (2005) Pulling out the intentional structure of action: the relation between action processing and action production in infancy, *Cognition*, 95(1): 1–30.

Sorce, J.F., Emde, R.N., Campos, J. and Klinnert, M.D. (1985) Maternal emotion signalling: its effects on the visual cliff behaviour of 1-year-olds, *Developmental Psychology*, 21(1): 195–200.

Steiner, R. (1965) *The Education of the Child: In the Light of Anthroposophy*. London: Rudolph Steiner Press.

Stern, D.N. (1985) *The Interpersonal World of the Infant: A View from Psychoanalysis and Developmental Psychology*. New York: Basic Books.

Stern, D.N. (2004) *The Present Moment*. New York: W.W. Norton & Co.

Stevens, R. (1912) *The Question as a Measure of Efficiency in Instruction*. Teachers' College Contributions to Education No 48. New York: Teachers College Press.

Stewart, N. (2012) Communication and Language, *Nursery World*, 20 August–2 September 2012.

Stone, L., Underwood, C. and Hotchkiss, J. (2012) The Relational Habitus: Intersubjective Processes in Learning Settings, *Human Development*, 55(2): 65–91.

Sure Start (2002) *Birth to Three Matters: A Framework to Support Children in their Earliest Years*. London: DfES, HMSO.

Sutter, A.L., Murray, L., Glatigny-Dallay, E. et al. (2003) Newborn behavior and risk of postnatal depression in the mother, *Infancy*, 4: 589–602.

Swift, J. and Gooding, C. (1983) Interaction of wait-time feedback and questioning instruction on middle school science teaching, *Journal of Research in Science Teaching*, 20: 721–30.

Sylva, K., Melhuish, E., Sammons, P. et al. (2004) *The Effective Provision of Pre-School Education (EPPE) Project: Final Report*. London: DfES.

Tassoni, P. (2013) So to speak, *Nursery World*, 2013: 24–6.

Thomas, S. (2002) *Familiar Things*. London: Thomson.

Tizard, B. and Hughes, M. (1984) *Young Children Learning, Talking and Thinking at Home*. London: Fontana Books.

Trevarthen, C. (1974) Conversations with a two-month old, *New Scientist*, 62: 230–5.

Trevarthen, C. (1993) The self born in intersubjectivity: an infant communicating, in U. Neisser (ed.) *The Perceived Self: Ecological and Interpersonal Sources of Self-Knowledge*. New York: Cambridge University Press.

Trevarthen, C. (1998) The concept and foundations of infant intersubjectivity, in S. Bråten (ed.) *Intersubjective Communication and Emotion in Early Ontogeny*. Cambridge: Cambridge University Press.

Trevarthen, C. (2002) Learning in companionship, *Education in the North: The Journal of Scottish Education*, 10: 16–25.

Trevarthen, C. (2011) What is it like to be a person who knows nothing? Defining the active intersubjective mind of a newborn human being, *Infant and Child Development*, 20(1): 119–35.

Trevarthen, C. and Aitken, K.J. (2001) Infant intersubjectivity, research, theory, and clinical applications, *Journal of Child Psychological Psychiatry*, 42(1): 3–48.

Trevarthen, C. and Hubley, P. (1978) Secondary intersubjectivity: confidence, confiding and acts of meaning in the first year, in A. Lock (ed.) *Action, Gesture, and Symbol: The Emergence of Language*. New York: Cambridge University Press.

Tronick, E., Als, H., Adamson, L. et al. (1978) The infant's response to entrapment between contradictory messages in face-to-face interaction, *Journal of the American Academy of Child and Adolescent Psychiatry*, 17: 1–13.

Underdown, A. (2007) *Young Children's Health and Wellbeing*. Buckingham: Open University Press.

Vaish, A. and Striano, T. (2004) Is visual reference necessary? Contributions of facial versus vocal cues in 12-month-olds' social referencing behaviour, *Developmental Science*, 7(3): 261–9.

Van de Pol, J., Volman, M. and Beishuizen, J. (2010) Scaffolding in teacher–student interaction: a decade of research, *Educational Psychology Review*, 22(3): 271–96. Available at http://dx.doi.org/10.1007/s10648-010-9127-6.

Vermes, S. (2008) What are the features of the adult's contribution which create good interactions during child-initiated activity? Unpublished MA dissertation, Oxford Brookes University.

Vygotsky, L.S. (1978) *Mind in Society: The Development of Higher Psychological Processes*. London: Harvard University Press.

Vygotsky, L.S. (2012) *Mind in Society: The Development of Higher Psychological Processes*, revised and expanded edition. London: Harvard University Press.

Weitzman, E. (1992) *Learning Language and Loving It*. Toronto, Ontario: The Hanen Centre.

Weitzman, E. and Greenberg, J. (2002) *Learning Language and Loving It*, 2nd edn. Toronto: Hanen Centre Publications.

Wells, G. (1983) Talking with children: the complementary roles of parents and teachers, in M. Donaldson, R. Grieve and C. Pratt (eds) *Early Childhood Development and Education: Readings in Psychology*. Oxford: Basil Blackwell.

Wells, G. (1985) *Language Development in the Preschool Years*. Cambridge: Cambridge University Press.

Wells, G. (2009) *The Meaning Makers: Children Learning Language and Using Language to Learn*, 2nd edn. Bristol: Multilingual Matters.

Wimmer, H. and Perner, J. (1983) Beliefs about beliefs: representation and constraining function of wrong beliefs in young children's understanding of deception, *Cognition*, 13: 103–28.

Winnicott, D.W. (1960) The theory of parent–infant relationships, *International Journal of Psychoanalysis*, 41: 585–95.

Winterbottom, M. and Wilkins, A. (2008) Lighting and discomfort in the classroom, *EARLI Practice-Based and Practitioner Research Conference on Learning and Instruction*, Bergen, Norway.

Wood, D. (1998) *How Children Think and Learn*, 2nd edn. Oxford: Blackwell.

Wood, D., Brunner, J. and Ross, G. (1976) The role of tutoring in problem-solving, *Journal of Child Psychology and Psychiatry*, 17: 89–100.

Wood, D., McMahon, L. and Cranstoun, Y. (1980) *Working with Under Fives*. London: Grant McIntyre.

Wood, D., Wood, H., Griffiths, A., Howarth, S. and Howarth, C. (1982) The structure of conversations with 6- to 10-year-old deaf children, *Journal of Child Psychology and Psychiatry*, 23(3): 295–308.

Wood, H. and Wood, D. (1983) Questioning the pre-school child, *Educational Review*, 35: 149–62.

Wood, H. and Wood, D. (1984) An experimental evaluation of the effects of five styles of teacher conversation on the language of hearing-impaired children, *Journal of Child Psychology and Psychiatry*, 25: 45–62.

Index

active listening 74–5
adult agenda, dealing with emphasis on 75
adult-initiated learning 90, 91–2, 176
adult interactions, child relaxation in 42–3
adult-led agendas, practitioner relaxation and
    43–4
adult-led learning
  balance between child-led learning and
    93–6
  difference between child-led learning and
    90–91
  interactions in 90, 91-2, 176
affirmation
  and consolidation of learning 14–15
  of positivity 178–9, 180
agenda following, child relaxation in 43
Ainsworth, M.D.S., Blehar, M.C., Waters, E.
    and Wall, S. 29
Alexander, Robin 2, 129
alternatives to questioning 155–8
Andrews, Mark 58
anxiety levels, reduction of 131–2
Asperger Syndrome 132–3
asymmetrical talk 171–2
Athey, C. 110
attachment
  babies and toddlers, interactions with
    20–21
  interactions, importance for learning 12
  security in 29
Attention Deficit Hyperactivity Disorder
    (ADHD) 132–3
attentiveness 164–5
  demonstration of 165
attunement
  babies and toddlers, interactions with 20
  tuning in to children 71–2
Autism Spectrum Disorder (ASD) 132–4
  categories of 132
  peer engagement in cases of 133–4

babies and toddlers 17–34
  attachment 20–21
    security in 29
  attunement 20
  being held 19
  boundaries, establishment of 28
  brain development, talk and 17
  communication, spoken language and 25,
    27, 30, 32
  conversation, environments conducive to
    52–3
    physical environments conducive to
      conversations 53
  deception, development of techniques of 33
  declarative pointing 31
  development of interactions 22–34
    from 2 to 6 months 22–5
    from 6 to 9 months 25–7
    from 9 to 12 months 27–30
    from 12 to 18 months 30–31
    from 18 to 24 months 32–4
  emotional meaning, touch and 19
  eye gaze 18
  faces, looking at 18
  foundations of interaction 18–21
  gestures, 'rainbow' of 17
  holding closely, effects of 19
  humour, development of sense of 33
  imitation 19–20
  imperative pointing 31
  interactions with infants (birth to 2
    months) 21
  interactions with infants (2 to 6 months)
    24–5
  interactions with infants (6 to 9 months)
    26–7
  interactions with infants (9 to 12 months)
    30
  interactions with infants (12 to 18 months)
    31

babies and toddlers (*continued*)
  interactions with infants (18 to 24 months) 33–4
  intersubjective communication 20, 22–3, 25–6
  knowing children well 36
  learning leadership 86–7
    learning capacity at birth 87
  loving communications 17
  marking 23–4
  mind, theory of 32
  mirroring and marking 23–4
  mobility, increases in 27–8
  negative responses in parents and practitioners, triggering of 20–21
  non-attachment, results of 21
  'party tricks,' development of repertoire of 26
  playing games 32–3
  pointing 31
  practitioner attributes 163–4
  primary intersubjectivity 22–3
  questions 144–5
  reluctance to interact, dealing with 127–8
  secondary intersubjectivity 25–6
  self-reflection 34
  sociability 19
  'social brain' 18
  social connections
    interaction and 30–31
  social interactions
    infants' facility for 17
  social referencing 28
  social sensitivity 24
  spoken language
    communication and (6 to 9 months) 25
    communication and (9 to 12 months) 27
    communication and (12 to 18 months) 30
    communication and (18 to 24 months) 32
  stranger anxiety 28–9
  Stranger Situation Test 29
  summary 34
  sustainment of interactions 108–9
  talk, brain development and 17
  theory of mind 32
  touch 19
  tuning in to children 69–70
    synchrony between actions and reactions, adeptness at sensing 70
  visual acuity, development of 23

Visual Cliff 28
  voice recognition 18
Baker, C. 134
Balint, M. 22
ball game, analogy of 172–3
Bandura, A. 13, 115, 170
Basic Skills Agency 9, 52
Beetlestone, F. 144
Behne, T., Carpenter, M. and Tomasello, M. 26
Benenson, J.F. and Dweck, C.S. 13
Bernstein, B 2
bilingualism, benefits of 134
Bion, W. 20
Bishop, J. 59
Blanden, J. 9
Blasi, A., Mecure, E., Lloyd-Fox, S. et al. 18
Bloom, Benjamin 150
body language
  interactions, sustainment of 122–3
  practitioner attributes 169
Boggs, S.T. 156
book corners 60
boundaries, establishment of 28
Bowlby, John 20, 128
Boyd, M.P. and Markarian, W.C. 171
brain development, talk and 17
Bredekamp, S. 96
British Sign Language (BSL) 138
Bronfenbrenner, U. 39
Brooker, L. 38
Brown, G.A. and Edmondson, R. 146
Bruner, Jerome 1–2, 43, 80, 109, 114

Cairns, K. 21
Carle, E. 121
Carroll, T. and O'Connor, A. 135, 136
Cazden, C. 172
Chapman, R.S. 6
child-led learning
  balance between adult-led learning and 93–6
  difference between adult-led learning and 90–91
  features on interaction in 97, 98
  interactions in 90, 92–3
  practitioner attributes 177
  tuning in to children 76
'Children's Minds' (Donaldson, M.) 76
Chilvers, D. 62

choices, supporting children in making of 115–16
'circle time' situations 62
Claxton, G. 120, 153, 171
Clegg, J., Hoiis, C. and Rutter, M. 8
clipboards 74
closed questions 149
co-construction 75–6
cognitive conflict 120
cognitive learning 4
commenting
    interactions, sustainment of 113
    questions 157
communication, spoken language and 25, 27, 30, 32
Communication and Language, Prime Area of Learning (EYFS) 9–10
'Communication Friendly Spaces Approach,' Jarman's concept of 56
communication skills, importance of 7–8
Communication Trust, research by 8
concepts, Piaget's theory of growth of 118
connecting
    connected discourse 1–2
    interactions, sustainment of 114
consolidation of children's learning 14–15, 117–18
control, questioning as 152
conversation, environments conducive to 52–68
    babies and toddlers, focus on 52–3
        physical environments conducive to conversations 53
    balance in emotional spaces 57
    Basic Skills Agency 52
    book corners 60
    child's emotional space 53–4
    'circle time' situations 62
    'Communication Friendly Spaces Approach,' Jarman's concept of 56
    conducive environments, features of interactions in 63
    emotional space 53–6
    equipment and furniture, positioning of 59–60
    Every Child a Talker (ECAT, DCSF, 2008) 57
    experiences 61–2
    'hot-spots' for children 57
    Key Persons Approach 54, 55–6
light 58–9
music, uses for 58
natural light, benefits of 59
noise 58
non-conducive environments, features of interactions in 63
Oxfordshire ACI Project 57, 61–2
parents and carers emotional space 54–5
partnership building 54–5
peaceful environments, need for 58
physical space 56–62
place 57
positioning 59–60
positive sense of selves, development of 54
practice, analysis of practitioners own work 63
practitioner's emotional space 55–6
reflective interaction, planning of spaces for 60
safe havens for interaction 61
self-reflection 68
spaces conducive to high-quality interaction, key features of 57–62
spontaneous interactions 62
stimulation 60–61
summary 67
time 61
transcripts 64–7
    outdoor play, engagement in 65–7
    sandpit as play area 64–5
'triangle of trust' 55
tuning in to children, sensitivity in 54
uniqueness of young children 54
welcome, sensitivity to warmth of 55
conversational exchange 35
conversational flow 42–3
conversational repertoire 152
conversational responses, effectiveness of 112–13
conversations with young children, studies on 3–6
Coster, F.W., Goorhuis-Brouwer, S.M., Nakken, H. et al. 8
creative thinking, language and 10
critical thinking, language and 10
Cross, T.G. 5
Csikszentmihalyi, M. 42
cultures and communities, knowing about 37–8
Cunningham, J. 26, 33

daily life, culture and 38
Dalton, J. and Smith, D. 150
dance, notion of 172
De Bono, E. 144
De Hann, M., Johnson, M.H., Maurer, D. et al. 18
deception, development of techniques of 33
decision-making
  on interactions, tuning in to children and 69, 80–81
  supporting children in 115–16
declarative pointing 31
development of interactions 22–34
  from 2 to 6 months 22–5
  from 6 to 9 months 25–7
  from 9 to 12 months 27–30
  from 12 to 18 months 30–31
  from 18 to 24 months 32–4
dialogic teaching 2
Dillon, Jim 146, 151, 155, 158, 166
The Discovery of the Child (Montessori , M., 1967) 94
dispositional learning 4
Dockrell, J., Sylva, K., Huxford, L. et al. 8
Donaldson, M., Grieve, R. and Pratt, C. 153
Donaldson, Margaret 76, 77, 110, 116, 166
Dowling, Marion 10, 76, 94, 110
Dubiel, J. 73
Dudek, Mark 59
Duffy, B. 114
Dweck, Carol S. 13

early education, importance of 94
Early Years Foundation Stage (DfE, 2012) 86
ease in company of children 170–71
  demonstration of 171
Edwards, C., Gandini, L. and Forman, G. 111
effectiveness
  attributes of 164–71
  definitions of 1–4
Elfer, P., Goldschmied, E. and Selleck, D. 41, 54, 55, 129
Emde, R.N. 17
emotional learning 4
emotional meaning, touch and 19
emotional space 53–6
engagement with young children, importance of 163, 171–4
english as an additional language (eal), children with 134–7

effectiveness of practitioners dealing with, requirements for 136–7
practitioner relationship with second language learners 135–6
second language learners, needs of 135–6
enhanced learning 3
equipment and furniture, positioning of 59–60
Every Child a Talker (ECAT, DCSF, 2008) 57
eye gaze 18

faces, looking at 18
families and histories, knowing about 37
fascination 76–7
feelings
  language and communication of 10
  talking about 115
Feinstein, L. and Duckworth, K. 9
Fisher, J. 15, 71, 90, 94
Flavell, J. 14
Flewitt, R. 39
Foundation Stage Profile (FSP) 94
Froebel, Frederich 71, 93, 94

Gable, S. 24, 33
Gall, M. 146
Galton, M., Hargreaves, L., Comber, C. et al. 146
genuineness 168–9
  demonstration of 169
Gerhardt, S. 20, 115
gestures, 'rainbow' of 17
Goddard Blythe, S. 10, 96
Goldschmied, E. and Jackson, S. 18, 19
Goleman, D. 20
Goouch, K. and Powell, S. 17
Gopnik, A., Meltzoff, A. and Kuhl, P. 8, 13, 124
guided participation 35

Hare Brain, Tortoise Mind (Claxton, G.) 153
Harrop, A. and Swinson, J. 144
Hart, B. and Risley, T. 6
Hart, K.I., Fujiki, M., Brinton, B. et al. 8
Hastings, N. and Schwieso, J. 59
Hedges, H. 13
Heschong, L., Wright, R.L., Okura, S. et al. 59
Heyman, G.D., Dweck, C.S. and Cain, K.M. 13
high-order questions 149–50
Hobson, P. 15, 17, 21, 22, 25, 109
home-based interactions 4–7
home conversations, origins of 5

home environment as learning culture 38
home visits, benefits of 39
'hot-spots' for children 57
House, R. 94
Hubbell, R.D. 156
Hughes, J.L. 94
humour, development of sense of 33
'Hundred Languages of Children' (Loris
        Malaguzzi poem) 77–8

ideas
    language and communication of 10
    planting of 157
imagining 114
imitation 19–20
imperative pointing 31
improvisation, interaction as 173–4
independence
    confidence and 41
    of specific learning areas 10
independent learning
    abandoned learning or 89–91
    benefits of 88–9
Ingersoll, B. 133
initiation of conversations 109–11
    adult-led learning 109–10
    child-led learning 110–11
inner speech, Vygotsky's notion of 13
interactions
    child known well, features of 46, 47–9
    child not known well, features of 46–7,
        49–51
    flow of 44–5
    foundations of 18–21
    importance for learning 1–16
        affirmation and consolidation of learning
            14–15
        attachment 12
        children entering school, importance of
            interactions for 9–11
        children's learning, affirmation and
            consolidation of 14–15
        cognitive learning 4
        Communication and Language, Prime
            Area of Learning (EYFS) 9–10
        communication skills, importance of 7–8
        Communication Trust, research by 8
        confidence with written word 10
        connected discourse 1–2
        consolidation of children's learning 14–15

context of talk at home, parents and 5
conversations with young children,
        studies on 3–6
creative thinking, language and 10
critical thinking, language and 10
development of child's own interests 5
dialogic teaching 2
dispositional learning 4
effective conversations with young
        children at home, crucial elements
        of 6
'effectiveness,' definitions of 1–4
emotional learning 4
enhanced learning 3
feelings, language and communication
        of 10
getting to know and understand children
        12–13
home-based interactions 4–7
home conversations, origins of 5
ideas, language and communication of 10
independence of specific learning areas
        10
inner speech, Vygotsky's notion of 13
interthinking 2
joint involvement episodes 2
knowledge and understanding by
        children, extension of 15
knowledge and understanding of
        children by practitioners 12–13
language in school, uses of 10–11
language learning at home 6–7
language modelling 13
language skills, development of 10, 11
learned helplessness 13–14
learning tool, language as 10
metacognitive learning 4
modelling language 13
modelling process of thinking 13–14
mutual learning encounters 2
non-verbal to verbal communication,
        movement between 7
Oxfordshire ACI Project, findings of
        12–13, 15
parental utterances, intuitive adjustment
        of 5
passages of intellectual search 2
poor communication skills, impact of 8,
        10–11
positive learning experiences 3–4

interactions (*continued*)
 practitioner enhanced learning 3
 practitioners, importance of interactions
  for 11–15
 prohibition of language at home 7
 questions from children at home 6
 relationship building, language and 10
 relationship building, practitioners and
  12
 *Researching Effective Pedagogy in the
  Early Years* (REPEY, DfES, 2002) 2
 responses of parents, contingency on
  children's competence 5–6
 scaffolding, concept of 14
 self-esteem 12
 self-reflection 16
 social learning 4
 Studying Pedagogical Effectiveness in
  Early Learning (DfES, 2002) 2
 summary 15–16
 sustained shared thinking 2
 talk at home, features of 5–6
 'Talk for Learning' research project 2
 thinking, modelling process of 13–14
 thinking skills, development of 10, 11
 time sensitivity 9
 universality 9
 vocabulary development, influences on 7
 vocabulary range 9
 written word, becoming confident with
  10
 interference and 174–5
 sustainment of 108–26
  babies and toddlers, focus on 108–9
  body language 122–3
   analysis of own practice on 123
  children, reflecting back to 115
  children's thinking, dealing with
   unexpected connections in 110
  choices, supporting children in making
   115–16
  cognitive conflict 120
  commenting 113
  concepts, Piaget's theory of growth of
   118
  connecting 114
  consolidating, extending and provoking
   learning, analysis of own practice
   on 122
  consolidating children's learning 117–18

conversational responses, effectiveness
 of 112–13
decision-making, supporting children in
 115–16
dialogue with children, importance of
 sustaining interaction 108
explaining 116
extending children's learning 118–19
feelings, talking about 115
imagining 114
informing 116
initiation of conversations 109–11
 adult-led learning 109–10
 child-led learning 110–11
knowledge (or coming to know),
 development of 120–21
learning momentum, maintenance of
 113–16
Oxfordshire ACI Project 111–12, 113,
 123–4
pondering 113–14
posing problems 116
practice, analysis of practitioners own
 work 122, 123, 124
provoking children's learning (and
 thinking) 120–21
quietness and staying quiet 116
reflecting back to children 115
self-reflection 126
staying quiet 116
summary 125–6
sustaining interactions 111–16
symbiotic interaction 111
talking about feelings 115
thinking aloud 114–15
tone of voice 123–4
 analysis of own practice on 124
transcripts 117–18, 119, 121, 124–5
 consolidating children's learning
  117–18
 extending children's learning 119
 provoking children's learning (and
  thinking) 121
 thinking and conversation, practitioner
  attentiveness to 124–5
'zone of proximal development,'
 Vygotsky's concept of 119
symbiotic interaction 111
see also babies and toddlers; questions;
 reluctance to interact, dealing with

interfering or interacting, difference between 80–81
interruptions, practitioner relaxation and 44
intersubjective communication 20, 22–3, 25–6
interthinking 2
intimate, participative exchanges, importance of 42
intimate information, respect for 39
Isaacs, N. 93, 144

Jarman, Elizabeth 56, 58, 59
Johnson, J. 145, 149
Johnson, M. and Jones, M. 129
joint involvement episodes 2

Karmiloff-Smith, A. 18, 58
Katz, L. 120
Kaye, K. 20
Key Persons Approach 19, 21, 169
  conversation, environments conducive to 54, 55–6
  knowing children well 40–42
Knez, I. 59
knowing children well 35–51
  adult interactions, child relaxation in 42–3
  adult-led agendas, practitioner relaxation and 43–4
  agenda following, child relaxation in 43
  babies and toddlers, focus on 36
  conversational exchange 35
  conversational flow 42–3
  cultures and communities, knowing about 37–8
  daily life, culture and 38
  families and histories, knowing about 37
  guided participation 35
  home environment as learning culture 38
  home visits, benefits of 39
  impact of 42–5
  independence, confidence and 41
  interactions, flow of 44–5
  interactions where child is known well, features of 46, 47–9
  interactions where child is not known well, features of 46–7, 49–51
  interruptions, practitioner relaxation and 44
  intimate, participative exchanges, importance of 42
  intimate information, respect for 39

Key Persons Approach, importance of 40–42
learning, assimilation of 35
learning about children, practitioners' needs 37–40
meeting new situations 35
outcomes, emphasis in recent years on 43–4
Oxfordshire ACI Project 42, 44
practice, analysis of practitioners own work 46–7
prior experiences and knowledge, knowing about 38–40
relaxation, children's most relaxing circumstances 42–3
relaxation, practitioners' most relaxing circumstances 43–5
Researching Effective Pedagogy in the Early Years (REPEY, DfES, 2002) 35, 45
secure attachment 41
self-reflection 51
sensitivities, understanding of 37
shared care 41
shared experiences, creation of 39–40
small group conversations, value of 45–6
speaking to adults, child relaxation in 43
speaking to children, practitioner relaxation and 44–5
Statutory Framework for the Early Years Foundation Stage (DfES, 2008) 40–41
summary 51
sustained shared thinking (SST), concept of 45
talking to someone, not everyone 45–6
thinking, contributions to 45–6
transcripts 47–51
  child not well known to practitioner 49–51
  child well known to practitioner 47–9
'Under Five in Britain,' Bruner's study on being 43
vulnerable children 37
knowledge (or coming to know), development of 120–21
known questions 150–51
Kogan, N. and Carter, A.S. 24
Kutner, L. 26

Laevers, Ferre 80, 165
Lancaster, Y.P. and Kirby, P. 75
language
  difficulties with, dealing with 130–31
  language modelling 13
  learning at home 6–7
  as learning tool 10
  in school, uses of 10–11
  skills in, development of 10, 11
  tuning in to children and 77–8
layering questions 157
learned helplessness 13–14
learning, assimilation of 35
Learning, Playing and Interacting (DCSF, 2009) 95
learning leadership 86–107
  adult-led learning
    balance between child-led learning and 93–6, 95–6
    difference between child-led learning and 90–91
    interactions in 90, 91–2
  babies and toddlers, focus on 86–7
    learning capacity at birth 87
  child-led learning
    balance between adult-led learning and 93–6
    difference between adult-led learning and 90–91
    features on interaction in 97, 98
    interactions in 90, 92–3
  The Discovery of the Child (Montessori, M., 1967) 94
  early education, importance of 94
  Early Years Foundation Stage (DfE, 2012) 86
  Foundation Stage Profile (FSP) 94
  independent learning
    abandoned learning or 89–91
    benefits of 88–9
  Learning, Playing and Interacting (DCSF, 2009) 95
  learning alongside an adult, benefits of 87–8
  National Assessment Agency (NAA) 94, 95
  Ofsted learning objectives 94–5
  Oxfordshire ACI Project 86, 91, 97
  play activities, Ofsted attitude to 94–5
  practice, analysis of practitioners own work 97–8

  practitioner-led learning, features on interaction in 98
  purpose of interaction 93
  self-reflection 107
  sensitivity in approach to children's play 92–3
  summary 106–7
  transcripts 98–106
    adult-initiated but child-controlled activity 101–2
    adult-led challenge 98–101
    child-led play, following children's thinking in 102–4
    sensitivity of practitioner within child-led activity 104–6
    Wait, Watch and Wonder, children's play and 92–3
    who leads learning? 96–7
learning momentum, maintenance of 113–16
Lee, W. 8, 30
Lees, J. and Unwin, S. 8
Leuven Involvement Scale (LIS) for Young Children 80
light 58–9
listening to children's answers 153–4
Listening to Four Year Olds (Cousin, J.) 150–51
Littleton, Karen 2
Locke, A., Ginsborg, J. and Peers, I. 9
loving communications 17
low-order questions 149–50
Lowry, L. 135

McColl, S.L. and Veitch, J.A. 59
McGurk, H., Caplan, M., Hennessey, E. et al. 41
Makaton language programme 138
making statements 155–7
Malaguzzi, Lois 71, 77, 78, 111, 172
managerial questions 151
Manning-Morton, J. 19, 36, 52, 54, 109
Manning-Morton, J. and Thorp, M. 36
marking 23–4
Matarazzo, J., Wiens, A., Matarazzo, R. et al. 158
Meadows, S. 38
Mehrabian, Albert 122, 123
Mercer, N. 2
Mercer, N. and Hodgkinson, S. 7–8, 10, 62
metacognitive learning 4

mind, theory of 32
mirroring and marking 23–4
misconceptions, dealing with 157
mobility, increases in 27–8
modelling language 13
modelling process of thinking 13–14
Montessori, Maria 93, 94
Morrell, J. and Murray, L. 21
Moses, L.J., Baldwin, D.A., Rosicky, J.G. and
    Tidball, G. 28
Mott, M.S., Robinson, D.H., Walden, A. et al.
    59
Moylett, H. and Stewart, N. 10
Murray, L. 18, 19, 20, 23, 24, 26, 28, 31, 32, 33
Murray, L. and Trevarthen, C. 70
music, uses for 58
mutual learning encounters 2

Nakamura, J. and Csikszentmihalyi, M. 42
National Assessment Agency (NAA) 94, 95
natural light, benefits of 59
negative reactions, awareness of potential
    for 129
negative responses in parents and
    practitioners, triggering of 20–21
noise 58
non-attachment, results of 21
non-conducive environments, features of
    interactions in 63
non-tuned-in practitioners, features of
    interactions with 81
non-verbal to verbal communication,
    movement between 7
Nutbrown, C. 110

observation 72–4
O'Connor, A. 10, 12, 20, 21, 28, 29, 36, 53, 54,
    55, 128
Ofsted 15
  learning objectives 94–5
open questions 149
Orlich, D., Harder, R., Callahan, R. et al. 150
outcomes, emphasis in recent years on 43–4
Oxfordshire Adult-Child Interaction Project
    (2010-14) 2–3, 174–5, 182–4
  aim of project 174
  conclusions 184
  conversation, environments conducive to
    57, 61–2
  effectiveness, analysis of 175

ethical considerations 183–4
findings 12–13, 15
interactions, sustainment of 111–12, 113,
    123–4
knowing children well 42, 44
learning leadership 86, 91, 97
methodology 182–3
positivity 175
practitioner attributes 174–5
purpose of project 174
questions 144–5, 146, 147, 149, 150, 151, 154,
    155, 156–7, 158–9
reluctance to interact, dealing with 127, 138
responsiveness 175
scope of 182–3
tuning in to children 72, 74, 77, 79–80, 81

Paradis, J., Genesee, F. and Crago, M. 134
Pascal, C. and Bertram, T. 111
pedagogy of listening 75
phatics 158
Phillips, A., Wellman, H. and Spelke, E. 26
physical space 56–62
Piaget, Jean 117, 118, 119, 120
place, conversation and 57
play activities, Ofsted attitude to 94–5
playing games 32–3
pointing 31
pointless questions 151
pondering 113–14
poor communication skills, impact of 8, 10–11
posing problems 116
positioning 59–60
positivity 169–70
  demonstration of 170
  positive learning experiences 3–4
  positive sense of selves, development of
    54
Poulin-Dubois, D., Blaye, A., Coutya, J. et al.
    134
practice, analysis of practitioners own work
  conversation, environments conducive to
    63
  interactions, sustainment of 122, 123, 124
  knowing children well 46–7
  learning leadership 97–8
  practitioner attributes 175–7
  questions 158–9
  reluctance to interact, dealing with 138–9
  tuning in to children 81

practitioner attributes 163–81
adult-led interactions 176
asymmetrical talk 171–2
attentiveness 164–5
demonstration of 165
babies and toddlers, focus on 163–4
ball game, analogy of 172–3
body language 169
child-led interactions 177
dance, notion of 172
ease in company of children 170–71
demonstration of 171
effectiveness, attributes of 164–71
engagement with young children,
importance of 163, 171–4
genuineness 168–9
demonstration of 169
improvisation, interaction as 173–4
interaction, not interference 174–5
Oxfordshire Adult-Child Interaction Project
(2010-14) 174–5
positivity 169–70
demonstration of 170
practice, analysis of practitioners own
work 175–7
reciprocity, importance of 171–4
respectfulness 167–8
demonstration of 168
responsiveness 166–7
demonstration of 167
see-saw (or scales), analogy of 172
self-reflection 181
sensitivity 165–6
demonstration of 166
social learning, imitative learning and
169–70
summary 180–81
tone of voice 169
transcripts 178–80
connection making 178–9, 180
independence, celebration of 178–9
knowledge, enhancement of 178–9, 180
modelling thinking 178–9
personal reference for mutuality in
exchange 178–9
positivity, affirmation of 178–9, 180
questioning, sustaining interaction with
178–9
self-esteem, contribution to 178–9
warm attentiveness 164–5

practitioner enhanced learning 3
practitioner-led learning, features on
interaction in 98
primary intersubjectivity 22–3
prior experiences and knowledge, knowing
about 38–40
prohibition of language at home 7
provoking children's learning (and thinking)
120–21

questions 144–62
alternatives to questioning 155–8
answers from children 152–4
babies and toddlers, focus on 144–5
Blooms, taxonomy of questions 150
from children at home 6
children's attempts to answer questions 153
closed questions 149
commenting 157
control, questioning as 152
conversational repertoire 152
disadvantages of asking questions 147
embellishing 157
fillers 158
future, talking about 157
Hare Brain, Tortoise Mind (Claxton, G.)
153
high-order questions 149–50
ideas, planting of 157
information, provision of 157
inhibiting stimuli, commands as 156
known questions 150–51
layering 157
listening to children's answers 153–4
Listening to Four Year Olds (Cousin, J.)
150–51
low-order questions 149–50
making statements 155–7
managerial questions 151
misconceptions, dealing with 157
offering alternative worldviews 157
open questions 149
Oxfordshire ACI Project 144–5, 146, 147,
149, 150, 151, 154, 155, 156–7, 158–9
personal reference for mutuality in
exchange 157
phatics 158
pointless questions 151
practice, analysis of practitioners own
work 158–9

question-answer relationship, dependency in 152
questioners 146–7
questioning, role of 144
questions that don't work 155
  features of interactions where questions don't work 159
questions that work 154–5
  features of interactions where questions work 159
rationale for asking questions 145–6
rhetorical questions 152–3
second silence 158
self-reflection 162
silence 158
summary 162
transcripts 147–8, 159–61
  dismissing children's thinking 147
  engagement with and questioning of children, need for sensitivity in 159–60
  interference by questioning 160–61
  interrupting children's thinking 148
  muddling children's thinking 147–8
  sidetracking children's thinking 147
types of questions 149–51
wait time in listening to children's answers 153–4
worldviews, offering alternatives to 157
quietness
  dealing with 129–30
  staying quiet and 116

Recchia, S.L. 28
receptivity, adaptations of interactions to 71–2
reciprocity, importance of 171–4
reflective interaction 60, 115
relationship building
  language and 10
  practitioners and 12
relaxation
  children's most relaxing circumstances 42–3
  practitioners' most relaxing circumstances 43–5
reluctance to interact, dealing with 127–43
  anxiety levels, reduction of 131–2
  Asperger Syndrome 132–3
  Attention Deficit Hyperactivity Disorder (ADHD) 132–3

autism, children with 132–4
Autism Spectrum Disorder (ASD) 132–4
  categories of 132
  peer engagement in cases of 133–4
babies and toddlers, focus on 127–8
bilingualism, benefits of 134
British Sign Language (BSL) 138
discouragement, features of interactions of 139
encouragement, features of interactions of 138–9
english as an additional language (eal), children with 134–7
  effectiveness of practitioners dealing with, requirements for 136–7
  practitioner relationship with second language learners 135–6
  second language learners, needs of 135–6
language difficulties, dealing with 130–31
Makaton language programme 138
negative reactions, awareness of potential for 129
Oxfordshire ACI Project 127, 138
practice, analysis of practitioners own work 138–9
quietness, dealing with 129–30
reluctant talkers 127, 128–32
selective mutism, dealing with 131–2
self-reflection 143
shyness, dealing with 129–30
signing communication 137–8
silence
  fear of saying wrong thing and 129–30
  rights of children in 130
speech difficulties, dealing with 130–31
summary 142
transcripts 139–42
  meaningful reasons for talking, need for 139–41
  one-to-one attentiveness as aid to reluctant talkers 141–2
written word, power of talk over 129
Researching Effective Pedagogy in the Early Years (REPEY, DfES, 2002) 2, 35, 45
respectfulness 167–8
  demonstration of 168
responsiveness 166–7
  demonstration of 167
Reszka, S.S., Odom, S.L. and Hume, K.A. 133, 134

rhetorical questions 152–3
Roberts, R. 12, 94
Robinson, M. 8, 10, 18, 19, 23, 26, 27, 28, 30, 115
Rogers, Carl 167
Rogoff, B. 35, 38, 115
Rojas, N.L. and Chan, E. 96
Rojas-Drummond, S., Torreblanca, O.,
          Pedraza, H. et al. 45
Rose, J. and Rogers, S. 20, 54, 71, 167
Rose, Jim 9
Roskos, K. and Neuman, S.B. 52
Rowe, M. 7, 153

safe havens for interaction 61
scaffolding, concept of 14
Schofield, G and Beck, M. 21
Schweinhart, L.J., Barnes, H. and Weikhart,
          D.P. 94
second silence 158
secondary intersubjectivity 25–6
secure attachment 41
see-saw (or scales), analogy of 172
selective mutism, dealing with 131–2
self-esteem 12, 94, 129, 131, 136, 179
self-reflection
    babies and toddlers, interactions with 34
    conversation, environments conducive to 68
    interactions, importance for learning 16
    interactions, sustainment of 126
    knowing children well 51
    learning leadership 107
    practitioner attributes 181
    questions 162
    reluctance to interact, dealing with 143
    tuning in to children 85
Selleck, Dorothy 41
Senju, A. and Csibra, G. 18
sensitivity 165–6
    in approach to children's play 92–3
    demonstration of 166
    social sensitivity 24
    understanding of sensitivities, knowing
          children and 37
shared care 41
shared experiences, creation of 39–40
shyness, dealing with 129–30
signing communication 137–8
silence 158
    fear of saying wrong thing and 129–30
    rights of children in 130
Siraj, I., Kingston, D. and Melhuish, E. 45

Siraj-Blatchford, I., Sylva, K., Muttock, S.
          et al. 13, 76
small group conversations, value of 45–6
Smith, P.K., Cowie, H. and Blades, M. 8, 23, 32
Snowling, M. and Stackhouse, J. 8
sociability 19, 23
'social brain' 18
social connections, interaction and 30–31
social interactions, infants' facility for 17
social learning 4
    imitative learning and 169–70
social referencing 28
social sensitivity 24
Sommerville, J. and Woodward, A. 26
Sorce, J.F., Emde, R.N., Campos, J. and
          Klinnert, M.D. 28
speaking to adults, child relaxation in 43
speaking to children, practitioner relaxation
          and 44–5
speech difficulties, dealing with 130–31
spoken language
    communication and (6 to 9 months) 25
    communication and (9 to 12 months) 27
    communication and (12 to 18 months) 30
    communication and (18 to 24 months) 32
spontaneous interactions 62
statement making 155–7
Statutory Framework for the Early Years
          Foundation Stage (DfES, 2008)
          40–41
Steiner, R. 93
Stern, D.N. 12, 25–6, 54
Stevens, R. 146
Stewart, N. 10
stimulation 60–61
Stone, L., Underwood, C. and Hotchkiss, J. 22
stranger anxiety 28–9
Stranger Situation Test 29
Studying Pedagogical Effectiveness in Early
          Learning (DfES, 2002) 2
summaries
    babies and toddlers, interactions with 34
    conversation, environments conducive to 67
    interactions, importance for learning 15–16
    interactions, sustainment of 125–6
    knowing children well 51
    learning leadership 106–7
    practitioner attributes 180–81
    questions 162
    reluctance to interact, dealing with 142
    tuning in to children 84–5

sustained shared thinking (SST), concept of 2, 45, 76
Sutter, A.L., Murray, L., Glatigny-Dallay, E. et al. 21
Swift, J. and Gooding, C. 153
Sylva, K., Melhuish, E., Sammons, P. et al. 94
symbiotic interaction 111

talk
    about feelings 115
    asymmetrical talk 171–2
    brain development and 17
    context of talk at home, parents and 5
    at home, features of 5–6
    'Talk for Learning' research project 2
    talking to someone, not everyone 45–6
Tassoni, P. 135
theory of mind 32
thinking
    child-led play, following children's thinking in 102–4
    children's thinking, dealing with unexpected connections in 110
    childrens' thinking, value of working out 79
    contributions to 45–6
    creative thinking, language and 10
    critical thinking, language and 10
    direct engagement with 73–4
    interthinking 2
    modelling process of 13–14
    provoking children's learning (and thinking) 120–21
    skills of, development of 10, 11
    sustained shared thinking (SST) 2, 45, 76
    thinking aloud 114–15
Thomas, Sally 52
time
    conversation, conducive environments and 61
    time sensitivity 9
Tizard, B. and Hughes, M. 2, 5, 6, 12, 144, 145, 146, 152
tone of voice 123–4
    analysis of own practice on 124
    practitioner attributes and 169
touch 19
transcripts
    conversation, environments conducive to 64–7
        outdoor play, engagement in 65–7
        sandpit as play area 64–5

interactions, sustainment of 117–18, 119, 121, 124–5
    consolidating children's learning 117–18
    extending children's learning 119
    provoking children's learning (and thinking) 121
    thinking and conversation, practitioner attentiveness to 124–5
knowing children well 47–51
    child not well known to practitioner 49–51
    child well known to practitioner 47–9
learning leadership 98–106
    adult-initiated but child-controlled activity 101–2
    adult-led challenge 98–101
    child-led play, following children's thinking in 102–4
    sensitivity of practitioner within child-led activity 104–6
practitioner attributes 178–80
    connection making 178–9, 180
    independence, celebration of 178–9
    knowledge, enhancement of 178–9, 180
    modelling thinking 178–9
    personal reference for mutuality in exchange 178–9
    positivity, affirmation of 178–9, 180
    questioning, sustaining interaction with 178–9
    self-esteem, contribution to 178–9
questions 147–8, 159–61
    dismissing children's thinking 147
    engagement with and questioning of children, need for sensitivity in 159–60
    interference by questioning 160–61
    interrupting children's thinking 148
    muddling children's thinking 147–8
    sidetracking children's thinking 147
reluctance to interact, dealing with 139–42
    meaningful reasons for talking, need for 139–41
    one-to-one attentiveness as aid to reluctant talkers 141–2
tuning in to children 81–4
    non-tuned-in interaction 83–4
    relaxation, tuning in in conditions of 81–3
Trevarthen, C. and Aitken, K. 23
Trevarthen, C. and Hubley, P. 26

Trevarthen, Colwyn 20, 23, 26, 109, 172
'triangle of trust' 55
Tronick, E., Als, H., Adamson, L. et al. 24
tuning in to children 69–85
   active listening 74–5
   adult agenda, dealing with emphasis on 75
   attunement 71–2
   babies and toddlers, focus on 69–70
      synchrony between actions and
         reactions, adeptness at sensing 70
   child as learner 70–72
   child-initiated learning 76
   'Children's Minds' (Donaldson, M.) 76
   childrens' thinking, value of working out 79
   clipboards 74
   co-construction 75–6
   decision-making on interactions 69, 80–81
   direct engagement with young children's
      thinking 73–4
   fascination, practitioner being fascinated
      by child 76–7
   'Hundred Languages of Children' (Loris
      Malaguzzi poem) 77–8
   interfering or interacting, difference
      between 80–81
   languages 77–8
   *Leuven Involvement Scale (LIS) for Young
      Children* 80
   non-tuned-in practitioners, features of
      interactions with 81
   observation 72–4
   Oxfordshire ACI Project 72, 74, 77, 79–80,
      81
   pedagogy of listening 75
   practice, analysis of practitioners own
      work 81
   receptivity, adaptations of interactions to
      71–2
   self-reflection 85
   sensitivity in 54
   strategies for 72–8
   summary 84–5
   sustained shared thinking (SST), concept
      of 76
   thoughts of children, value of working out
      79
   transcripts 81–4
      non-tuned-in interaction 83–4
      relaxation, tuning in in conditions of
         81–3

tuned-in practitioners, features of
   interactions with 81
Unique Child 71
'what, when and whether,' mantra for 73

'Under Five in Britain,' Bruner's study on
   being 43
Underdown, A. 20, 71, 128
Unique Child 71

Vaish, A. and Striano, T. 28
Van de Pol, J., Volman, M. and Beishuizen, J.
   14
Vermes, Sue 164
visual acuity, development of 23
Visual Cliff 28
vocabulary development, influences on 7
vocabulary range 9
voice recognition 18
Vygotsky, L.S. 13, 14, 118, 119, 171

Wait, Watch and Wonder, children's play and
   92–3
wait time in listening to children's answers
   153–4
warm attentiveness 164–5
Weitzman, E. and Greenberg, J. 23, 25, 133,
   172
Weitzman E. 70
welcome, sensitivity to warmth of 55
Wells, Gordon 2, 5, 6, 12, 34, 146, 171
'what, when and whether,' mantra for tuning
   in to children 73
Wimmer. H. and Perner, J. 32
Winnicott, D.W. 20, 35
Winterbottom, M. and Wilkins, A. 59
Wood, D. 5, 114, 119, 120
Wood, D., Brunner, J. and Ross, G. 14
Wood, D., McMahon, L. and Cranstoun, Y. 1–2,
   152
Wood, D., Wood, H., Griffiths, A., Howarth, S.
   and Howarth, C. 156, 158
Wood, H. and Wood, D. 156, 158
worldviews, offering alternatives to 157
written word
   becoming confident with 10
   power of talk over 129

'zone of proximal development,' Vygotsky's
   concept of 119

STARTING FROM THE CHILD
Fourth Edition

Julie Fisher

ISBN: 9780335246519 (Paperback)
eBook: 9780335246526
2013

Starting from the Child supports early years practitioners to be advocates for young children and their learning needs. In the fourth edition of this highly influential and inspirational book, Julie Fisher outlines the important theories and research which should underpin best early years practice. She takes a robust and principled stand against downward pressure to formalize young children's learning too soon, and offers practical and meaningful ways to develop high quality learning and teaching in the early years.

Starting from the Child challenges all early years practitioners to consider:

- How to build on children's innate desire to learn and their competence and autonomy as effective early learners
- How to plan environments indoors and out that make learning irresistible
- How to plan for high quality child-initiated learning to take place seamlessly alongside learning that is a dult-initiated
- The role of the adult in supporting and extending young children's learning
- How daily observation of children informs and underpins planning for their individual and unique learning needs

www.openup.co.uk

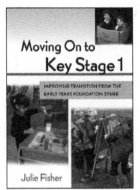

MOVING ON TO KEY STAGE 1
Improving Transition from the Early Years
Foundation Stage

Julie Fisher

ISBN: 9780335238460 (Paperback)
eBook: 9780335268477
2010

The author considers recent evidence about how children learn and questions whether current practice in Key Stage 1 optimises these ways of learning. Challenging the reliance on teacher-directed activity, she asks whether introducing more child-initiated learning could offer children a more appropriate balance of learning opportunities.

Key issues include:

- The place of play in Key Stage 1
- Organizing the learning day to include child-initiated activity
- Observation and assessment
- Planning
- The role of the teacher

www.openup.co.uk

The Excellence of Play

Moyles

ISBN: 9780335264186 (Paperback)
eBook: 9780335264193
2014

Play as a powerful learning and teaching experience remains key to effective early childhood education. Retaining its popular approach and style, this new edition reflects the contemporary context of early childhood education and care as well as emerging research on young children's development.

Key features include:

- A chapter overview giving a brief outline of aims and purpose
- Lively and meaningful cameos to help bring the themes and issues to life
- Content drawing on the cameos to help link research, theory and practice
- Reflective questions to raise awareness of, and reflection on, the issues
- Useful websites and further reading

www.openup.co.uk

CHARACTERISTICS OF EFFECTIVE EARLY LEARNING
Helping young children become learners for life

Helen Moylett

9780335263264 (Paperback)
2013

eBook also available

The key argument of *The Characteristics of Effective Early Learning* is that how children learn is as important as what they learn. This book helps you understand how to support the learning and development of young children through promoting the characteristics of effective early learning: play and exploring, active learning, and creating and thinking critically.

Key features:

- Investigates how children engage in learning through playing and exploring, and are motivated through active learning
- Explores how children become creative and critical thinkers able to review their own learning and thinking, imaginatively solving problems and excited by their own
- Examines appropriate approaches to observation, assessment and planning

www.openup.co.uk

OPEN UNIVERSITY PRESS
McGraw - Hill Education

Printed and bound by CPI Group (UK) Ltd, Croydon, CR0 4YY

27/03/2025

01837458-0002